THE GROLIER LIBRARY
OF
INTERNATIONAL
BIOGRAPHIES

PRODUCED BY THE PHILIP LIEF GROUP, INC.

MANAGING EDITOR
KITTY COLTON

EDITOR
JONATHON BRODMAN

EDITORIAL STAFF
JUSTINE FRIEL
GARY KREBS
CHRISTIAN NAGY
GARY SUNSHINE
HEIDI VON SCHREINER

WRITTEN AND RESEARCHED BY:
HOWARD JACOBSON

STEPHEN COLE
ROBERT COLEMAN
ROBERT DELAURENTIS
STEPHANIE GIRARD
ROBERT MILLER
GEORGE ROBINSON
ROBERT SCHNAKENBERG
JAY STEVENSON

THE GROLIER LIBRARY
OF
INTERNATIONAL
BIOGRAPHIES

Activists

VOLUME 1

Grolier Educational Corporation
Sherman Turnpike, Danbury, Connecticut 06816

Published 1996 by
Grolier Educational Corporation
Danbury, Connecticut 06816

Published by arrangement with
The Philip Lief Group, Inc.
6 West 20th Street
New York, New York 10011

The following copyrighted photographs appear in this volume:

Arafat: The Nobel Foundation. Biko: Library of Congress. Blum: French Press Services. Booth: Library of
Congress. Cassin: French Press Services. Chattopadhyay: Library of Congress. Corrigan: The Nobel Founda-
tion. Daw Aung San Suu Kyi: Library of Congress. Dolci: Library of Congress. Fawcett: Library of Congress.
Gandhi: Library of Congress. Geldorf: Library of Congress. Gonne: Library of Congress. Guevera: Library of
Congress. Hammarskjold: Library of Congress. Ichikawa: Library of Congress. Kubler-Ross: Washington Post.
Laing: Washington Post. Luthuli: The Nobel Foundation. Luxemburg: Library of Congress. Makarios III:
Washington Post. Mandela: Washington Post. Mother Teresa: The Nobel Foundation. Pankhurst: Library of
Congress. Sadat: Washington Post. Tutu: Washington Post. Zapata: Library of Congress.

ISBN 0-7172-7527-2
Library of Congress Catalog Number: 95-078649
Cataloging Information to be obtained directly from Grolier Educational Corporation.
First Edition
Printed in the United States of America

Contents

Introduction

Polish-born chemist Marie Curie, one of the greatest scientists of all time, once said, "One never notices what has been done; one can only see what remains to be done." This spirit has spurred every outstanding individual profiled in the GROLIER LIBRARY OF INTERNATIONAL BIOGRAPHIES. Perhaps these doers and thinkers did not themselves pause to reflect on their past achievements, but it is well worth our while to do so, as there is much to be learned from the examples of these enterprising and talented individuals. Included in this ten-volume set are profiles of twentieth-century achievers as diverse as South African anti-apartheid leader Desmond Tutu, a persecuted advocate for racial unity; British singer and songwriter Peter Gabriel, who has exposed millions of people to the music of diverse cultures; twice-elected Pakistani Prime Minister Benazir Bhutto, a powerful woman in a country in which men had long dominated politics; German-born physicist and humanist Albert Einstein, whose theories forever changed our view of the world and who was an outspoken critic of the arms race; the pain-stricken but indomitable Mexican painter Frida Kahlo; and influential French feminist writer and philosopher Simone de Beauvoir, who devoted her talents to improving women's lives.

Creating a mosaic that spans time and geography while overcoming the boundaries of gender, race, and class, the GROLIER LIBRARY OF INTERNATIONAL BIOGRAPHIES displays the rich heritage of our world's diverse cultures. It also demonstrates just how valuable the contribution of one individual can be to family, community, nation, and world. "It is better to be making news than taking it; to be an actor rather than a critic," said British statesman Sir Winston Churchill (1874–1965), speaking for all those who believe in the power of their own abilities.

Each biographical entry describes how a subject came to be a person of historical significance—detailing how that person grew up and emphasizing important childhood events and inspirational figures, as well as deeply held values and beliefs. His or her noteworthy discoveries, inventions, and achievements are placed in a historical context to show their influence during the period in which that individual lived. The lasting impact of each subject's contribution is then explained, providing a sense of how these individuals have affected all of our lives, directly or indirectly.

Many of the challenges met by the women and men chronicled in the INTERNATIONAL BIOGRAPHIES can inspire young readers today. As students relate to these exceptional individuals, they can begin to discover that even the most far-reaching goals and professions can be realized in their own lifetime:

Volume 1: Activists Inspirational and devoted advocates of social and political change

Volume 2: Athletes Skilled players of a variety of sports from basketball and boxing to soccer and skiing

Volume 3: Entrepreneurs, Inventors, and Discoverers Enterprising business leaders, engineers, and pioneers of discovery

Volume 4: Explorers Bold prospectors of land, sea, air, and space

Volume 5: Performing Artists Talented actors, dancers, comedians, and musicians

Volume 6: Political and Military Leaders Influential government leaders, including presidents, prime ministers, and generals

Volume 7: Scholars and Educators Innovative thinkers of philosophy, mathematics, literature, history, economy, and the law

Volume 8: Scientists Tenacious researchers in the fields of social and physical science

Volume 9: Visual Artists Creative painters, photographers, sculptors, architects, and filmmakers

Volume 10: Writers Stirring voices of poets, prose writers, playwrights, and journalists

The GROLIER LIBRARY OF INTERNATIONAL BIOGRAPHIES reveals the range and power of our rich cultural heritage, providing students with a greater knowledge of the remarkable achievements and successes of the world's past and present, while encouraging their dreams and aspirations for its future.

Adams, Gerry

(1948–   )

IRISH POLITICAL LEADER AND WRITER

Gerry Adams is the leader of the Irish Republican Army's political wing, Sinn Féin (pronounced "shin fane"). The Irish Republican Army (IRA) is a resistance movement to British rule in Northern Ireland. Adams has been a leader of Sinn Féin since the late 1970s. He spent most of the 1970s in prison or in hiding. In 1994, he emerged as the Irish Republican negotiator for a peaceful settlement to the conflict in Northern Ireland.

Adams was born in West Belfast, a working-class Catholic neighborhood of Belfast, the capital of Northern Ireland. He was one of thirteen children. His mother's family were well-known Irish **nationalists**. They had been fighting for many years to get the British government and army to leave Ireland. Since the nineteenth century, many Irish were in favor of **home rule.** Ireland would remain part of Great Britain, but would have its own Parliament and could make its own laws. But Protestants in Ireland did not want to be ruled by a Catholic majority. Two home rule bills were defeated in the British Parliament in 1886 and 1892.

In 1905, an organization called Sinn Féin was created. The name means "we ourselves" in Gaelic, the traditional language of the Irish people. Sinn Féin members fought for Irish independence from England. In 1920, Great Britain passed a law creating the Republic of Ireland, an independent country in the south of Ireland with a large Catholic majority. The remaining part of Ireland, in the north, still was ruled by Britain. Northern Ireland was two-thirds Protestant, and many Protestants felt that the only way to protect their rights was to remain under British rule. They were known as Unionists. The Catholics in Northern Ireland who wanted an independent country were known as Republicans. Adams's mother's family had been fighting on the Republican side for many generations.

When Adams was a boy, his father was shot and imprisoned by the Royal Ulster Constabulary, the Unionist police force in Northern

Ireland. Adams received a Catholic education, and he identified very strongly with Irish culture. As a teenager, he worked as a bartender in pubs (bars that also serve light meals) in Belfast, and he developed good relationships with both the Catholic and Protestant workingmen who visited the pubs. He became politically active during the Davis Street riots of 1964, which broke out after the British forbade the showing of the Irish Republican flag in public. Adams joined Sinn Féin and organized action groups that fought for the rights of the Catholic minority of Belfast. He protested the unfair treatment of Catholics by the government, and he complained that the police would not protect Catholic demonstrators from Protestant **paramilitary** groups (unofficial groups that acted like small, independent armies).

Adams was suspected by the government of leading the Belfast Brigade of the IRA, a Catholic paramilitary group that used **terrorism** tactics to drive the British from Northern Ireland. He denied this charge, but he spent years in prison in the 1970s. He led discussion groups in prison, and he read about the theories of **Marxism**. In 1972, he was flown secretly to London to attend ceasefire talks between the IRA and the British army. While in prison, he wrote a book about prison life called *Cage Eleven*.

Upon his release from prison in the late 1970s, Adams was made vice-president of Sinn Féin. He emphasized political, rather than military, action to achieve independence. In 1982, he was elected to the Northern Ireland Assembly. He was also elected to the British Parliament for the years 1982–1992, but he never took office. He refused to swear an oath of loyalty to the British crown. In 1984, he was severely wounded in an assassination attempt by Unionist gunmen. Since then he has worn a bulletproof vest underneath his clothes. In the late 1980s, he led Sinn Féin's overtures of peace.

In Britain from 1988–1994 it was illegal to play Adams's voice on radio or television. Someone else had to read his words in a voiceover narration. It was difficult for him to get his message to the world. In 1994, however, U.S. President Bill Clinton broke a long-standing tradition when he allowed Adams to visit the U.S. for three days. Despite protests by the British government, Adams came to the U.S. from January 31 to February 2. He appeared on talk shows and news programs, and his ideas were printed in countless newspaper columns. The publicity that he generated by his passionate, intelligent bearing put pressure on the British to come to terms with Sinn Féin and the IRA. On August 31, 1994, Adams negotiated a ceasefire between the Unionist forces in Northern Ireland and the IRA. It is possible that peace is on the horizon in Ireland for the first time in many years.

Arafat, Yasir

(1929–   )

CHAIRMAN OF THE PALESTINE
LIBERATION ORGANIZATION

Yasir Arafat has been the leader of the Palestinians' struggle to be granted their own state. He currently heads the Palestinian government in the Gaza Strip and Jericho, Israel.

Arafat was born in Jerusalem in 1929. What is now Israel—Jordan, Gaza, and the West Bank—was then a part of the British empire known as Palestine. It was ruled by an English high commissioner and was inhabited by two main groups of people. Arabs had been the majority of the population since the seventh century. Jews viewed it as their ancient biblical homeland. From the time when Theodor Herzl had founded political **Zionism** (the movement to create a Jewish state in Palestine) in 1897, Jews had been arriving from Europe in ever-increasing numbers. By the time Arafat was eleven years old, Arab leaders had succeeded in convincing the British authorities to severely limit the number of Jews who could come to Palestine.

Unfortunately, this was precisely the time when the Jews of Europe most needed a safe place to go. From 1933 to 1945, Germany's Adolf Hitler carried out a brutal war of **anti-Semitism** against the Jews. They became desperate to leave Germany. With most of the world in an economic **depression** at the time, few countries were willing to accept Jewish refugees from Germany and the countries that Germany had conquered in the early days of World War II. Palestine, with a growing Jewish settlement, **collective farms**, Hebrew-language universities, and an unofficial Jewish government, was a logical place for European Jews to go.

The British attempted to keep the peace in Palestine, a task that became increasingly difficult as Arabs and Jews fought for control of the territory. In 1948, the British left Palestine, which the United Nations divided into a Jewish state, Israel, and a Palestinian state, Jordan. The Jews accepted this plan; the Arabs did not, and they immediately launched an attack on the new state of Israel. Israel survived the war, and actually increased the geographic territory that it held.

Palestinian Arabs living in what had become Israel faced what many saw as a number of unpleasant choices. They could remain within Israel as a minority, with rights of citizenship but without their own nation. They could leave the country and dedicate themselves to the Palestinian struggle to regain it. They could leave and try to create a new life elsewhere. Arafat moved to Cairo, Egypt, and earned a degree in civil engineering. In the 1950s, he helped to create a number of Arab **guerrilla** groups that were dedicated to the destruction of Israel. One of these groups, El Fatah, became a central part of the Palestine Liberation Organization (PLO), which was founded in 1964. The PLO is the umbrella organization for many of the smaller Arab groups that have used diplomacy, negotiation, and **terrorism** to create a Palestinian state.

The PLO, in its **charter** of 1969, called for the liberation of "all of Palestine" from the state of Israel. In effect, this meant eliminating (destroying) Israel entirely. Arafat coordinated terrorist activities against Israel and Jewish organizations and individuals around the world. From 1965 to 1971, the PLO operated against Israel from their base in Jordan. The Jordanian king, Hussein, drove the PLO out of the country in 1971, after Arafat challenged Hussein's right to rule. Arafat moved the PLO to Beirut, Lebanon, north of Israel, where he continued the guerrilla war against Israel. He attempted to make alliances with other countries. He spoke often at the United Nations, which in 1974 recognized the PLO as the "sole, legitimate representative of the Palestinian people."

In 1982, Israel invaded Lebanon in an attempt to stop the terrorist attacks on its northern cities. The PLO abandoned Lebanon, and Arafat set up the PLO offices in Tunisia, in North Africa. Arafat spent much of the 1980s fighting off challenges to his leadership from other Palestinians. In 1983, the Syrian government supported PLO rebels who tried unsuccessfully to remove Arafat from power. Despite the many power struggles, the PLO remained extremely popular among the Palestinian people. In December 1987, a Palestinian uprising began in Arab East Jerusalem, and it quickly spread to the West Bank and Gaza. Israel had captured these lands in the 1967 war with neighboring Arab countries, and the Palestinians who lived in them did not have rights of citizenship in Israel. Many Palestinians from these occupied territories had been jailed by Israeli soldiers, and there was a strong feeling that the Palestinians were being denied equality and basic **human rights**.

The uprising led Arafat to declare a Palestinian state in 1988. In the declaration, for the first time, he accepted Israel's right to exist. He said that his goal was a Palestinian state existing side by side with Israel. Under heavy pressure from the United States, he also said that the PLO would no longer use terrorism to achieve its goals. In 1993, Israel and the PLO signed a peace treaty in Washington, D.C. Arafat shook hands with Yitzhak Rabin, the prime minister of Israel, in a historic ceremony. The Palestinian and the Israeli pledged to work together to create a just and lasting peace in the Middle East. Israel agreed to the creation of an **autonomous** (limited self-governing) Palestinian territory made up, at first, of the West Bank town of Jericho and the Gaza Strip. Arafat has ruled over these areas since the signing of the treaty. He continues to negotiate with Israel to expand the territory and the amount of independence that the Palestinian area and its people will have.

Recently, Arafat's popularity with the Palestinian people has slipped. As a fighter, he was a symbol of their struggle and their will. As a peacemaker and a nonelected ruler who cannot tolerate disagreement, he has made many enemies among his former supporters. Many Palestinians felt that he should not have made peace until a Palestinian state was declared, and they now consider him to be a puppet of Israel and the United States. Israel still holds Arafat responsible for acts of terrorism against Jews. He is in a more difficult situation now, as a ruler, than he ever was as a fighter. *See* ASHWARI, HANAN; AWAD, MUBARAK; SADAT, JIHAN

Aristide, Jean-Bertrand

(1953–   )

PRIEST AND PRESIDENT OF HAITI

> Can we continue to find this situation of violence that is imposed
> on the poor normal? No. We must end this regime where the don-
> keys do all the work and the horses prance in the sunshine, a regime
> of misery imposed on us by the people in charge. They are vora-
> cious and insatiable dogs who go their own way, each one looking
> out for himself.
>
> —Jean-Bertrand Aristide, in a sermon

Jean-Bertrand Aristide, the most well known priest in Haiti, was elected president of Haiti in February 1991. He has dedicated his life to helping the poor of his country gain rights and fight their way out of poverty. After he was in office for only eight months, the army and the secret police forced him to flee during a bloody rebellion. In late 1994, international pressure, led by the threat of invasion by the United States armed forces, brought Aristide back to power in Haiti.

Aristide was born in 1953 in Port-Salut, a small town on the south coast of Haiti, which is the eastern portion of an island in the Caribbean; the Dominican Republic is its western, adjoining neigh-bor. His father, an **illiterate** (unable to read or write) farmer, died when Aristide was three months old, and his mother moved the fam-ily to Port-au-Prince, the capital of Haiti. She became a merchant. When Aristide was six, his mother sent him to the Catholic school run by the Salesian order of monks, who were dedicated to serving the poor. He did very well in school, and in 1974 he decided to join the priesthood. In 1979, he earned a psychology degree from the State University of Haiti, and then studied in Israel, Egypt, England, and Italy. In addition to speaking French, the official language of Haiti, and Creole, his native language and the language of the peas-ants, he became fluent in Hebrew, English, Arabic, Italian, and Span-ish.

Even while he was deep in his studies, Aristide became more and more concerned about the conditions of the poor, uneducated people in his country. Haiti is the poorest country in the **Western Hemi-**

sphere, and most of the wealth is controlled by a very small number of rich people. During the 1970s and 1980s, Aristide wrote articles for Haiti's Catholic newspaper *Bon Nouve*, in which he criticized the greed and cruelty of the **dictator** of Haiti, Jean-Claude ("Baby Doc") Duvalier. In 1982, Aristide returned to Port-au-Prince from his travels abroad. There he became the priest of St.-Jean-Bosco, a church attended by some of the poorest people in Haiti. In his sermons, he told his congregation that if they wanted a better life, they would have to stand up to the military dictatorship that ruled the country.

This was not an easy thing for the people to do. Duvalier ruled by keeping his subjects in a state of terror and ignorance, just as his father, François, had done before him. His private, secret army, the Tontons Macoutes, threatened and killed many citizens who criticized the government. Shortly after one of Aristide's sermons, Duvalier forced the leaders of the Haitian Roman Catholic Church (whom he had appointed) to send Aristide into **exile** in Canada. After three years in Montreal, where he studied the Bible, Aristide returned to Port-au-Prince in 1985. He led the **liberation theology** movement of priests who believed that it was their job to fight injustice. These priests organized the poor to fight against their oppressors.

Although the Catholic Church in Haiti kept trying to silence Aristide, he played a big part in Duvalier's removal from power in 1986. The leaders who took over, however, were no better, and they were very afraid of Aristide's ability to organize the poor. In 1988, about one hundred Tontons Macoutes, armed with sticks, knives, and guns, burst into the St.-Jean-Bosco church just as Aristide was beginning mass. They attacked the congregation and burned down the church. Aristide escaped, but he was badly shaken by the attack. The Salesian order expelled him from the priesthood, but the people of Port-au-Prince protected him night and day. They would not let him be sent into exile again. During the next few years, Aristide worked to better the lives of the poor, by creating a school for them to learn trades, and establishing other organizations. In October 1990, he announced his candidacy for the presidency in the first-ever democratic elections in Haiti. He won with almost 70 percent of the vote. As president, he tried to dissolve the Tontons Macoutes, and tried to break the power of the **elite** groups that had ruled Haiti for almost two hundred years. He donated his own salary, $25,000 a year, to charity. On October 1,

1991, he was deposed in a **coup d'état**. He spent the next three years in the United States, until his return to Haiti in November 1994. *See* AUGUSTE, ROSEANNE

Ariyaratne, Ahangamage Tudor

(1931–   )

SRI LANKAN MONK AND SOCIAL WORKS ORGANIZER

A.T. Ariyaratne, a science teacher, founded a self-help organization in 1958 in Sri Lanka, an island nation off the southeast coast of India. It quickly spread across the island and became a national movement of service and self-reliance. Using Mohandas Gandhi's **pacifist** principles of nonviolence and respecting all people, Ariyaratne's movement began transforming the economy and soul of Sri Lanka. Once, powerful enemies of change hired the head of organized crime in Sri Lanka to assassinate Ariyaratne during a speech at a **Buddhist** center in Colombo, the capital of Sri Lanka. Ariyaratne heard of the plan the day before he was to give the speech. He went to the crime boss's house that night and asked that he be killed there and then, so that his blood would not desecrate the Buddhist house of learning. The would-be killer looked into Ariyaratne's eyes and refused to kill him. Instead, he became a great admirer of Ariyaratne's and a supporter of his movement.

Ariyaratne was born in a village on the southern coast of Sri Lanka in 1931. His father was a local businessman who later became a leader of the village. Ariyaratne studied Buddhism even before attending primary school, and learned to read Sinhalese, the language of Sri Lanka, from a local Buddhist monk. As he went through school, he combined the spiritual teachings of Buddhism with his regular education, always involving himself in some sort of social work in the community.

Ariyaratne earned a degree from Mahinda College in the city of Galle, Sri Lanka, and another degree in science that enabled him to teach in a prestigious Buddhist high school in Colombo. Soon after establishing himself as a teacher, Ariyaratne began to fulfill his dream of service to others. He organized a "vacation work camp" for some of the students at the school. They went to a terribly poor village far from the city that was inhabited by the lowest **caste** (social class) of Sri Lankans. Ariyaratne wanted his students to, as he explained later, "understand and experience the true state of affairs that prevailed in the rural and poor areas, and develop a love for their people, utilizing the education they received to find ways of building a more just and happy life for them."

Ariyaratne did not want his students, with their advanced education, to feel superior to the people they were helping. They lived in the village, shared the people's huts and food, and learned from the villagers what their needs were. When they found that poor sanitation was the biggest problem, the students formed a plan to dig latrines (outdoor toilets). To build the latrines, Ariyaratne organized a work camp, which he called *shramadana* (*shrama* means "labor," or "energy," and *dana* means "to give"). Many high-caste (upper class) residents of neighboring villages were offended at the thought of wealthy students digging latrines for poor villagers, and they sabotaged (attempted to destroy) the project several times. Nevertheless, after two weeks the latrines were completed, and the students and villagers had become friends.

Other schools heard about the idea, and they instituted their own *shramadanas*. Students would spend weekends and vacations living with and helping poor communities all across Sri Lanka. Many poor villages were inspired to become part of the *shramadana* movement themselves, and they completed their own projects without outside help.

Ariyaratne felt that the movement could do much more, however, and he traveled to India to seek the inspiration of one of Gandhi's disciples, Vinoba Bhave. Bhave had started a movement that he called *sarvodaya*, or "all-awakening." He walked for thousands of miles across India, speaking to thousands of people, getting rich people to donate land to the poor. In twenty years, Bhave had collected about four million acres of land for poor people in India. Ariyaratne brought the principles of the *sarvodaya* movement back to Sri Lanka. He helped set up education programs, health clinics, roads, farming projects, and technologies for producing energy cheaply and efficiently.

Sarvodaya built more roads in Sri Lanka than the government did.

It created more than one hundred centers around the country, each one serving a number of villages. Many African and Asian countries also began organizing *sarvodaya* campaigns. Leaders organized international conferences that were aimed at bringing rich and poor countries into equal partnerships, in the same way that Ariyaratne's students and the poor villagers had cooperated in 1958. One of the most important parts of the movement is the definition of "development," which economists usually use to refer to making poor countries just like rich ones. Ariyaratne considers development to be the increasing of human fulfillment. The three million Sri Lankans who are part of *sarvodaya* meditate daily, all at the same time. Buddhist monks have always played a large role in carrying out the projects.

At the same time that he was building a national movement, Ariyaratne was still working full-time as a science teacher. In the early years, his salary supported the movement, his wife, mother, and six children. By 1972, *sarvodaya* was known around the world, and enough donations came in so that Ariyaratne could resign from teaching and devote himself to the movement full-time. In a country suffering from great poverty, at risk of civil war, and torn between the many poor and the few wealthy, one man has inspired millions to help each other and themselves. *See* GANDHI, MOHANDAS

Ashrawi, Hanan

(1946–   )

PALESTINIAN POLITICAL LEADER

> We wish to address the Israeli people, with whom we have a prolonged exchange of pain: Let us share hope instead. . . . We have seen you look back in deepest sorrow at the tragedy of your past and look on in horror at the disfigurement of the victim turned oppressor. Not for this have you nurtured your hopes, dreams, and your offspring. . . . Let us end the Palestinian-Israeli fatal proximity in this unnatural condition of occupation, which has already claimed too many lives. . . . Set us free to reengage as neighbors and equals in our holy land.
>
> —Hanan Ashrawi, in a speech

Hanan Ashrawi is a Palestinian college professor who became the spokesperson of the Palestinian delegation to the Middle East peace talks in Madrid, Spain, in 1991. She succeeded in putting into motion events that have led to a peace treaty between the Palestine Liberation Organization (PLO) and Israel, and to talks leading toward eventual Palestinian statehood.

Ashrawi was born in 1946 in the town of Ramallah, in what is now the Israeli-occupied West Bank. In 1948, Ramallah became part of Jordan, until Israel conquered it during the 1967 war it fought with neighboring Arab countries. Ashrawi's father was a prominent political leader, and he inspired her to devote her life to the Palestinian struggle for **self-determination**. She attended the American University in Beirut, Lebanon, in the late 1960s, where she met Yasir Arafat, leader of the PLO. She studied literature, and she was involved in Palestinian politics. She accepted a teaching job at Bir Zeit University in the West Bank in 1973, but she left to earn a Ph.D. (doctorate degree) in English literature from the University of Virginia, in the United States, in 1981. She returned to Bir Zeit that same year and resumed her activity on the Human Rights Action Project.

The conditions of Palestinians living in the West Bank worsened in the late 1970s and 1980s. Israel had won the territories from Jordan in the 1967 war, but under a right-wing government elected in 1977, it began encouraging large-scale Jewish settlement in the area, pressuring Palestinians to leave, and preparing to **annex** the territories into Israel permanently. As Palestinian discontent grew, the Israeli military occupation became stronger and harsher. In 1982, in response to **guerrilla** attacks upon its northern cities, Israel invaded Lebanon. When Israel's Lebanese Christian allies massacred Palestinian refugees in Sabra and Shatilla camps, while Israeli soldiers watched, Ashrawi was moved to protest vehemently. She led demonstrations on the Bir Zeit campus against the Israeli occupation of the West Bank.

For many in the Western world and in Israel, the word *Palestinian* meant the same thing as *terrorist*. Indeed, the PLO and other organizations have used terrorism against Israel, and Jews around the world, in their efforts to win statehood. These acts have damaged the Palestinian cause in the eyes of the world. Ashrawi, a mother of two, a professor of English, a woman who wore Western clothes and went to a beauty parlor, changed that image. She spoke to Israeli women about their common desire for peace. Starting in 1988, she appeared often on the American ABC television news show *Nightline*. She spoke gently, yet forcefully, about **human rights** and justice, and not about ancient history and violent struggle.

With the fall of communist Eastern Europe in 1989, the PLO lost its main source of funding and support. The PLO's international image was also hurt when leading PLO officials, including Arafat, refused to condemn Iraq's 1990 invasion of Kuwait. When the Madrid conference on Middle East peace began in August 1991, the Palestinian delegation appeared too weak to achieve any of its goals. Many observers expected that the conference would just be one more chance for Israel and its Arab neighbors to repeat their uncompromising statements. But, led by Ashrawi, who officially was not even part of the delegation because of her support for the PLO, the Palestinian delegation stole the show. They agreed to accept a period of **autonomy** (limited self-rule) before becoming a state. They compromised on a number of other issues. Ashrawi spoke to the international press, and repeated the Palestinians' desire for peace and justice. Now Israel appeared to be the stubborn, unreasonable nation. Israeli officials even threatened to arrest Ashrawi for meeting with PLO officials in Geneva, a crime for Palestinian residents of Israel, but she refused to be intimidated. Many in Israel's Labour Party were embarrassed by their government, and they called for the law to be repealed. U.S. President George Bush publicly expressed sympathy for Ashrawi.

Ashrawi continues to take a leading role in the Palestinian movement toward statehood. She has close contacts with Israeli peace groups and women's groups, and she tries to reassure them that Palestinians are not their enemies. She expresses an understanding of Jewish history, including the tragedy of the **Holocaust**, in which six million Jews were killed between 1933 and 1945, and she vows to work with the Israelis for a just peace in the Middle East. Patiently and impatiently, as she puts it, she educates people and builds bridges of trust and peace. *See* ARAFAT, YASIR; AWAD, MUBARAK

Auguste, Roseanne

(1964–   )

HAITIAN NURSE AND HUMAN RIGHTS ACTIVIST

Even before Roseanne Auguste graduated from nursing school in 1987, she had decided to fight to provide health care to poor women in Haiti, the poorest country in the **Western Hemisphere**. While still in school, she organized a student union of nurses that lobbied for better health care for patients who could not afford to pay for it. After graduation, she interned at Hôpital Sainte-Thérèse in Hinche, Haiti. She also worked with community members and nongovernmental agencies to help the poor receive needed medical and preventative services. She called her patients' lack of access to health care a **human rights** abuse, and she challenged the Haitian government to take care of its poor. Since the overthrow of the feared dictator Jean-Claude Duvalier (nicknamed "Baby Doc") in 1986, Haiti had been ruled by a series of dictators who owed their power to the terrorizing tactics of the Haitian secret police, the Tontons Macoutes. After a brief period of improvement in 1991, during the democratically elected government of Jean-Bertrand Aristide, the situation worsened in September 1991. Aristide, who had won 70 percent of the popular vote, was overthrown by yet another military dictatorship. The poor had supported Aristide, and so they became the targets of violence and threats from the military. Auguste, as a human rights **activist** for the poor, found her life in danger. Nevertheless, she continued her work.

After the military **coup**, soldiers entered the State University Hospital where Auguste worked and murdered several patients who were suspected of being Aristide supporters. Doctors were too frightened to return to work, so the hospital closed down. Because of the fighting, more Haitians than ever needed medical treatment. Auguste tried to reopen the hospital, but she found that the doors had been locked. This did not stop her. She found the next-best thing to a key: an ax, with which she opened the doors and found the medical supplies and hospital records. She herself declared the hospital open again, and she convinced some doctors and nurses to return to work with her.

Her bravery inspired many health workers to staff the hospital, which she ran until the military removed her from the building.

In 1992, Auguste turned her attention to the poorest and most dangerous section of the Haitian capital of Port-au-Prince, Kafou Fey. Many residents of Kafou Fey were strong Aristide supporters, and the military carried out violent attacks on them frequently. Auguste found an abandoned house and turned it into Haiti's first clinic for poor women. She expected to see twenty to thirty women a day. The clinic was to provide basic health care, education, and family planning. Because of the violence, however, children and men also began streaming into the clinic for treatment for injuries. Soon, Auguste was treating more than two hundred people a day.

Auguste focused world attention on the human rights abuses in Haiti. She edited a magazine that dealt with women's rights until the Haitian government banned it, and she helped to found the Ad Hoc Committee on Violence Against Women. In an act of bravery and defiance, she worked with this organization to hold a conference, after the coup, on violence against women. International human rights observers reported on the proceedings. Many of the women who were fighting for human rights for themselves and their families were targeted for violence by the government. Auguste helped women to hide from authorities, and she assisted them in their attempts to escape from Haiti. She herself went into hiding, although she continued in her efforts to organize poor women to fight for their rights, and to alert the world to the human rights abuses carried out by the Haitian government. When Aristide was returned to power in 1994, Auguste returned to her grueling days at the clinic. Now a mother of two, she provides health care to the residents of Kafou Fey during the day, and in her spare time she lobbies the government to help pay for the clinic's operation. Even though the threat of violence has diminished, hundreds of people still line up every day for emergency medical treatment. Auguste's battle to bring health to the poorest of the poor has just begun. *See* ARISTIDE, JEAN-BERTRAND

Awad, Mubarak

(1943–   )

PALESTINIAN ACTIVIST

> One day a young Palestinian boy, maybe thirteen years old, came to me crying. He was from one of the refugee camps and he had been throwing stones at an Israeli soldier. Three times he had thrown stones at the soldier, and three times the soldier had beaten him up, the third time quite badly. On the fourth time, the boy again threw the stones, and again the soldier chased him. When he was finally caught by the soldier, the boy expected to be really severely beaten this time, but instead the soldier hugged him. This boy came to me weeping, angry, not understanding. He said to me, "He hugged me." I said to the boy, "That Israeli soldier was a human being."
>
> —Mubarak Awad, on Arab-Israeli relations

Mubarak Awad is a nonviolent leader of the Palestinian uprising against Israel. His influence is clearly seen in the intifada, or popular uprising against Israeli rule, which he calls "75 percent nonviolent." After establishing a center for the Palestinian study of nonviolence in Jerusalem, he was harassed, arrested, and tortured by Israeli authorities. Despite protests by U.S. President Ronald Reagan, Awad was **exiled** from Israel in 1988. He moved to the United States, where he has continued to work for the establishment of a Palestinian state through nonviolent means.

Awad was born in 1943, just as Jews and Palestinians were coming into frequent conflict over the land they shared. After the State of Israel was declared in 1948, many Palestinians left in order to fight with the invading Arab armies of Egypt, Iraq, Syria, Jordan, and Lebanon. Others were forced out during the fighting. Awad's father was killed during a battle, when he tried to carry a wounded friend to safety. Awad's mother saw Israeli soldiers threaten to shoot her seven children, and she feared both for their safety and for her ability to provide for them. She sent all but two of them to orphanages. Mubarak stayed in an orphanage all through high school, and then attended St. George's School in Jerusalem, one of the most prestigious Christian schools in Israel. His mother remained a part of her children's lives, teaching them not to seek revenge, but to make the world a better place so that no mother in the future would suffer as she had.

Awad became interested in Christianity, and in 1959 he won a scholarship to study for the ministry in Lee College in Cleveland, Tennessee. He quickly disapproved of the treatment of black people in the American South, and he did not like Lee College's attempts to convert other people to its brand of Christianity. He went back to Jerusalem and taught English, math, and religion in a Mennonite orphanage for boys until 1969. From 1970 to 1983, he lived in Ohio, earned a master's degree in counseling, and worked as a group and family therapist for delinquent children. He set up a program to help troubled children by providing support for them at home and in school. His work with these children was very successful, and Awad began thinking about applying what he had learned to his homeland.

In 1983, Awad returned to Jerusalem and began helping troubled Palestinian youths by setting up the Palestinian Counseling Center. Many of the young people were involved in protests against Israeli occupation. At first, Awad was proud of them for throwing stones at Israelis, but later he felt that "stones make people run away." He soon realized that the political situation took up Palestinian people's attention, and they weren't interested in solving their own behavioral problems. They blamed the Israeli occupation for everything, including poor health care and juvenile delinquency. Awad realized that the Palestinians would not solve their personal or political problems unless they took responsibility for their own lives. He wrote an article suggesting many nonviolent ways that Palestinians could fight against Israel. He argued that Palestinians could choose not to be under occupation, and could refuse to pay taxes and deal with the Israeli government. Awad had visited India a number of times, and he used the inspiration of Mohandas Gandhi to map out his plan for Palestinian **civil disobedience** against Israel. He organized a workshop in Jerusalem on nonviolent protest, and he was surprised to find in attendance Palestinians who had once supported an armed struggle. A Palestinian-American professor in the United States, Hisham Sharbi, provided funding, and in 1985 Awad established the Palestinian Center for the Study of Nonviolence. He wanted to show Palestinians the teachings of nonviolence and peaceful protest from within Arabic literature and Islamic holy books.

The study center proved to be threatening to the Israeli government. Beginning in 1985, Awad was harassed by soldiers, and often arrested. He was tortured several times. It seemed that the Israeli government of right-wing Prime Minister Yitzhak Shamir understood the power of a nonviolent Palestinian movement. After years of conducting **guerrilla** warfare against Israelis and Jews, the Palestinians had a negative image in the world press. Awad represented a greater danger to Shamir: that the world would see Israelis as the aggressors, and Palestinians as the victims. Awad wrote, "We need to make it economically, psychologically, and morally expensive for Israel" to continue to rule over the Palestinians.

Awad was in and out of prisons and torture chambers from 1985 to 1987, but his nonviolent ideas spread throughout the Palestinian community in Jerusalem and the West Bank. In December 1987, the uprising known as the intifada began. Despite numerous incidents of rock-throwing and tire-burning, Awad said that the intifada was "75 percent nonviolent." Arab shops and businesses went on strike, people demonstrated, and thousands were arrested, shot, and killed. The harder the Israeli government tried to stop it, the stronger the protest became. The intifada was a threat not only to Israel, but also to other Arab states, and to the leadership of the Palestine Liberation Organization (PLO). The intifada had no leader, no government. It represented a popular uprising, one that PLO leaders could not control or take credit for.

In the 1990s, secret peace talks between the Israeli government and Palestinian leaders finally led to a peace agreement. In 1993, Israeli Prime Minister Yitzhak Rabin, who had been in charge of the Israeli military response to the intifada, and PLO leader Yasir Arafat shook hands on the White House lawn, and both agreed to stop the fighting. They would work together for a solution that would allow both Israelis and Palestinians to feel secure and justly treated. Despite acts of terrorism by extremist Jews and Palestinians, the majority of both peoples still appear to be committed to ending the struggle, and sharing the land with each other. Awad, as one of the first Palestinian voices for a nonviolent solution, deserves much of the credit. *See* ARAFAT, YASIR; ASHRAWI, HANAN; GANDHI, MOHANDAS

Aylward, Gladys

(1903–1970)

ENGLISH MISSIONARY IN CHINA

Gladys Aylward worked with Chinese refugees and orphans and tended the sick during China's war with Japan in the 1930s. She once led one hundred children on a long march over mountains to escape from an oncoming Japanese army. She was made famous by a film starring actress Ingrid Bergman that was based on her life, *The Inn of the Sixth Happiness*.

Aylward was born in Edmonton, London, England, in 1903. She left school when she was fourteen and found work as a parlor maid, dusting and cleaning the living rooms of her wealthy employers. She wanted to become a **missionary**, someone who traveled around the world spreading Christianity. By the time she was twenty-seven, she had saved enough money to buy a train ticket to make the grueling voyage from England to Tientsin, in northern China. From there she traveled to Yangzheng, in southern Shanxi province. With a Scottish missionary, Miss Dawson, she established the Inn of the Sixth Happiness, a place for travelers to stay. While the travelers rested and ate, the two women taught them the Christian gospel.

Aylward soon learned the local dialect of Chinese and won the respect and trust of the local people. She also made friends with the Mandarin, or local ruler, and worked for him. She became the area foot inspector, an important job in protecting women's rights in China. Foot binding was an ancient Chinese tradition whereby a young girl's feet were doubled over, and broken, then bound tightly, so that she could fit into tiny shoes and appear very dainty. Wealthy families bound their daughters' feet so that they would be beautiful, and could be married off easily. This custom was outlawed after the Chinese revolution of 1912, and it became Aylward's job to make sure that none of the local families still performed it.

One year after her arrival in China, Aylward became a Chinese citizen. In 1938, the Japanese army overran Shanxi province, and Aylward took one hundred local children to safety through the mountain passes. She joined the Chinese nationalists who were fighting the

Japanese, and she traveled with them as they fled from village to village, taking care of the wounded. In 1948, she returned to England for five years. She told people what she had seen and done, and she preached about Christianity. In 1953, Aylward moved to Formosa (now Taiwan, a small island off the southeast coast of mainland China), the country that the Chinese nationalists had established after being defeated by the **communists** in 1949. She worked with orphans and refugees from mainland China until her death in 1970.

Baden-Powell, Olave

(1889–1977)

ENGLISH GIRL SCOUT ORGANIZER

Lady Olave Baden-Powell helped organize the Girl Scouts in England, and she led the international Girl Scout movement until her death. After World War II, she focused on the building of world peace through international Girl Scout associations, conferences, and camps. She flew a total of almost five hundred thousand miles between 1930 and 1970.

Baden-Powell was born in England in 1889. Her father was a wealthy man who could not stay in one place for long. Baden-Powell lived in seventeen different homes as a child. She lived the typical life of a rich English girl in other respects, going to school only until she was twelve, going to parties, hunting, traveling, and learning to play the violin. After her debutante party, which introduced her to society as a young woman eligible for marriage, she traveled with her father to the West Indies in 1912. On the boat was "the only interesting person on board," as Baden-Powell wrote to her mother at the time, the "Scout Man," General Robert Baden-Powell. Robert was the founder of the Boy Scouts, and Chief Scout of the world.

Olave and Robert were married that same year, and they spent their honeymoon in the Algerian desert, in North Africa. They returned to England, where he worked to build up the Boy Scouts internationally, and she raised three children and helped him with his work. She was also asked to become the local Girl Scout commissioner in 1916. She showed a talent for organization, and she convinced many people to become Girl Scout leaders. When people responded that they were too busy, she convinced them that training Girl Scouts was important war work. She was so successful in organizing the English Girl Scouts that she turned her attention to the rest of the world. She organized international conferences, created an international council, and in 1924 established a Girl Scout summer camp for girls from all over the world.

The Baden-Powells traveled around the world frequently. As Chief Scout (he) and Chief Guide (she) of the World, they visited scouting groups in India, Italy, the Mediterranean Sea region, the Baltic Sea area, and many other places. In 1938, they moved to Kenya, in East Africa, because of Robert's ill health. He died in 1941, and Olave continued to expand the international Girl Scout movement. During World War II, the scouts in countries fighting against Adolf Hitler's Nazi regime devoted their time to helping with the war effort. They worked in blood-bank campaigns, raised money, sold bonds, collected food and clothing for needy people in Europe, and helped young children leave dangerous areas and get to safety. They also helped in hospitals, child care settings, and on farms. In countries invaded by the Nazis, Girl Scouts took part in resistance activities.

After World War II, Baden-Powell devoted her time to molding the Girl Scout movement into an instrument of world peace and harmony. In 1946, she arranged for Girl Scout groups from countries that had been enemies in the war to meet with one another and create bonds of peace. She continued to work energetically with scout groups all over the world.

On her doctor's orders, she stopped traveling in 1970. By that time she had been made a Dame of the British Empire, and had won many international awards as well. Under her leadership, the Girl Scouts numbered 6.5 million worldwide at the time of her death, in 1977.

Benenson, Peter

(1921–   )

ENGLISH FOUNDER OF AMNESTY INTERNATIONAL

Peter Benenson, a successful lawyer, was riding on the London Underground (subway system) one day in early 1961 when he read a newspaper article that made him angry. It was about the arrest of two Portuguese students who had drunk a toast to the independence of Portugal's overseas colonies. By the time Benenson reached his stop, the idea for **Amnesty** International, an organization dedicated to fighting against torture and the holding of political prisoners, had taken shape in his mind.

As a young man, Benenson was groomed for success. He attended Eton, one of the most prestigious secondary schools in England, and went from there to the equally prestigious Oxford University. He studied law, and upon graduation he set up a successful practice in business law. He developed an early interest in **human rights** around the world, and found himself interrupting his law practice to take trips to countries like Hungary, South Africa, Cyprus, and Spain. He would defend political prisoners, and sometimes attend their trials as a legal observer. In the 1950s, he helped set up the English branch of the International Commission of Jurists. This organization monitored human rights violations around the world and tried to enforce the rule of law. Benenson divided his time between his commercial law practice and his passion for human rights, until he received a large inheritance at the end of the 1950s. He gave up his practice and devoted himself full-time to the cause of people imprisoned by their governments for their opinions and statements. As a lawyer, Benenson knew that he could do some good, but he realized that without a lot of publicity, most governments could afford to mistreat their political prisoners. When he read about the arrest of the Portuguese students, Benenson made up his mind to form an international organization that would tell the prisoners' stories to the world. If English citizens found out about other countries' human rights abuses, they might put pressure on the English government to stop trading with those nations, or to demand in the United Nations that the abuses stop.

Benenson spent the next few months after his Underground ride contacting people who could help to publicize human rights abuses. He worked with other lawyers, writers, and publishers, and together they decided on a strategy. They launched a worldwide media campaign in which they focused attention on a few "prisoners of conscience," as they called the men and women locked in prisons worldwide for speaking their minds. The Appeal for Amnesty, as Benenson called the campaign, was kicked off with an article that Benenson wrote for the May 28, 1961, London Sunday *Observer* newspaper. The article, titled "The Forgotten Prisoners," also appeared in many other newspapers and magazines around the world. More than one thousand people responded to the article. Many had questions about political prisoners. Others wanted to know what they could do to help. One American enclosed a check for a thousand dollars with his reply. Newspaper editors around the world also began to spread the word about human rights abuses in prisons all over the world.

On May 29, Benenson cleared an office in his law firm for the Appeal for Amnesty. There, Benenson, a secretary, and volunteers began collecting information on prisoners of conscience. They worked to publicize individual cases, and gave information to people who wanted to join the Appeal. Within two months, they had collected information on more than two hundred prisoners around the world. Now that the information was available, Benenson and his fellow activists had to decide what to do with it. Benenson hit upon the idea of dividing up the work of representing and trying to free prisoners. He challenged volunteer groups that were forming all over England to choose three prisoners and work for their release. Benenson was concerned that the Appeal not play politics by selecting only prisoners of **communist** countries, or Western ones. He recommended that one prisoner from each "Group of Three" be from a communist country, one from a **capitalist** country, and one from a country that was not allied with either the United States or the Soviet Union.

"Groups of Three" began forming throughout Europe. The Appeal seemed as if it had the potential to become a permanent organization. By involving more people, Benenson decided, more work could be done. The work of publicizing the plights of the prisoners was the key to winning their release. In the summer of 1961, representatives from six European nations created Amnesty International as a permanent body. They wrote letters to governments everywhere in the world, asking for copies of their laws, questioning the legal rights of citizens and prisoners in their countries, and asking for travel visas to attend trials of "political enemies of the states."

As knowledge about political prisoners spread throughout Europe and the United States, Benenson decided to take advantage of the momentum. He wrote a book, *Persecution 1961*, about nine political prisoners. He arranged for large-scale demonstrations to commemorate Human Rights Day, December 10. At St. Martin in the Fields Cathedral in London, two famous performers, the singer Cy Grant and the actress Julie Christie, were tied together with handcuffs made of rope. A candle wrapped in barbed wire was lit, and the flame was used to burn through the handcuffs and "release" the prisoners. Benenson chose one prisoner, Christopher Payi, in prison in the Portuguese colony of Guinea, in Africa, to represent all prisoners of conscience at the ceremony. Payi was released shortly after Human Rights Day.

Amnesty International grew tremendously during its first few years. Benenson ran the day-to-day operations from his London office, and he also traveled to other countries to establish chapters of the organization there. The research branch collected information on more than 1,200 prisoners. A number of countries proclaimed amnesty for political prisoners, including Czechoslovakia, Ireland, France, Ghana, the Sudan, and Yugoslavia. Benenson did not allow Amnesty International to take credit for these amnesties. He saw how much work remained, and how hard Amnesty International would have to work to protect prisoners of conscience in the future. Benenson remained with Amnesty International for a few more years, until differences with other leaders led him to resign. The organization that originally grew out of his vision on the Underground is more active than ever today. It produces reports on most countries of the world, and has chapters all around the globe. Its symbol, the candle surrounded by barbed wire, is recognizable everywhere. The work that Peter Benenson began in 1961 is still going strong.

Biko, Steven

(1946–1977)

SOUTH AFRICAN BLACK CONSCIOUSNESS ACTIVIST

Black consciousness is in essence the realization by the black man of the need to rally together with his brothers around the cause of their sub-jection—the blackness of their skin—and operate as a group in order to rid themselves of the shackles that bind them to perpetual servitude . . . It seeks to infuse the black community with a newfound pride in themselves, their efforts, their value systems, their culture, their religion, and their outlook to life. The interrelationship between the consciousness of self and the emancipatory programme is of paramount importance.

—Steven Biko, speaking of his Black Consciousness philosophy

Steven Biko is remembered both for his call to South African blacks to take pride in themselves and not rely on whites for **liberation** (freedom), and for his gruesome death at the hands of South African police. His life story was told in the 1987 movie *Cry Freedom*.

Biko grew up in King William's Town, on South Africa's east coast. His mother worked as a housemaid, and his father was a clerk. In 1963, Biko was expelled from high school because his older brother had been thrown in prison by the South African police for op-posing **apartheid** (the strict separation of people based on their race). Biko was then sent to St. Francis College as a boarding student, and after he graduated in 1966 he enrolled in the University of Natal's black medical section. He was one of the first South African blacks allowed to study at a large South African university.

Biko became active in the anti-apartheid struggle, and became one of its leaders when the African National Congress (ANC) was banned and its head, Nelson Mandela, was imprisoned by the government. Biko became a member of the National Union of South African Stu-dents (NUSAS), to which both whites and blacks belonged. Biko soon became frustrated with the NUSAS, which he saw as all talk and no action. He also criticized the blacks in the organization for letting liberal whites speak for them and tell them what to do. According to Biko, blacks in South Africa would gain true freedom only if they relied on their own leaders and their own community. Biko started the Black Consciousness movement in South Africa, arguing that blacks had to break out of the psychological prison of thinking themselves inferior to whites. He founded the all-black South African Students' Organization in 1969, and told the anti-apartheid whites that their job in the movement was to prepare other whites for black rule. At first, many whites were hurt by Biko's rejection of their help, but later they understood that blacks did need to control their struggle if they were ever to rule the country.

Biko spread his message of black self-reliance around the country. The South African government tried to stop him by forbidding him from leaving King William's Town and from seeing more than one person at a time. His words could not be repeated in the press. However, the government succeeded only in making Biko famous around the world. He wrote pamphlets that were sent throughout the country, and gave interviews to foreign journalists. The United States government told South Africa that before relations between the two countries could improve, the South African prime minister had to meet with Biko, among others. But South Africa did not give in to outside pressure. Instead, the government imprisoned Biko for 137 days without charging him or holding a trial.

Biko's philosophy of black consciousness was put into practice in 1976. The South African government forced black schools to teach some of their classes in Afrikaans, the language of the Afrikaner rulers of South Africa. The black students protested that Afrikaans was a language of oppression, and anyway, English was far more useful. When the government refused to take back the order, black students took to the streets of Soweto township, outside the large city of Johannesburg. The police killed a thirteen-year-old girl, sparking black demonstrations all over the country. The police again responded violently, killing hundreds of blacks. Many of them were schoolchildren.

Biko was arrested again in August 1977. He was taken to a police station in the city of Port Elizabeth. The police stripped him naked, saying it was so that he did not hang himself. Biko was tortured and interrogated from September 6 until he died sometime before the announcement of his death on September 13. The South African government implied that he had died because of a hunger strike. Protests came in from all over the world. Biko had weighed more than two hundred pounds. How could he have died of malnutrition in less than a week? Furthermore, Biko had told his friend, white journalist Donald Woods, that he would never go on a hunger strike. An autopsy revealed head injuries, which the police said Biko suffered when he attacked them.

The South African government tried to stop the protests over Biko's death by holding a hearing to see if his captors had killed him. Despite overwhelming evidence that Biko had been murdered, all of the policemen and the doctors who examined him after his death were found not guilty. Afraid of increasing unrest, the South African government cracked down on the anti-apartheid protesters by declaring the South African Students' Organization illegal, and by jailing prominent black leaders. The United Nations then put into place a worldwide prohibition on sending arms to South Africa.

Biko's death provided the anti-apartheid movement with a symbol and a martyr, while his life, and his thinking, helped shape the struggle that finally toppled apartheid in 1994. *See* MANDELA, NELSON

Blum, Léon

(1872–1950)

FRENCH SOCIALIST AND HUMANIST

In critical times men can save their lives only by risking them.
—Léon Blum, on the importance of following one's conscience

On February 13, 1936, Léon Blum was riding in a car that unfortunately turned down a street where a **fascist** demonstration was taking place. Blum, who was sixty-three years old, was recognized by the mob as the leader of the French **socialist** movement. He had spent his life fighting for democracy and against **fascism**, which sought to replace the voting power of the people with the **dictatorship** of one leader. He was pulled from the car and beaten until he was unconscious. Four months later, Blum became the first Jewish person ever to be elected premier of France. His government was toppled by the **Nazi** invasion in 1940, and he was imprisoned in a concentration camp. After the war, he led the French provisional government and helped to rebuild the French economy.

Blum was born in Paris in 1872, the second of five sons of a silk and ribbon manufacturer and his liberal wife. The Blums were Jewish, and they believed that education was the best way for France's Jews to become good French citizens. Blum's mother's mother had owned a bookstore, and she held salon (gatherings of intellectual people) discussion groups for the exchange of radical ideas. Blum excelled in school, and he was expected by his family to become a great lawyer or a great writer. He entered the top private school in Paris, the École Normale Supérieure, in 1890, and met many of the future leaders in French government, industry, and the arts. He failed two exams, however, and transferred to the Sorbonne, where he received a law degree with highest honors in 1894. During this time, Blum attended the literary salons of Paris, and met a number of famous authors. He began to make a name for himself as a writer and an intellectual. He wrote magazine articles, poems, and works of literary criticism. He loved the theater, and wrote the horseracing column for *La Revue Blanche*, a rather elite French magazine. He wrote articles on law and politics, and became interested in **socialism** after the librarian at the École Normale had introduced him to that movement. He was exposed to **anti-Semitism** during the Alfred Dreyfus affair (1894–1899), in which a Jewish French army captain was accused of spying. France was split by this affair, with the liberals on one side and the anti-Semitic right wing on the other. The liberal writer Émile Zola wrote a famous public letter in 1898, in which he accused the French military of framing Dreyfus as an excuse to attack Jews and liberals and to set up a military dictatorship to replace the republic. Zola was accused of **libel** (telling public lies), and ordered to stand trial. Blum assisted Zola at the trial, but it soon became obvious that it would be impossible for Zola to receive a fair trial. Zola fled to

England, and Blum then knew for certain what his political path would be.

Blum saw that the socialists were the ones who had fiercely de-'fended Dreyfus, even before he was proved innocent in 1899, and Blum became a devoted follower of the socialist Jean Jaurès. Blum met Jaurès in 1897, and was deeply influenced by his strong personality, as well as his interpretations of the work of the political philosopher and socialist Karl Marx. Jaurès was impressed by Blum, and he urged Blum to run for public office. However, Blum felt that his family, consisting of his wife, Lise Bloch, whom he had married in 1896, and a son, would suffer if he entered politics. He also saw himself as an author, not a political **activist**.

Blum wrote several books as a young man. One of them, *Marriage*, published in 1907, gave the then-shocking opinion that women should have sex before marriage. Many of his other writings were equally controversial. After insulting a playwright, Blum fought the man in a duel in 1912. Blum entered politics in 1914, after his mentor, Jaurès, was assassinated for his opposition to World War I. Blum took over the leadership of the French socialist party, and he opposed the view that the government had to be overthrown. Instead of having a revolution, as occurred in Russia in 1917, Blum believed that socialists could take power peacefully and legally in European countries. In 1919, Blum was elected to the French Parliament, and in 1921 he was elected head of the French socialist party (SFIO). In 1921, the SFIO split over whether to join the **communist** third international party. Blum led the group that did not wish to join an organization that supported revolution. He founded a socialist newspaper, *L'Humanité*, which became a powerful political force in France.

In Parliament, Blum opposed the ruling parties, and was defeated by the communists in 1928. One year later, he was reelected in a different district. During the 1930s, as fascism spread throughout Germany and Italy, it appeared that France might be next. Blum and the communist leaders formed a "Popular Front" against fascism in 1934. Following the attack on Blum's life in February 1936, the Popular Front won a landslide victory in the June 1936 elections. Blum became premier of France, the first Jew and the first socialist to hold that office. Blum settled workers' strikes, and he enacted laws that protected and strengthened workers' rights. These included the forty-hour work week, paid vacations, and the right to form unions. He fought fascism by **nationalizing** the weapons industry, and dissolving the fascist organizations. During the **Spanish Civil War**, which started in July 1936, Blum declared that France would remain neutral. His opponents on the right accused him of secretly supplying weapons to the Spanish anti-fascist Loyalists, and the communists accused him of not helping them. Additionally, big business disliked Blum for his laws to help workers. All this opposition forced Blum to resign in the summer of 1937. When Adolf Hitler marched into Austria on March 12, 1938, Blum again became head of the government when the premier resigned. Blum tried to unite France against fascism, but he was unable to form a stable government. When World War II broke out in 1939, Blum declared that both fascism and communism were dangerous for France. In June 1940, the Nazis invaded France and set up a fascist government, led by Marshal Pétain, in Vichy. Pétain arrested Blum and put him on trial. Blum was then sent to Buchenwald concentration camp until the Nazi defeat in 1945. While in Buchenwald, Blum, at age seventy-three, wrote *For All Mankind*, his political testament that tried to combine socialism with **humanism**. Upon his release, he visited the United States to negotiate economic help for France, and in December 1946 and January 1947 he headed a temporary French government that helped to put into place the fourth French republic.

Throughout his life, Blum engaged in political compromise to try to achieve his goals. He himself recognized his weaknesses as a politician when he said, "For thirty years I have done precisely that thing for which I was least fitted. What I really love is solitude and books." Despite this, he served the French people, his Jewish roots, and freedom-loving people everywhere with his courage and brilliance. When he died in 1950, the people of Paris took to the streets to pay their respects. The funeral procession was led by hundreds of mine workers, wearing mining helmets with the lights on. This symbolized the leadership Blum had shown in helping the working people of France earn a decent living and have the time to enjoy it.

Bonhoeffer, Dietrich

(1905–1945)

GERMAN THEOLOGIAN

Dietrich Bonhoeffer was a German Lutheran pastor and **theologian** (religious thinker). He was arrested and sent to Buchenwald concentration camp in 1943 by the **Nazi** government for plotting to kill Adolf Hitler, Germany's leader. He was hanged by the Nazis in 1945.

Bonhoeffer was born in the German town of Breslau in 1905. He studied religion in Berlin and New York, and was influenced by his German teacher Karl Barth. Religion, to Bonhoeffer, had to be something *lived*, not just written, preached, and thought about. He began his ministry in the 1930s, at the same time that Hitler began ruling Germany. Bonhoeffer joined the "confessing Church," a group of Lutherans opposed to the evils of Hitler and his regime. He taught theology in Berlin, but he fled to the United States in 1939 so that he would not have to serve in the German army. A month later, however, he returned to Germany. According to Bonhoeffer, being a true Christian meant fighting Hitler, not escaping him. He joined a group of people who were plotting to overthrow Hitler, and he continued writing about the duties of a Christian. In 1943, he was arrested for taking part in a plot to kill Hitler. While in prison, he wrote letters and diaries, which were eventually published after his death. He condemned the organized churches of his day, because they had not taken a stand against Hitler. He felt that human beings had to create a religion that did not rely on a supernatural God to make them behave. He was hanged by the Nazis in 1945, shortly before Hitler took his own life. Bonhoeffer's life, even more than his writings and preaching, had a huge impact on Christianity in the second half of the twentieth century.

Bonner, Yelena

(1923–   )

RUSSIAN HUMAN RIGHTS ACTIVIST

Yelena Bonner, the wife of 1975 Nobel Peace Prize winner Andrei D. Sakharov, fought for **human rights** within the Soviet Union from the 1960s until the collapse of the Soviet Union in the late 1980s. Despite constant harassment by the KGB (the Soviet secret police), and ill health, Bonner was able to serve as Sakharov's contact with the outside world, and she received the Nobel Peace Prize in his name in 1975.

Bonner was born in Moscow in 1923. Both of her parents were active in the **Communist** Party of the Soviet Union. When Bonner was fourteen, both of her parents were arrested during the dictator Joseph Stalin's purges (attempts to rid the country of those who did not believe in or follow his philosophy). Her father was killed, and her mother was imprisoned until 1954. Bonner and her brother moved in with their aunt and uncle, but they, too, were soon purged. The children were raised by their grandmother, and Bonner worked as a maid and a file clerk while in high school. In 1940, she became involved with Communist Party youth groups, and she volunteered for the army after Germany's leader, Adolf Hitler, invaded the Soviet Union with his army in 1941. She was injured in the war, and nearly lost all her vision. She finished World War II as a lieutenant. After spending two years struggling to regain her sight, Bonner enrolled in medical school in Leningrad (now St. Petersburg). There she met her first husband and had two children. Following her graduation, she worked as a pediatrician (children's doctor), and then in Iraq as a foreign-aid health worker. She also edited a book of poems of Vsevolod Bagritsky, her first love, who had died in World War II.

In 1965, Bonner joined the Communist Party only after it denounced (condemned) Stalin. She wrote that she never believed that her parents had done anything wrong, and never forgave Stalin for what he had done. Also in 1965, she separated from her husband and began pursuing political interests. When the Soviet Union invaded Czechoslovakia in 1968, she began to oppose the Communist Party.

She started publishing underground (secret) newspapers, and she met fellow **dissident** Andrei Sakharov at the trial of another dissident in 1970. They were married in 1971, and Bonner resigned from the Communist Party.

For the next fifteen years, Bonner and Sakharov were harassed by the KGB for their work to end human rights abuses in the Soviet Union. They were spied on by secret police, questioned endlessly about their work, prohibited from attending dissident trials, forbidden from owning a telephone, and not allowed to travel within or outside the country. They formed a watchdog group in Moscow, along with other dissidents, to monitor the human rights abuses in the Soviet Union. They often used the hunger strike as a means of political protest, for the couple was well known in the West and it would have been a great embarrassment to the Soviet government had they been allowed to die of hunger. Several times, Bonner and Sakharov were taken to a hospital and force-fed to end their strikes. Alone among the dissidents, Bonner was not arrested. She reported that she was spending her political prisoner's day all by herself, because all the people who had protested against the holding of political prisoners had become political prisoners themselves.

Bonner had to fight to receive the exit visas (a special form of passport) she needed to travel to Europe and the United States for medical treatment. On one of her trips, in 1975, she was in Italy when the Nobel Committee announced that her husband had won the Peace Prize. She traveled to Norway to accept it in his name, and she put the $143,000 prize money in a Western bank, so the KGB would not confiscate it.

Sakharov was **exiled** to Gorky in 1980, and he was not allowed to leave that city. Bonner visited him frequently and carried his messages to the world. On one trip to the United States, she managed to write her memoirs in a hospital bed while recovering from heart surgery. In 1984, Bonner was arrested by the KGB as an evil influence on her husband, and she was sentenced to internal exile in Gorky, along with her husband. She received a travel visa in 1985, after another hunger strike, and while in the United States she met with government officials and received a pledge from President Ronald Reagan that he would do everything he could to free Sakharov. On the same trip she met with British Prime Minister Margaret Thatcher and French President François Mitterand.

In 1986, one day after their first telephone was installed, Bonner and Sakharov received a phone call from Soviet Premier Mikhail Gorbachev, doing away with their exile and inviting them back to Moscow, to live as free citizens. The couple returned to Moscow and threw themselves once again into human rights work. Their efforts paid off. Many dissidents were released from Soviet jails, and those Soviet citizens who wished to **emigrate** (leave the country) were being allowed to do so. In 1989, shortly before his death, Sakharov was elected to the Congress of People's deputies. Yelena Bonner has continued to represent courage and strength in the face of great opposition. In January 1995, Bonner asked U.S. President Bill Clinton to pressure Russian President Boris Yeltsin to stop his military attacks on Chechnya, a breakaway Russian republic. *See* SAKHAROV, ANDREI; SHARANSKY, NATAN

BOOTH FAMILY

Booth, William

(1829-1912)

Booth, Catherine

(1829–1890)

Booth, Evangeline Cary

(1865–1950)

Booth, Catherine Bramwell

(1883–1987)

FOUNDERS AND LEADERS OF THE SALVATION ARMY

Catherine and William Booth founded the Salvation Army in the 1850s. Catherine's parents were deeply religious, and they taught her at home due to her ill health. In 1844, when Catherine was fifteen, her family moved to London. She joined the Wesleyan Methodist Church and met William Booth at a prayer meeting. They eventually married, and Catherine convinced her husband to leave the comforts of the Methodist Church. Instead, she urged, he should teach the gospel of Christianity to the poor people living in the slums and on the streets of London. They began preaching on street corners and formed what they called a "Hallelujah Band" from among former criminals. They founded the Salvation Army, combining ministry and charity work in what they saw as a war on poverty and immorality. Catherine Booth worked especially to improve the lives of women and children, and her husband helped turn the Salvation Army into a large international organization. All eight of their children became Salvationists. One of the most prominent was Evangeline Cary Booth.

Evangeline, born in 1865, was William's favorite child. She was very much like him in her ability to attract crowds and win people's attention. She worked in the slums of London, and the poor people there called her "the White Angel." At the age of fifteen, she became a sergeant in the Salvation Army, and two years after that she was made a captain. Like a regular army, the Salvation Army promoted its "soldiers" because of their service to the cause. Eventually, Evangeline was given charge of the entire London operation.

In 1895, she traveled to Canada. She commanded the Salvation Army in Canada for nine years, including a mission to the Klondike gold fields. She then took charge of the Salvation Army's American operations. She helped it expand until it became one of the country's biggest charity organizations. One of her most important contributions was making the organization more like a democracy, and less like a real army. In 1934, she was made general of the International Salvation Army, a position she held until her retirement five years later. She moved to the United States, where she lived until her death in 1950.

Catherine Bramwell Booth, born to Bramwell and Florence Booth in 1883, was the granddaughter of William and Catherine. She grew up in the East End of London, the city's worst slum. Her parents worked for the Salvation Army; her mother managed a home for prostitutes who were trying to change their lives. Catherine studied, and later taught, at the Salvation Army Training College. During World War I, she became international secretary for the Salvation Army in Europe, and following the war she led relief efforts for children in need. As leader of Women's Social Work from 1926 to 1937, she helped unmarried women and abused children. She worked with needy children after World War II as well, and after her retirement from the Salvation Army she wrote biographies of her grandmother and father. In 1978, she was given the Best Speaker award by the Guild of Professional Toastmasters, a tribute to her witty and moving stories. On her one hundredth birthday, she was interviewed on English television, touching the hearts of millions. She lived to be 104. Her work, and the work of her entire family, has given hope and a fresh start to millions of people around the world since the 1850s.

Breytenbach, Breyten

(1939–   )

SOUTH AFRICAN POET, PAINTER, AND ACTIVIST

> I'd never reject Afrikaans as a language, but I reject it as part of the
> Afrikaner political identity. I no longer consider myself an
> Afrikaner. Actually, I prefer to consider myself a citizen of the
> world. I feel at home in Paris. I'm a Parisian! But Afrikaans—I've
> long felt there was hope for it only if it were used in resistance to
> apartheid, but I think it is now too late. For blacks, it is a denial of
> reality and a humiliation.
>
> —Breyten Breytenbach, on the language of apartheid

Breyten Breytenbach is the most famous living writer using the
Afrikaans language, the tongue of the white settlers who came to
South Africa in the seventeenth century. Based on Dutch, Afrikaans
is perceived in South Africa as the language of **apartheid,** oppression
of blacks and other nonwhites. Breytenbach was imprisoned in South
Africa for more than seven years for his activities against the state.
Breytenbach continues to write in Afrikaans, but he rejects the label
"Afrikaner," and prefers to think of himself as "albino," rather than
"white."

Breytenbach's family were Afrikaner farmers who lived in the
wheat- and wine-growing region of the Cape Province. One of his
brothers became "a trained [and enthusiastic] killer" in a South
African anti-**guerrilla** unit, while another became a reporter with
ties to the secret police. Breytenbach himself began to question his
family's **racist**, right-wing beliefs when he attended the English-
language University of Cape Town. He studied poetry there until
1959, when, at the age of twenty, he traveled to Europe on a freight
ship. He took many jobs in Europe to support himself in his travels,
including one as a cook on a private yacht in France. He settled in
Paris in 1961. He taught English, and also began to paint. He married
Yolande Ngo Thi Hoang Lien, the daughter of a man who had once
been South Vietnam's finance minister.

Breytenbach became a successful painter, exhibiting his work
throughout Europe. His poetry, written in Afrikaans, began attracting

the attention of South African audiences. His first book of poems was titled *The Iron Cow Must Sweat* (1964), and, along with a collection of short stories, this won him the Afrikaans Press Corps prize. He won many other South African literary prizes during the 1960s and 1970s, and during that time he began to show the influence of Senegalese poet and statesman Léopold Senghor and other poets of the **négritude** (French black consciousness) movement. Breytenbach tried to return to South Africa to collect prizes in 1967 and 1969, but was refused an entry visa for his wife because she was nonwhite. He himself was threatened with arrest in South Africa for violating the country's Immorality Act by marrying a nonwhite. Finally, in 1973, the couple were granted three-month visas. During their trip, Breytenbach told a group of Afrikaner writers that they were doomed because of their isolation from the rest of the world. "Do something," he thundered at them. The government informed Breytenbach that he was no longer welcome in South Africa.

Breytenbach joined the illegal African National Congress (ANC), and founded an organization that provided white militants with basic training outside of South Africa to help them fight apartheid once they returned. Breytenbach went back to South Africa in 1975, in disguise and traveling under a false passport, to make contact with radical trade unionists. The South African security forces had known that he was coming, and they arrested him at the airport just before his flight back to France. He was accused under the Terrorism Act, and might have received the death penalty had not certain documents "miraculously disappeared," according to his friend and fellow writer André Brink. Instead, Breytenbach agreed to apologize for what he had done if the others arrested with him were set free, and if he were given only five years in prison. The government did not honor this deal, however, and sentenced him to nine years in jail.

Breytenbach spent the next two years in solitary confinement. He hallucinated that he was sharing his cell with the nineteenth-century Russian novelist Fyodor Dostoevsky, who had also been imprisoned. While in prison, Breytenbach wrote poems and his memoirs, *The True Confessions of an Albino Terrorist*, and they reached the world despite the South African **censors**. He continued to win international literary prizes, and after two years he was moved to a much more comfortable prison. In 1982, he was suddenly set free, and was allowed to fly to Paris. He has continued to write in Afrikaans, al-

though he feels that it can never be a language of world literature after its connection with apartheid. He returned to South Africa in 1986 to receive a literature prize and mocked the contribution of the Afrikaner heritage to the world: "Erecting and enthroning racism as an ideal state and then, as a sacrament to this idolatry, apartheid."
See BIKO, STEVEN; MANDELA, NELSON

Bukovsky, Vladimir

(1942–   )

RUSSIAN DISSIDENT AND HUMAN RIGHTS ACTIVIST

> Our society is still sick. It is sick with the fear that we inherited from the time of Stalin's terror. But the process of society's spiritual regeneration has begun and there is no stopping it.
>
> —Vladimir Bukovsky, on the rebirth of human rights in Russia

Vladimir Bukovsky was imprisoned by the Soviet Union for a total of eleven years between 1963 and 1976 for his **human rights** protests. During this time he managed to inform the world about the abuses of psychiatry in the Soviet Union, where former "political prisoners" were said to have become "criminally insane."

Bukovsky was born in 1942 into a home soon torn by divorce. He lived with his mother, who in 1972 expressed amazement that her son had become such a rebel. She described herself to an Amnesty International worker as "a hen who has given birth to an eagle." Bukovsky, the "eagle," first got in trouble for publishing a satirical magazine while in high school. He was suspended, but allowed to graduate. He was expelled from Moscow University, where he was studying physics, for behavior that did "not correspond to the character of a Soviet student." The activities of which he was guilty included praising abstract art, reading poetry in public, and behaving like a Westerner.

Bukovsky was first arrested in 1963 for owning two copies of a banned (forbidden) book. He was placed in solitary confinement in a Moscow prison, where in his interrogation he refused to name the person who gave him the book and helped him to copy it. He was declared mentally ill and sent to a hospital for the criminally insane in Leningrad (now St. Petersburg). Bukovsky discovered that because Soviet Premier Nikita Khrushchev had announced in 1959 that there were no longer any political prisoners in the Soviet Union, those who were held by the state for their political activities had to be called something else. Soviet psychiatrists were told that opposing the state was a form of mental illness, and they were ordered to "cure" **dissidents** (those who disagreed with state policies) with dangerous, mind-altering drugs. Bukovsky himself was not treated with the drugs, but he witnessed a number of his fellow dissidents "turned into vegetables," as he later said, with the drugs.

Bukovsky was released in February 1965, and in December of that year he led the first student demonstration in the Soviet Union since 1927, to protest the arrests of two dissidents. He was arrested, but the psychiatrists who examined him in Leningrad refused to label him as mentally ill. Despite this, he was kept for "observation" in a psychiatric institute until Amnesty International obtained his release in August 1966.

Six months later Bukovsky was arrested again, this time for leading a demonstration against the imprisonment of political enemies of the state. He served three years in a labor camp, working as a carpenter. In 1970, he gave an interview to a correspondent for *The Washington Post* newspaper, in which he described the Soviet abuses of psychiatry. He also smuggled out of the Soviet Union case histories of the punishment of political prisoners. He was arrested for these acts, and sentenced to two years in prison, followed by five years in a hard-labor camp, and then five years in **exile**. He went on a hunger strike to protest the treatment of his fellow prisoners, so he was put into a solitary cell so he could not see what was going on. After two years, he moved to the hard-labor camp, where he wrote *A Dissident's Guide to Psychiatry* with another inmate. They smuggled the document out of the country, and it was published in England in 1975.

Through his writings and the work of Amnesty International, which stayed in touch with Bukovsky through his mother, the world came to know of Bukovsky. Famous American writers, actors, and union leaders signed petitions calling on the Soviet Union to release him. Andrei Sakharov suggested that Bukovsky be exchanged for a

communist political prisoner, Luis Corvalán Lepe, who was being held in Chile. In 1976, the exchange took place in Switzerland, a neutral country. Bukovsky's mother, sister, and a nephew were allowed to join him. It was the first public admission by the Soviet Union that it still held political prisoners.

Bukovsky became active in the international struggle to bring human rights to the Soviet Union. He supported an amendment to a U.S.–USSR trade bill that linked free trade with **emigration** rights for Soviet Jews. He lectured on the Soviet abuse of psychiatry, and urged Western psychiatrists to support honest Soviet ones. His book, *To Build a Castle: My Life as a Dissenter*, was published in 1978.
See BENENSON, PETER; SAKHAROV, ANDREI

Caldicott, Helen

(1938–   )

AUSTRALIAN PEDIATRICIAN AND ANTINUCLEAR ACTIVIST

> The incidence of congenital diseases and malignancies will increase in direct ratio to the radioactive contaminants polluting our planet. . . . I'm a conservative. . . . I'm for conserving lives.
>
> —Helen Caldicott, describing the medical effects
> of nuclear testing

Helen Caldicott is an Australian pediatrician (children's doctor) who has fought against nuclear testing and the spread of nuclear weapons as part of her campaign to save human lives. She organized successful opposition to French nuclear testing in the South Pacific, and also to the export of uranium. She breathed new life into an antinuclear organization, Physicians for Social Responsibility.

Caldicott was born on August 7, 1938, in Melbourne, Australia. At the age of fourteen, she was deeply impressed by *On the Beach,* a novel by Nevil Shute that explored the possibility of nuclear war and the destruction of life on Earth. In 1961, she graduated from Adelaide Medical School with degrees in medicine and surgery. She and her husband, whom she married in 1962, spent three years in Boston in the late 1960s, and returned to Adelaide in 1969. While she was pregnant with her first child, Caldicott began to have nightmares about a nuclear catastrophe killing her children. Caldicott worked in a hospital and almost died of hepatitis after pricking her finger with an infected needle. When she recovered, she "felt she owed the world something." She became a pediatrician, or children's doctor, and specialized in the study and treatment of cystic fibrosis, a fatal genetic disease that attacks the lungs and intestines. While directing a cystic fibrosis clinic, she became involved in what she called "the ultimate form of preventive medicine," the fight against nuclear weapons. She reasoned that nuclear radiation damages human genes, and helps cause diseases like cystic fibrosis. She led a popular campaign in Australia against French nuclear weapons testing in the South Pacific. She wrote letters to newspapers and appeared on television and radio, describing the high levels of radiation in Australian drinking water and the dangers this posed, especially to children. She organized protest marches, boycotts of French products, and even convinced postal workers to stop handling French mail. The first result of the protest was the 1972 election victory of the Labour Party, which opposed the testing. In 1973, the Labour government and the government of neighboring New Zealand took France to the World Court, and pressured France to stop above-ground nuclear testing.

In 1974, the Australian government began selling the highly radioactive element uranium on the world market. When Caldicott protested this time, she was not given time on television and radio. In this instance the issue was money for Australia, and the scientific and government communities did not want to stop selling the very profitable uranium. Caldicott was not discouraged. She took her case directly to the uranium miners, and she convinced them that their health was endangered. Even though they needed their jobs, Caldicott's warnings about the effects of uranium on their testicles, sperm, and children had a powerful effect. The Australian Council of Trade Unions voted in 1975 to refuse to mine, transport, or sell uranium.

In 1978, the Caldicotts moved permanently to the United States, where Helen took over the leadership of a tiny organization, Physicians for Social Responsibility (PSR). Following a nuclear accident at Three Mile Island in Pennsylvania in 1979, PSR took out an ad in the *New England Journal of Medicine*. Hundreds of doctors joined PSR immediately, and the organization quickly became a powerful antinuclear voice. Led by Caldicott, PSR attacked the nuclear power industry. A 1982 documentary film, *If You Love This Planet,* which featured Caldicott encouraging an audience to shut down a New York air command base, won an Academy Award. The U.S. Department of Justice called the movie "political propaganda" and demanded a list of all organizations that wanted to see it. Caldicott has criticized many U.S. presidents for their lack of interest in true nuclear arms reduction, and she even met privately with President Ronald Reagan for more than an hour, at his daughter's request.

Caldicott was nominated for the Nobel Peace Prize in 1985. She continues to spread the message of the danger of nuclear weapons and nuclear power. She gives lectures around the world, and tries to break through people's attitudes of denial about the threats that nuclear materials pose to planet Earth and its inhabitants. Her speeches are often very emotional. As she once noted, "To be unemotional about the end of the world is sick."

Cardenal, Ernesto

(1925–   )

NICARAGUAN POET, PRIEST, AND REVOLUTIONARY

> Manrique said our lives were rivers
> going down to the sea which is death
> but the death they flow down to is life.
> —Ernesto Cardenal, from a poem on revolution in Nicaragua

Ernesto Cardenal began his career writing violent revolutionary poetry and plotting to overthrow the Nicaraguan dictatorship of Anastasio Somoza. Later, after a spiritual struggle, he renounced violence and hatred in favor of love. He became a Catholic priest, and set up a Christian community in Nicaragua dedicated to simple living and service to others. When the Nicaraguan dictatorship was overthrown by the Sandinista rebels in 1979, Cardenal was named minister of culture.

Cardenal attended high school in Granada, Nicaragua, and at the age of eighteen left to study at the National University in Mexico.

When he was twenty-four, he received a doctorate (Ph.D.) in philosophy from Columbia University in New York City. He returned to Nicaragua, which was ruled by the ruthless **dictator** Anastasio Somoza. Somoza dealt with his political opposition through terror and brutality, hiring "death squads" to roam the countryside and murder his opponents. Cardenal wrote poetry about the revolution that he hoped would end Somoza's rule, and he joined secret groups plotting to overthrow him. One of these groups, Unidad Nacional de Accion Popular (National Union for Political Action), prepared an April 3, 1954, attack on Somoza's palace, but someone betrayed the group and gave its plans away to the National Guard. Cardenal was one of the only group members who was not caught and killed. He went into hiding, and he wrote one of his most famous poems, "La Hora 0" ("Zero Hour").

In 1956, Somoza was assassinated, but his son, Anastasio Somoza de Bayle, replaced him as dictator. Cardenal began to doubt the power of violence to bring about real change. He had a spiritual crisis, and decided to explore his religious longings at Thomas Merton's Trappist monastery in Kentucky. Merton, a Catholic priest and scholar, preached a nonviolent approach to social problems. Cardenal became a devoted follower of Merton, and he returned to Nicaragua determined to work for revolutionary change through love and nonviolence.

In 1957, Cardenal moved to a Benedictine monastery in Cuernavaca, Mexico. He wrote a book of poetry based on his experiences in Kentucky. In contrast to his early poems about violent struggle, the poems in *Gethsemane, Kentucky* focused on God's love for the entire universe. Cardenal also became interested in the history and culture of the communities who lived in Central America before the European invasion of the fifteenth and sixteenth centuries. The descendants of these people, the so-called "Indians" of Central America, were among the most oppressed peoples of the region. Cardenal wrote a poem titled "Lost Cities," which examined the destructive effects of European culture and modern **capitalism** on the Indians. He criticized Western culture in such poems as "Prayer for Marilyn Monroe."

Cardenal had been planning for many years to establish in Nicaragua a community like the Trappist monastery in Kentucky. In preparation, he entered La Ceja seminary in Colombia, South America, in 1961, and was ordained as a priest in Managua, Nicaragua, four years later. He spent much of this time researching the past and present culture of the Colombian Indians. In 1966, he established a Christian community near Managua. Called Solentiname, it provided Cardenal and his followers with the chance to live a life of hard manual labor, study, good deeds, quiet meditation, and poetic expression. Cardenal's research while at Solentiname focused on a comparison of the moneyless culture of the Inca Indians of Central America with the money-obsessed culture of modern capitalism. He increasingly saw capitalism as the biggest obstacle to freedom and happiness in Nicaragua.

In 1970, Cardenal visited Cuba, which had become the first **communist** country in Latin America, in 1959. He spent three months there, noting the successes and failures of Fidel Castro's revolution. He felt that the Cuban system of government had made many improvements in the lives of its citizens, but was doing some harm because it was not based upon Christian compassion. He called his trip to Cuba his "second conversion," and he returned to Solentiname determined to convert all of Nicaragua into a large version of his tiny Christian commune. While love and compassion were still at the core of his revolutionary philosophy, after he returned from Cuba his poetry had more violence in it. Cardenal came to believe that some violence would have to happen for society to change itself in important ways.

In 1972, a huge earthquake rocked Nicaragua. Pictures and stories of the suffering of the people of Managua and other cities moved many people around the world to send money, medicine, blankets, clothing, and other donations. It soon became widely known in Nicaragua that Somoza de Bayle was stealing the relief money and supplies. Popular anger against him turned into an unstoppable rage. Nicaragua was plunged into civil war, with the government fighting against the **Marxist** Sandinista rebels and more and more Nicaraguan people. In 1979, the Sandinistas overthrew Somoza and established a Marxist government in Nicaragua. Cardenal was appointed minister of culture. He was a strong supporter of the government in the beginning, and he compared the revolutionaries to Jesus in what was known as **liberation theology**: Just as Jesus had helped the poor and oppressed of his society, the job of Christians in the modern world, Cardenal believed, was to overthrow unjust governments and help the weak and downtrodden. In the early 1980s, the Sandinista government itself was found to be violating the **human rights** of the Nicaraguan Indians. Cardenal and the Nicaraguan Church stopped supporting the Sandinistas, and worked to help the oppressed people against their new government. Cardenal continues to use poetry to bring about social change, and to warn dictators of all types that the people will eventually rise up and overthrow the cruel and greedy.

Cassin, René

(1887–1976)

FRENCH HUMAN RIGHTS ADVOCATE AND LAWYER

All human beings are born free and equal in dignity and rights. They are endowed with reason and conscience and should act towards one another in a spirit of brotherhood.

—from the Universal Declaration of Human Rights

René Cassin is best remembered for his work on behalf of **human rights** for the United Nations (U.N.). He helped write the Universal Declaration of Human Rights in 1948, and participated in the founding of the United Nations Education, Scientific, and Cultural Organization (UNESCO). He worked for international human rights as a lawyer, serving as president of the European Court of Human Rights. He received the Nobel Peace Prize in 1968.

Cassin was born in France in 1887 into a distinguished Jewish family. One of his ancestors had been honored for his service in the Napoleonic wars. He studied in Nice, and attended the University of Aix-en-Provence to study law and humanities. In 1914, he was admitted to the Paris bar (passed exams to practice law). That same year, he fought with the French army in World War I, and was severely injured by German shrapnel in October 1914. He made a remarkable recovery, but was troubled by that injury for his whole life. He returned to France, married, and began teaching law courses and working for the victims of World War I. He helped set up the Federal Union, which provided services to veterans, the disabled, and widows. He taught law at the University of Lille and then at the University of Paris.

Cassin spent the years after World War I trying to organize former soldiers from different countries to work toward keeping the peace. Through the International Labor Organization, the League of Nations (the organization that later became the United Nations), and the Geneva Disarmament Conference, he worked to create a peaceful political climate in Europe. Cassin was also a committed Jew, very sympathetic to **Zionism** (a movement to establish a Jewish state in Palestine, the historical homeland of Jews), and when Adolf Hitler rose to power in Germany, Cassin fully supported confronting Hitler, even at the risk of going to war. When France was overrun by Germany in 1940, Cassin escaped to London and served in Charles de Gaulle's government-in-**exile**. The Vichy government that the Germans set up in France sentenced Cassin to death in 1942, but he responded by documenting war crimes by French Vichy leaders. He also became president of the Alliance Israélite, the major Jewish organization in France. After the war, Cassin returned to France and served in many important government posts.

Cassin worked on behalf of the U.N. to set up standards for human rights around the world. As vice-president of the U.N. Commission on Human Rights, he used his experience as a lawyer to draft the Universal Declaration of Human Rights in 1948. He tried to make sure that the terrible human rights abuses that had occurred in World War II would never be repeated. The **charter** prohibited countries from engaging in torture, slavery, arrest without a good reason, exile, and detention. It also guaranteed the rights of prisoners and people accused of crimes. Cassin was also concerned about economic, social, and cultural rights of U.N. member states. He helped form UNESCO to assure that these rights would be protected.

Cassin served on other international bodies. During the 1950s he sat on the Court of Arbitration in The Hague, Netherlands. He later presided over the European Court of Human Rights. Throughout his long career, he always insisted that human rights could and must be protected by international law. In 1968, Cassin was awarded the Nobel Peace Prize. He said in his acceptance speech that international bodies such as the U.N. had the responsibility to protect the human rights of individuals within a country. No country had the right to oppress its own citizens.

Cassin continued to work for human rights until he died. He sponsored a conference that led to the inclusion of important human rights provisions in the Helsinki Declaration of 1975. He published his memoirs in 1975, married for the second time in November, and died two months later.

Chai Ling

(1966-   )

LEADER OF CHINESE DEMOCRACY MOVEMENT

> This nation is our nation, these people are our people, this government is our government. If we do not speak, who will? If we do not act, who will?
>
> —Chai Ling, on bringing democratic principles to China

Chai Ling was one of the student leaders of the Chinese democracy movement that was crushed by the Chinese army in Tiananmen Square in 1989. She convinced the protesters to demonstrate peacefully and gave speeches encouraging them to remain firm. Now living in New Jersey, she continues to coordinate international efforts to bring democracy to China.

Chai was born in Shandong, China, in 1966. She grew up in a family that supported the Chinese government. Both of her parents are doctors for the Chinese army and are members of the Chinese **Communist** Party. She had no interest in protest politics until she attended Beijing University. There, she met young Chinese students who wanted to turn China into a democracy, instead of maintaining the communist dictatorship that has ruled the country since 1949. She went to demonstrations and she married an **activist**, Feng Congde.

She continued her studies in child psychology at Beijing Normal University, where she was studying when the sit-in in Tiananmen Square began.

Tiananmen Square is located in the center of Beijing, the capital and largest city in China. It is a large open space, and it seemed to be a perfect place to demonstrate and attract people's attention. In April 1989, three thousand students went on a hunger strike to protest government corruption and to demand democratic reforms. Many students joined the protest, including Chai, until the total number of protesters reached at least one million. Chai was moved to write a speech explaining the demands of the democracy movement. The speech was taken up as the official position of the demonstrators, and Chai was elected their leader. She later said that she had no intention of becoming a leader and was probably chosen for the reason that ". . . I had less ego than the men."

Chai worked to keep the protest peaceful. It was growing day by day, and was sparking other demonstrations all over China. If the students could remain nonviolent, perhaps the Chinese people would be inspired to join in the millions and force the present government to give up power. To avoid bloodshed, Chai negotiated with army troops sent in to stop the protests. She and other leaders walked among the demonstrators and convinced them to give up their bricks, guns, and homemade weapons. She later recalled, "At the last moment, I spoke to the students, reminding them that ours is a peaceful movement. We had the Goddess of Democracy, the beautiful statue that we made. To take up arms would turn it all into tragedy."

The Chinese government had no desire to avoid tragedy. They acted to stop the protest on June 3, 1989. The lights in the square were turned out, and suddenly gunfire was heard throughout the square. Tanks and soldiers attacked the protesters, killing many and wounding a lot more. They were looking for Chai and the other leaders, many of whom were caught. Chai and her husband escaped from the square and went into hiding for ten months. Hundreds of Chinese people helped her move around the country to flee the troops trying to capture her. On April 3, 1990, she and her husband appeared on French television, safely out of China.

Chai settled in New Jersey, while her husband moved to Boston; neither is sure if their marriage can survive the events they experienced. Chai's family still lives in China, and she fears for their safety.

She has become a visiting scholar at Princeton University, and is working on a book telling her side of the Tiananmen Square protest and massacre. She fights for the release of Chinese political prisoners, and hopes for the day that she can return to a democratic China. Her love of the Chinese people and her "poor, miserable country," as she puts it, give her strength as she faces long years of **exile**.

Chattopadhyay, Kamaladevi

(1903–1988)

INDIAN LEADER OF CRAFTS MOVEMENT

Traditional crafts reflect the landscape, the seasons, the moods of the day. Into the crafts are woven the epics, the legends, the romantic heroic tales of the countryside. They heighten the big events in human life: the wonder of birth, the joy of marriage, the mystery of death. In each event the crafts play a special role, for they live and grow and have their being in everyday life.

When we wander away from creation and fill it with sheer mechanics, we get out of our depth. The answer is creativity, not in the isolation of the poet in the ivory tower, but as part of a living community with a dynamic tradition. This is what the traditional crafts represent and bring home to us.

—Kamaladevi Chattopadhyay, on the importance of, and pride derived from, craft work

Kamaladevi Chattopadhyay founded the Indian Cooperative Union (ICU) in 1948, the year following India's independence from Great Britain. The ICU organized refugees and helped them build their own new cities, and provided markets and skills to hundreds of thousands of crafts people all over India. Chattopadhyay's work has become the model for craft **cooperatives** all over the world.

Chattopadhyay was born in Mangalore, India, in 1903. She began her schooling in her hometown. At the age of sixteen she got married, to the poet and playwright Harindranath Chattopadhyay. After studying in London, at Bedford College and the London School of Economics, she returned to India and became involved in the country's independence movement. She was elected to the All-India Congress in 1927, and led the women's branch of that organization. She was imprisoned by the British (who controlled India as a foreign colony at the time) four times between 1930 and 1942.

India won its independence from Britain in 1948. The country was divided into India, a mostly **Hindu** state, and Pakistan, a largely Muslim country. Terrible fighting broke out as the partition went into effect, and millions of refugees left their homes in both new countries and escaped to the other. Chattopadhyay founded the ICU in 1948 to provide housing and jobs for some of these refugees. The first cooperative was created in the city of Chattarpur, near the Indian capital of New Delhi. It helped local crafts people by providing them with loans, tools, and markets for their goods. It was part bank, part employer, part educator, and part social network. The cooperatives helped the refugees make new lives for themselves, and taught them the value, both economic and spiritual, of their handicrafts. They also allowed India to develop an economy that did not have to depend on the West for necessities of life.

Chattopadhyay helped build the city of Faridabad for 300,000 refugees. She established many large cooperatives for weavers and consumers. Once the refugees were able to settle into their new lives, Chattopadhyay had to find a way to sell the cloth and other crafts that they were making. She established the Cottage Industries Emporium, which marketed the crafts in India and around the world. More than seven hundred cooperatives used the Cottage Industries Emporium to sell their goods.

In 1952, Chattopadhyay was made Chairman of All-India Handicrafts Limited, and became vice-president of the World Crafts Council, which she had helped to create. Her belief that rural and city crafts people could lead happier, more productive lives by creating their own original handiwork than by laboring in a factory was proved correct by the success of the ICU. The monetary success of the ICU made it a model for cooperatives in developing countries all over the world.

Chattopadhyay has published books on **socialism**, Indian crafts, and American, Japanese, and Chinese society. She became the president of the Indian Theater Center, and from 1978 to 1980 she served as vice-president of the India International Center. Because of her dedication and vision, millions of people are leading creative, productive lives around the world through the pursuit of their own handicrafts heritage.

Chaudhary, Dilli Bahadur

(1970–   )

NEPALI HUMAN RIGHTS ACTIVIST

Dilli Chaudhary was born into the Tharu ethnic minority, in the Dang region of western Nepal. Most of the 400,000 Tharu are farm laborers, and 100,000 are enslaved, or bonded, laborers. They are working to pay off their or their families' debts, and almost never earn enough to win their freedom. Chaudhary, whose father was a government official, began working to help his fellow Tharus when he was only fifteen. One of the rituals of a traditional Tharu festival involves teenagers going from hut to hut, singing and dancing for coins. Chaudhary, who alone among them had gone to school, told them that instead of spending the money on Tharu beer, they should buy pens and paper, and he would teach them to read and write. Eight of them agreed, and so was born the Backward Society Education Organization (BASE), which is now dedicated to helping the bonded laborers and other poor workers learn about their rights and fight for a better life.

BASE quickly grew to become the largest and most important **human rights** organization in Nepal. More than one thousand people work for BASE, eighty-five thousand Nepalis are members, and twenty-five thousand students take part in BASE activities every year. The most important work is education. Although a law was passed in Nepal in 1992 that made bonded labor illegal, many farm owners and Nepali politicians look the other way, and most workers do not know about their rights. BASE conducts seminars and workshops all over Nepal, teaching the poor people that bonded labor is illegal. Another Nepali law states that no one in Nepal should be without his or her own land. People who can prove that they are landless are entitled to a small plot of land. BASE helps people go through the application process, and it helps them document their claims.

BASE has moved beyond human rights and land rights of bonded laborers. It conducts programs to teach people how to prevent the spread of AIDS (Acquired Immune Deficiency Syndrome), and offers courses in earning and saving money. Chaudhary has also moved BASE into direct action, including water irrigation programs so that the small farmers will be able to grow crops for food and sale, tree-planting programs to preserve the environment, and family planning services that provide sex education and **contraception** so that women can choose if and when they will have children. He also initiated the building of hospices (special hospitals for those who are dying) for children, and has started teaching poor Nepali children and adults how to read and write. Once community members are literate, they can use the information that BASE provides on health, cleanliness, and community building.

Once without power and without a voice, the poorest people in Nepal are becoming a strong political force, thanks to Chaudhary. The people who exploit the poor are aware of Chaudhary's influence. He has been threatened, harassed, and jailed a number of times. In 1993, he was arrested, but when two thousand people surrounded the prison where he was being held and protested, he was released unharmed. Wealthy landowners hired thugs to beat him up, but he was not seriously harmed.

Chaudhary has been offered prestigious jobs in other organizations in Nepal and around the world, but has decided to remain with BASE. He has been described as extremely modest, focusing attention away from himself and on to the work that BASE is doing. After traveling to the United States to receive the Reebok Foundation Youth-in-Action Award, he returned to his homeland and was given a medal by the king of Nepal, who pledged $200,000 in government money to end bonded labor in agriculture. At a very young age, Chaudhary has become one of the world's most effective, respected, and courageous **activists** for justice and hope.

Chazov, Yevgeni

(1929–   )

RUSSIAN PHYSICIAN AND ANTINUCLEAR ACTIVIST

> The world is closer to nuclear catastrophe today than it used to be.
> But I think more people are aware of the effects of nuclear war.
> And maybe that will restrain the politicians and the military.
>
> —Yevgeni Chazov, warning of the dangers of nuclear war

Yevgeni Chazov, personal doctor to three former Soviet premiers, and a high-ranking and honored member of the **Communist** Party in the 1970s and 1980s, decided in 1980 that it was ridiculous to work as a doctor to save people's lives when the government was actively pursuing technologies and policies that could kill every person on the face of the earth. He voiced his concerns to doctors from other countries, including Bernard Lown from the Harvard School of Public Health in the United States. In 1980, the two of them founded International Physicians for the Prevention of Nuclear War (IPPNW). In 1985, the IPPNW won the Nobel Peace Prize for its efforts to educate the world about the medical effects that a nuclear war would have on the human race.

Chazov was an unlikely nuclear **activist**. He had been a member of the Communist Party since 1962, and had never criticized Soviet policy. He was named a Hero of Socialist Labor, and won the Soviet Union's Lenin Prize three times. He directed the USSR Cardiology Research Center. As one of the world's leading cardiologists (heart specialist), he made frequent contact with doctors from Western countries. One of them, Bernard Lown, had become a close friend. They thought that it was ironic that their governments were supporting their work to save lives while both the United States and the Soviet Union were building more and more weapons of mass destruction. In 1980, the two friends decided to form an international organization of doctors who would oppose nuclear war.

They convened a meeting of six interested doctors from the Soviet Union and the United States in Geneva, Switzerland, in 1980. But the newly created IPPNW almost died before it was born. The Soviet delegation threatened to walk out of the talks many times. The two sides disagreed on almost everything, from the Soviet invasion of Afghanistan to the United States's policies in Central America. When they saw that they were getting nowhere, the participants decided on an important rule if IPPNW were to survive: no politics. They agreed that nuclear war was more of a threat to the world than anything else, and that their differences about other issues would not be discussed.

Unlike other Soviet officials who spoke in favor of peace, Chazov did not try to convince the world that the Soviet Union could be trusted with its nuclear weapons while the West could not. In his statement that the government and military needed to be "restrained," he attacked the official Soviet view that both of those institutions in the Soviet Union always acted responsibly. Chazov refused to criticize the West, and spread the antinuclear message as a doctor, not a Soviet propagandist. IPPNW focused on spreading information to the world about the medical consequences of nuclear war. The doctors explained the effects of a nuclear explosion, the radiation, the "nuclear winter" that would follow as the sun's light would be disrupted by all the floating debris, and the starvation that would result from an inability to grow crops in contaminated soil.

Chazov was one of a small group of Soviet citizens who had been allowed to travel to the West and meet its people. He felt that if the two superpowers (the Soviet Union and the United States) were to avoid nuclear war, it would be because their citizens trusted each other more than they believed their governments. He promoted the idea of citizens' exchanges, in which Soviets and Americans could meet each other as human beings. In the West, discussions of nuclear war were more common than in the Soviet Union and its satellites (countries under Soviet control). Chazov and Lown went on Soviet television and told viewers that the "official" Soviet position—that civil defense measures would protect them in case of nuclear war—was a lie. They also opposed the idea that nuclear weapons have prevented war by making it so dangerous. Chazov said in 1984, "We go against the theory of mutual nuclear destruction. We don't think that heaps of nuclear arms protect the world."

IPPNW grew quickly. Partly because it avoided political disputes, and partly because its message was so simple, within five years it was operating in forty-one countries, and had 135,000 members. In 1985, Chazov and Lown were honored when IPPNW was awarded the

Nobel Peace Prize in Geneva, Switzerland, where IPPNW was born. It was the first East-West citizens' group ever to win the prize.

Corrigan, Mairead

(1944–   )

and Williams, Betty

(1943–   )

IRISH PEACE ACTIVISTS

We are for life and creation and we are against war and destruction, and in our rage in that terrible week, we screamed that the violence had to stop.

—Betty Williams, on the continuing war in Northern Ireland

Mairead Corrigan and Betty Williams won the 1976 Nobel Peace Prize for their work in reducing the violence in Northern Ireland. The two women were brought together by the accidental killing of three children in fighting between the Irish Republican Army (IRA) and British forces in Belfast, the capital of Northern Ireland. Corrigan, a secretary, and Williams, a housewife, began a **grass-roots** campaign for peace that quickly swept the country.

Corrigan was born in Belfast to a poor, working-class Catholic family. She was one of seven children. Her father was a window washer, and he could not afford to send Mairead to Catholic school after she turned fourteen. She worked as a baby-sitter, and learned secretarial skills so that she could earn a living one day. She grew up disliking the IRA, which was made up of Northern Irish Catholics like herself and used terrorism to try and force the British to leave Northern Ireland, and she hated the British soldiers, who themselves used terror to control the Catholics.

At age sixteen, Corrigan became an assistant bookkeeper at a textile factory, and when she was twenty-one she got a job as a secretary at the Guinness brewery. She rose quickly at Guinness, and soon was the private secretary of the director. While she was working her way up the career ladder, she was also devoting her evenings to charity work for the Legion of Mary, a Catholic community organization. As a teenager, she led groups of poor children and teens in activities, and set up a nursery school.

In 1968–1969, violence broke out in Northern Ireland. Catholics protested for increased political rights, and the marches and demonstrations led to confrontations with the British. To protect themselves, members of the Protestant majority set up the Ulster Defense League. This organization and the IRA turned Belfast into a war zone. Each section of town was protected by its own small army, and all legal authority broke down. Corrigan spent much of 1969 working with the Legion of Mary to keep children safe from the fighting. She also visited prison camps in which Catholic revolutionaries were being held, and tried to turn the angry young men into **pacifists** (those advocating nonviolence). She became involved in the international religious community as well. In 1972, she attended a meeting of the World Council of Churches in Thailand, and in 1973 she traveled to the Soviet Union to make a documentary film for the Legion of Mary on religious life in that country.

Betty Williams was also born in Belfast, but her mother was Catholic and her father was Protestant. People in both communities saw this marriage as treasonous (a crime against the country), since the two religious groups had been enemies in Northern Ireland for centuries. Her mother's father was a Polish Jew whose family had been wiped out by the **Nazis**, and Williams learned from him and her father not to hate other people because of their differences. Her father once told her off because she described a girl she had met as a Protestant. Even though prejudice was everywhere around her, Betty Williams was raised to respect all people.

When Williams was thirteen, her mother suffered a stroke and could no longer move around. While her father worked in a butcher shop, Williams took care of the house and her younger sister. She attended Catholic schools, and learned secretarial skills as well. At the age of eighteen, she married an English Protestant, a merchant marine engineer. Because of his job, the couple traveled frequently, and Williams took an interest in world affairs. She resolved to work outside the home, and in 1976 she was working in a consulting firm by day and waiting on tables at a restaurant at night.

On August 10, 1976, an event occurred that brought Williams and Corrigan together. Eight years after the Catholics and Protestants had begun their civil war, an IRA getaway car swerved out of control when its driver was shot by British troops. The car ran over a Catholic mother, Anne Maguire, and her three children. The children were killed instantly. Williams had witnessed the accident. Anne Maguire was Corrigan's sister.

Williams was angered and horrified at what she had seen. That same day, she wrote a petition that demanded peace and walked all through her neighborhood collecting signatures. Two days later, she read the petition, which had six thousand signatures on it, on television. She asked all Irish women, Catholic and Protestant, to join her in a peace march in the area where the children had died. Corrigan heard her appeal, and she invited Williams to the children's funeral. Ten thousand women joined them on August 14 as they marched, singing and praying, to the children's graves. Members of the IRA attacked the demonstrators, especially the Protestants, but the women remained united.

Corrigan and Williams joined Ciaran McKeown, a politically clever reporter who was also a pacifist, and formed an organization to bring about peace in Northern Ireland. The organization was first named Women for Peace, and was later broadened be called the Community of Peace People. Thirty thousand people joined them on their third march, at the end of August, in which Catholic women crossed the dividing line and were welcomed by Protestant women. The three leaders devoted themselves to the cause full-time. They planned and led rallies, including one in London that included American folk singer Joan Baez. They traveled around the world, gaining support and collecting money. In October 1976, they visited the U.S. to convince Irish-Americans not to give their money to the IRA even if they supported their cause. The money, Corrigan and Williams explained, would still be used to kill people in Northern Ireland.

In just two months, Corrigan and Williams had created an international peace movement for Northern Ireland. Violence declined, mostly because fewer weapons were finding their way into Northern Ireland. The Community of Peace People started community projects designed to bring together Catholics and Protestants, and began rebuilding war-damaged schools and factories. They were leading candidates for the 1976 Nobel Peace Prize. There were two problems, however. They were too late to be nominated, since the deadline for the Nobel Committee was February 1. Also, for the past few years only political leaders had been awarded the prize. When it appeared that Corrigan and Williams would not receive it, groups in Norway created the Norwegian Peace Prize and awarded it, along with $340,000, to the two women. In October 1977, the same day the 1977 Nobel Prize was awarded to **Amnesty** International, Corrigan and Williams were given the 1976 prize, which had been held open for them. *See* BENENSON, PETER

Coudenhove-Kalergi, Count Richard Nicholaus

(1894–1972)

INTERNATIONALIST

> More terrifying than anything, perhaps for centuries to come, is the awakening of the aggressive tendency of nationalism.
> —Count Coudenhove-Kalergi, on the dangers of nationalism.

Count Richard Nicholaus Coudenhove-Kalergi was the leader of the movement to create a "United States of Europe," or Pan-Europe. He believed that **nationalism**, or extreme pride and identification with one's own national group, would lead the world into terrible war and suffering. The two world wars of the twentieth century convinced many people that he was right, and many of his ideas were at the center of the attempts at European unification going on in the 1990s.

Coudenhove-Kalergi was not only a believer in **internationalism**, he was also a living example of it. On his father's side, the Couden- hoves were Fleming nobles who could trace their title to the 1099 crusade, and the Kalergis were Greek-Russians. His mother was an upper-class Japanese woman fifteen years younger than her husband. Coudenhove-Kalergi was born in Tokyo, where his father was working in the Austro-Hungarian embassy. He grew up in Bohemia, in his family's ancestral Ronsberg Castle. In the household were people of nine different nationalities. His father, who spoke sixteen languages, taught him Russian and Hungarian, as well as philosophy and politics. When Coudenhove-Kalergi was twelve, his father died, and he was raised as an Austrian Catholic by his strict mother.

He graduated from the Theresianische Akademie in Vienna in 1913, and received his doctorate (Ph.D.) in philosophy in 1917. While living in Vienna before and during World War I, he became frightened by the **anti-Semitic** nationalism of the Austrian middle class. Many Austrians wished to combine with Germany to form Pan-Germany, and saw the Jews as enemies of a united German people. When the League of Nations was created after World War I, Coudenhove-Kalergi felt "conscious of being a citizen of the world," as he described it.

The League of Nations was not able to keep the peace in Europe. Coudenhove-Kalergi became convinced that only a united Europe—with a single army, currency, bank, government, and transportation system—could avoid living under what he termed "the law of the jungle." He failed to interest European leaders in the idea of a Pan-Europe, and he decided to create it on his own. He published a book, *Pan-Europe*, in 1923. It was soon translated into most European languages. He traveled around Europe, gaining supporters, and in 1926, called the first Pan-European congress in Vienna, where he was elected president of the Pan-European Union.

The rise of **Nazism** in Germany caused Coudenhove-Kalergi to temporarily abandon his dreams of a unified Europe. Instead, he led his organization to fight German nationalism and Hitlerism, and tried to convince Italy's dictator, Benito Mussolini, to fight against Hitler. As German armies marched across Europe, Coudenhove-Kalergi was forced to flee to the United States. He led the movement to unite Europe following the war, and he gained the support of leaders such as Great Britain's Prime Minister Winston Churchill.

Coudenhove-Kalergi wrote many books on the subject of internationalism. He was nominated for the Nobel Peace Prize in 1931, 1945, and 1949. Near the end of his life, he worked to turn the European Common Market into a political organization. The efforts to create a unified Europe that began in the 1980s and continue to this day are a direct result of the work of Coudenhove-Kalergi, who envisioned a world without national divisions, in which all people could live in harmony as "citizens of the world."

Courtney, Kathleen

(1878–1974)

IRISH FEMINIST AND PACIFIST

Dame Kathleen Courtney devoted the first part of her life to the **suffragist movement** (giving women the right to vote) in Great Britain. Once this right was won, she became active in the international peace movement. She helped draw up the United Nations **charter** in 1945, and chaired the British branch of the United Nations Association. She was made a Dame of the British Empire in 1952.

Courtney was born in Dublin in 1878. Her father was a major in the British army. She attended Oxford University, where she studied foreign languages. While at Oxford, she joined the suffragette movement, and led the Oxford branch of the National Union of Women's Suffrage Societies for three years. She traveled to The Hague, Netherlands, for a Women's Congress in 1915, and helped form the Women's International League for Peace. She was chairperson of the British branch of this organization for ten years.

When World War I broke out in 1914, Courtney decided that she had to do something to help the innocent victims. She helped Serbian refugees, and worked with the Quakers to bring aid to people in Austria, Poland, and Greece. Following the war, she threw herself into the work of the League of Nations, the international body whose job it was to prevent future wars. In 1939, she became vice-chairperson of the British League of Nations Union. During World War II she worked for the British government. She traveled around the United States twice, giving speeches for the British Ministry of Information. When the war ended, she participated in the creation of the United Nations, the new international organization that would try to succeed where the League of Nations had failed. She remained active in the British delegation to the United Nations, becoming chairperson of the British Association in 1949. The London *Times* described her style of leadership as being able to cut through confusion "like a knife cutting through butter." She remained active and energetic for many years, enjoying traveling and walking. She died in 1974, at the age of ninety-six.

Daw Aung San Suu Kyi

(1945–   )

BURMESE ACTIVIST AND
DEMOCRATIC REFORMER

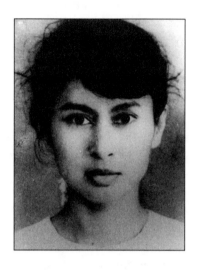

We have a **fascist** government in power. Like all fascists, the only language they understand is confrontation. Nonviolence does not mean we are going to sit back weakly and do nothing.

—Daw Aung San Suu Kyi, in a speech to her followers, describing the military junta that rules Burma

Daw Aung San Suu Kyi is a Burmese political **activist** who was held under **house arrest** from July 1989 through July 1995, literally a prisoner in her own home. She was allowed no contact with the outside world, and she was probably not even aware at the time that she had won the 1991 Nobel Peace Prize for her work to bring democracy to Burma (renamed Myanmar by the ruling military government), a Southeast Asian nation that shares its large border with India, China, and Thailand.

Suu Kyi was born in 1945. Her father, Aung San, was the founder of modern Burma. He was assassinated when Suu Kyi was two years old. Suu Kyi studied at Oxford University, England, and lived in Bhutan (a tiny kingdom in the Himalayan mountains) and Japan before settling down in England with her husband, college instructor Michael Aris. The couple had two children. Suu Kyi left her family in England when she returned to Burma in 1988 to take care of her sick mother. She soon became involved in a campaign to bring democracy to Burma.

The country of Burma won its independence from the British in 1948, led by the Anti-**Fascism** People's Freedom League. This organization, led by Suu Kyi's father, Aung San, had opposed the Japanese-imposed Burmese government set up during World War II, when Japanese forces invaded and occupied much of the country. Burma has been ruled by a single party since 1962, when military leader Ne Win overthrew the elected government. Since that time, the military has run the country, severely limiting the freedom of the Burmese people. Burma, which, ironically, is vastly rich in natural resources (gem deposits, timber), became one of the poorest countries in the world, with the average person earning under $200 per year. Rebel groups, including **communists** and ethnic minorities, have waged war against the governments of Burma since the 1950s. Students joined them in protesting against government repression and almost brought down the **dictatorship** (absolute rule). In 1988, however, General U Saw Maung took over the government and brutally crushed all opposition. In 1989, he changed the name of the country to Myanmar.

When Suu Kyi returned to Burma, she soon became the leader of the National League for Democracy (NLD), a political party that uses nonviolent protest to bring about a democratic revolution. The government scheduled elections for 1990, and Suu Kyi campaigned all around the country for her party. In 1989, she was taken prisoner by the government. Soldiers put up a sign around her house telling people to stay away. During her incarceration, Suu Kyi read, studied Japanese, did aerobics, and meditated. On rare occasions, she was allowed to have a brief visit from her husband or sons, but the government saw to it that even those family visits were monitored closely. In the May 1990 elections, her party won 392 out of 485 seats in the parliament, but the military government refused to step down. Many NLD candidates and Buddhist monks were arrested, and Suu Kyi was offered the option of going into **exile** if she stayed out of politics. In response, she demanded that the government release the political prisoners and let the NLD take power. In 1990, Suu Kyi won the Sakharov Prize, and she was nominated by Czech President Vaclav Havel for the Nobel Peace Prize, which she was awarded in 1991.

Sui Kyi was suddenly released from house arrest on July 10, 1995. News of her freedom spread quickly, both in Myanmar and around the world. Her immediate plans are not set, but she seems to want to work jointly with the military to bring democratic reforms to Myanmar.

Dimitrova, Blaga

(1922–   )

BULGARIAN POET, DISSIDENT, AND VICE-PRESIDENT

> That's why
> there are so many poets
> among women in my land.
> The mute whose speech
> is suddenly restored
> will rend the air
> with a moan or a shout—
> centuries of silence
> crying to come out.
>
> —Blaga Dimitrova, in a poem celebrating women's strength

Blaga Dimitrova became vice-president of Bulgaria in 1992, at the age of seventy. She is a poet and novelist whose works were banned (forbidden to be published or read) by the **communist** government of Bulgaria, and who organized a women's opposition movement.

Dimitrova traveled to Vietnam during the war there, experienced bombing raids, and returned to Bulgaria with an adopted Vietnamese child. She became critical of the Bulgarian communist regime after she survived cancer in 1974. She recalled, "After I met death and survived, I lost all my human doubts and fears. I came back ready for the battle with the system. I swore that if I survived the illness I would never compromise on truth or risk." She wrote books that were banned by the government, and got involved in politics after seeing a documentary film about the chemical poisoning of a Bulgarian city. Starting in 1981, a Romanian factory had been releasing chlorine gas into the air. The poisonous gas crossed the Danube River into Rousse, Bulgaria, where residents started developing different forms of cancers, breathing problems, and headaches. Pregnant women mis-carried; the fetuses died before they were born. But because the Bulgarian government did not want to anger the Romanian government, it did nothing.

In 1988, Dimitrova organized a committee that held the first opposition rallies in Bulgaria in forty-four years. She was forbidden to give poetry readings in public, and her mail and phone calls were monitored by the government. She fought back by forming the Club for Glasnost (openness) and Democracy. She also defended the rights of Turkish **immigrants** to Bulgaria.

In 1989, the communist government fell. Dimitrova decided to run for vice-president, because, as she put it, "To be a poet is my real profession, to be a politician is my temporary duty. We are all dilettantes [amateurs] in politics, but being **dissidents**, we started this job a long time ago and now we are responsible for the results." She won the election despite being ridiculed as too old, a woman, and a poet. She has appointed many women to positions of power in Bulgaria, and devotes much of her energy to children's health, cultural matters, and the status of women. She has made both adoption and abortion easier, to reduce the number of children in overcrowded orphanages.

Dimitrova looks to the future when a united women's movement will emerge in Bulgaria. She believes that true democracy will be achieved only when women are truly equal to men, with the same job opportunities and quality of life. Her revolution, she hopes, will come about "not [through] bloodshed, but a blood transfusion."

Dolci, Danilo

(1924–   )

ITALIAN SOCIAL ACTIVIST
AND WRITER

[When] people are convinced that their region needs a large dam . . . and when a mere request brings no results, the people must be prepared to engage in a struggle to get their dam.

The struggle must be nonviolent, taking the form of active or passive strikes; refusal to cooperate on what is deemed to be harmful; protests and public demonstrations in all the many forms that may be suggested by the circumstances, one's own conscience, and the particular need . . . The struggle must be carried on peaceably but energetically, until common sense and sense of responsibility have won the day.

—Danilo Dolci, on the importance of nonviolent protest

Danilo Dolci, social **activist** on the Italian island of Sicily, south of the mainland, has been described as "the ideal twentieth-century saint." Since 1952, he has led nonviolent protests in poor Sicilian towns to lessen the problems of unemployment, hunger, **illiteracy**, poverty, and hopelessness. He has forced the government to build dams, hospitals, roads, and community centers. Perhaps most important, he has given hope to the Sicilian people that they have the power to improve their own lives. He has received many international prizes for his social activism and his writing, and has been nominated for the Nobel Peace Prize several times.

Dolci was born in northern Italy. He spent his teenage years waking up three hours before school began so that he could read the great works of world literature. He studied Shakespeare, the Bible, **Hindu** writings, Russian novelists, German poets, and many others. When World War II broke out, Dolci declared himself a **conscientious objector** (someone opposed to all war on moral grounds) and was imprisoned for refusing to fight. He escaped, and returned to Italy after the war to study architecture. He did not complete his degree, how-ever, as he was more interested in people than buildings. He joined a religious organization that worked with homeless children, and learned the importance of community life through the group's agri-culture and house construction projects. He left the group in 1952 for the island of Sicily, the poorest part of Italy.

Dolci settled in a fishing village called Trappeto, which he later called "the most wretched piece of country I had ever seen." Many of the inhabitants had no homes, not enough to eat, no education, and no jobs. Dolci became a fisherman, and worked and lived in Trappeto to earn the people's trust. He quickly saw that the biggest problems in Sicily were the Mafia, an organized crime web that consisted of most of the politicians and wealthy families; and the hopelessness of the inhabitants themselves. They believed that their situation would never change, so they never had tried to improve it.

Dolci set to work to improve the lives of the people of Trappeto, and to show them that they had power over their own lives. He and some volunteers who worked for food built dwelling places for the homeless. He heard of a young girl who had died of starvation. He began a hunger strike (refusal to eat) in her bed to protest the poverty of the town. The publicity that Dolci received embarrassed the local politicians, who sent money to the village. Through more fasts and other protests, Dolci succeeding in forcing officials to build a dam to improve the agricultural production of Trappeto, a nursery school, and a "people's university," as he called it. For Dolci, education was one of the keys to lifting the residents out of poverty and helpless-ness. Not all of his protests were successful at getting what he was asking for, but with each collective action, more and more people came to see that they could defend their rights and work together to get things done.

After three years Dolci left Trappeto, once he felt that the inhabi-tants could go on without him. He settled in Partinico, a town near the Sicilian capital of Palermo. The Mafia was very strong in Partinico. Dolci moved into a section of town with no sewage (there was only one place in the entire town with running water, and that for only two hours a day), and where eight to ten people lived in each room. While few people had jobs and most people turned to crime just to survive, the police practiced shooting their rifles in the nearby barracks. Dolci led protests in Partinico to improve the residents' lives. His most famous action was a "reverse strike," in 1956. Dolci led a few hundred unemployed fishermen and peasants to a road that had become impassable, where they began repairing it. The police tried to force them to stop, but the protesters lay down on the muddy road and refused to move. The police dragged them away and locked them in their paddy wagons, while Dolci shouted, "Denying work to those who want to work, according to the spirit and letter of the constitution, equals murder." Dolci was arrested and spent several months in prison. The townspeople were inspired to continue fighting to improve their lives, and the world's attention was focused on Partinico. When Dolci received the Soviet Union's Lenin Peace Prize, he took the money and used it to established community centers in five Sicilian towns.

Many famous people became supporters of Dolci and his efforts. He was honored all over the world, and activists have used his tactics to energize communities without hope. He has written many works of fiction and nonfiction, as well as several volumes of poetry. He is regularly nominated for the Nobel Peace Prize, and continues to inspire the people of Sicily and all those over the world to form communities to care for one another and struggle for justice.

El Saawadi, Nawal

(1931–   )

EGYPTIAN PSYCHIATRIST, WRITER, AND FEMINIST

> The authorities claimed that I was instigating women toward absolute sexual freedom and immorality even though in everything I wrote I tried to combat reducing women to being sex objects fit only for seduction and consumption. I was even opposed to women wearing makeup. I encouraged them to be intelligent human beings and not mere bodies to satisfy men, to produce children, or to be slaves.
> —Nawal El Saawadi, on the concerns of Arab women

When Nawal El Saawadi was six years old, she, like millions of women in **Third World** countries (those that are the least developed economically, socially, and politically) underwent **female circumci-**

sion. Now one of the strongest opponents of this practice, El Saawadi is also a successful Egyptian psychiatrist, award-winning writer, and **feminist** leader.

El Saawadi was born in Cairo, Egypt, in 1931. She wanted to become a doctor, and at age twenty-four she graduated from the University of Cairo. She studied at Columbia University in New York for one year, then returned to Egypt to work at Cairo University Hospital, as a doctor in rural areas, and later as a psychiatrist. In 1958, she became the director of health education in the Egyptian Ministry of Health, and in 1968 she was named editor in chief of the Egyptian magazine *Health*. She lost both of those jobs in 1972 because of the publication of her first book, *Women and Health*. In the book, El Saawadi wrote about the oppression of women in Arab society, and argued for the political and sexual **liberation** of Arab women. She made the point that the lack of political rights for women was linked to the restrictions on women's sexual freedom.

El Saawadi was no longer able to work as a physician in Egypt. She turned to writing full-time, and has written ten novels, seven collections of short stories, and seven works of nonfiction. Most of her books were banned in Egypt for a time, and are still banned in many Arab countries. Nevertheless, copies of the books did enter most of these countries. She based many of her ideas on the philosophies of Karl Marx (the German political philosopher and socialist) and Sigmund Freud (the famous Viennese psychoanalyst), and saw the **capitalist** system as a model of male domination. In the West, she wrote, women are metaphorically circumcised; even in "free" countries like the United States, women still are not free to express their sexuality, still are paid less than men, and have fewer rights.

El Saawadi has devoted most of her attention to the plight of Arab women. Her first work available in English, *The Hidden Face of Eve: Women in the Arab World* (1989), opens with her account of the circumcision she and her sister underwent when she was a child. She wrote about how she and her sister felt right after the operation: "Now we know what it is. Now we know where lies our tragedy. We were born of a special sex, the female sex. We are destined in advance to taste of misery, and to have a part of our body torn away by cold, unfeeling cruel hands." She then describes how, as a doctor to women, she found many of them still haunted by the memory of their own circumcisions. She treated many girls who were brought, bleeding, into her clinic after being circumcised. She writes of the many girls who died because of the amputation, and others who were infected, and still others who were psychologically scarred for life.

As part of El Saawadi's fight to win equal rights for Egyptian women, she has tried to educate Egyptians about the dangers of female circumcision. She published a feminist magazine, *Confrontation*, in 1981, and was jailed by Egyptian President Anwar el Sadat. He charged her under the "Law for the Protection of Values from Shame." International protests led to her release two and a half months later. In 1982, El Saawadi founded the Arab Women's Solidarity Association, of which she is still president. The group fights for women's rights in all Arab countries.

El Saawadi has won literary awards in Egypt, Australia, France, and Libya. She continues to write, and she lectures all over the world. She is one of the few writers in the Arab world who has influenced a whole generation of young people by writing the "unwritable."

Enoki, Miswo

(1939–   )

JAPANESE FEMINIST

In 1972, thirty-three-year old Miswo Enoki was working as a pharmacist in Japan when she became enraged over the fact that Japanese women were not allowed to use birth control pills. She saw this as a symptom of the fact that women had very little power in traditional Japanese society. They were raised to obey their husbands, never question authority, and put everyone's needs ahead of their own. If women wanted to be able to control their own bodies and become sexually free, Enoki reasoned, they had to organize and show Japanese men that they were willing to fight for their rights. Enoki organized the "Pink Panthers," an extremely radical **feminist** group. The women in this organization wore white military uniforms and pink helmets. They used confrontational tactics, such as sit-ins, marches, and protest rallies. Although most women did not join the Pink

Panthers, the **feminist** movement in Japan became a powerful force in the 1970s.

Enoki also pushed for a woman's right to an abortion, equality in the job market, fair divorce settlements, and equal rights in marriage. Under her leadership, the Pink Panthers numbered more than four thousand women by the mid-1970s. Enoki then declared that she was forming a new political party, the Japan Women's Party. Enoki and her party, which ran in the 1977 elections, proved too radical for Japan. They received less than half of one percent of the vote, and Enoki returned to her former life as a suburban housewife. While her radical feminism did not gain many followers, the issues Enoki raised have continued to surface in Japanese politics. In a country as conservative as Japan, even this change can be seen as a great accomplishment. In surveying her work as a feminist, Enoki said that she showed Japan that a woman could be a "determined, assertive fighter" without losing her beauty and femininity.

Fang Lizhi

(1936–   )

CHINESE ASTROPHYSICIST AND ADVOCATE FOR HUMAN RIGHTS

> There is a social malaise in our country today, and the primary reason for it is the poor example set by party members. Unethical behavior by party leaders is especially to blame. . . . Many of us who have been to foreign countries to study or work agree that we can perform much more efficiently abroad than in China. . . . Some of us dare not speak out. But if we all spoke out, there would be nothing to be afraid of.
>
> —Fang Lizhi, urging democratic reform in China

During the Chinese government's crackdown on students demonstrating for democracy in Tiananmen Square in 1989, Fang Lizhi and his wife, Li Shuxian, escaped from Chinese troops and sought refuge in the U.S. embassy in Beijing, China's capital. Fang was considered the father of the modern Chinese freedom movement because of his many years of criticism of the Chinese state. As one of the country's most famous scientists, he led efforts to reform the Chinese educational system to allow and encourage independent thinking.

Fang was born in 1936, the son of a railway clerk. He began to attract attention for his brilliance at Beijing University, where he enrolled in 1952. He joined the university's **Communist** Youth League, and criticized the organization at its first meeting for trying to get all of its members to think alike, instead of "training people to think independently." After graduating with straight A's, he entered the Chinese Academy of Science, where he worked in the Institute of Modern Physics Research. He studied nuclear reactor theory, but responded to the Chinese dictator Mao Zedong's invitation to let intellectuals offer opinions about Chinese society. He wrote a paper criticizing China's educational system for letting **Marxism**, the nineteenth-century political theory of Karl Marx and Friedrich Engels, dominate the sciences. In 1957, Fang was expelled from the Communist Party because of this paper. Thousands of intellectuals were sent to labor camps, tortured, and killed during this period, but Fang was allowed to remain at the science academy because of his brilliant and important research.

In 1966, however, Fang was not so lucky. He was imprisoned in a cow shed, a form of solitary confinement used for intellectual enemies of the state. After one year, he was sent for "reeducation" (a form of brainwashing) to a communal farm, where he had no contact with scientists, and was allowed to have only one scientific book, which he read over and over. The book, Lev Landau's *Classical Theory of Fields*, influenced Fang to switch his field from physics to cosmology, the study of the origins and fate of the universe. In 1969, he was allowed to resume teaching, but he had to publish his papers under a false name because he feared further punishment. In 1978, when Deng Xiaoping took over the **dictatorship** in China, Fang returned to political favor. He traveled abroad, wrote hundreds of papers, and won numerous science prizes.

In 1985, encouraged by the freedom he had to write and study, Fang and his colleague Guan Weiyan, president of the University of Science and Technology, re-formed their university. They allowed academic freedom, let faculty members vote on how the university was run, and established foreign-exchange programs with the United States, Italy, Japan, France, and England. Fang made academic freedom in China his first priority, and he gave speeches at universities all over the country, arguing that the Communist Party line was wrong, and had to be challenged by free thinking.

Beginning in 1986, Chinese students began acting on Fang's words. They protested in the streets for democracy, and by January 1987, more than ten thousand students were involved. Fang was elected to the local people's congress during the protests. He supported the students' right to march but disapproved of the marches themselves. He personally was held responsible for the protests by local Communist Party officials, and he was fired from the university and transferred to Beijing. His wife, Li Shuxian, won a seat in the People's Congress in Beijing. Deng Xiaoping criticized Fang, and sent copies of his writings to members of the Communist Party, so that they might see how wrong and dangerous he was. The result was that Fang won many more supporters who had never heard his opinions before.

Fang was not put in jail, but was harassed and followed by police. He called for the release of political prisoners, and demanded political reforms to make China a more free society. In April 1989, more than one million students, led by Chai Ling, gathered in Beijing's vast Tiananmen Square to protest the lack of freedom in China. On June 4, tanks and armed troops attacked the students, killing at least five thousand of them in just a few hours. The government ordered Fang to turn himself in, so that he would not be treated harshly. Instead, Fang and Li headed for the American embassy in Beijing and asked for **asylum**. The Chinese protested that the United States could not keep them from arresting two of their own citizens, while the U.S. refused to turn the couple over to the Chinese. *See* CHAI LING

Fawcett, Millicent

(1847-1929)

ENGLISH FEMINIST

When English women were first given **suffrage** rights (the right to vote) in 1918, it was due in large measure to the constitutional work of Dame Millicent Fawcett, the president of the National Union of Women Suffrage Societies (NUWSS). From the age of twenty on, she devoted her life to winning equal rights for women in England.

Fawcett was born in Suffolk, England, in 1847. Her father, a merchant, sent her to school only from ages of eleven to fourteen. Her sister, Elizabeth Garrett Anderson, got her interested in the women's suffrage movement, which had begun in the 1860s. She married Henry Fawcett, a blind economics professor and member of Parliament, in 1867. By working as her husband's political secretary, Fawcett learned a great deal about politics that would serve her well in later years.

She first became active in the suffrage movement in 1867. She also worked to pass laws that would protect a married woman's right to hold on to her own property, and started Newnham College as an outgrowth of a women's lecture series held in her own home. When her husband died in 1884, she threw herself into the suffrage movement with all her energy. She founded a suffrage society in 1886, and combined it with others to form the NUWSS, of which she became president in 1897. She also fought against Northern Ireland's independence from England as a member of the Liberal-Unionist group. She traveled to Ireland frequently. During the Boer War in South Africa (between the British and the Boers, who were South Africans of Dutch descent), reports came to England that British soldiers had put thousands of Afrikaner (South Africans of European descent) women and children in concentration camps to force the Afrikaner men to surrender. Disease and hunger swept through these camps, killing twenty-eight thousand people, most of them children. Fawcett led a women's commission to investigate the conditions in the concentration camps.

The suffrage movement changed in the twentieth century. Under the leadership of the Pankhurst family, women began marching, protesting, and committing acts of **civil disobedience**. Fawcett continued to work for women's suffrage through legal means. She traveled around the country, lobbied members of Parliament, and helped make deals with political parties. She lost some of her support in the NUWSS because she supported the British troops in World War I, and she resigned from the presidency at the end of the war.

In 1918, women were first given the right to vote in England, but they had to be over thirty years old. Fawcett continued to fight for equality for women, and in 1928 women were given the same voting rights as men. She wrote a number of books on famous women, and convinced many people that women should be given the same opportunities as men. She died in 1929, four years after being made a Dame of the British Empire. *See* PANKHURST FAMILY

First, Ruth

(1925–1982)

SOUTH AFRICAN ACTIVIST AND JOURNALIST

The world was outraged and saddened on August 17, 1982, when South African journalist and revolutionary Ruth First was blown to bits by a letter bomb sent to her home in **exile** in the African country of Mozambique, adjoining South Africa on the Indian Ocean coast. It was widely believed that the South African government was responsible for First's death, as she had been one of the most powerful opponents of **apartheid** (the government's strict separation of races), as practiced by South Africa.

First was born into a Jewish family in Johannesburg, South Africa, in 1925. Her family was wealthy; her father, Julius, was a successful furniture manufacturer. Despite their wealth, her parents were founding members of the **Communist** Party of South Africa. Julius was its first treasurer. The Communist Party and the African National Congress (ANC) worked together to win rights for blacks. Ruth was deeply influenced by her parents' **activist** activities. She studied at the University of Witwatersrand, in Johannesburg, where she formed a student organization made up of people of many races. At the age of twenty-one, she was one of a small group of whites who helped black miners in a strike in 1946. One year later, she traveled to the town of Bethal, in the province of Transvaal, and wrote about the terrible situation of the black farm laborers there. She was harassed by the South African police for her political activities, and was not allowed to publish anything critical of the South African government or society.

In 1949, she married fellow revolutionary Joe Slovo. The couple had three children. During the 1950s, First edited a revolutionary literary magazine, *Fighting Talk*, and was the Johannesburg editor for the newspapers *Guardian* and *New Age*. She investigated the living and working conditions of blacks in South Africa, and wrote a number of reports that directed the world's attention to their plight. For disobeying the South African government's order not to criticize South Africa in the press, First was arrested in 1963. She spent almost four months in solitary confinement, and was tortured in prison. She wrote about her experience in her autobiographical *One Hundred and Seventeen Days*, which was published two years later. Upon release from prison, First **immigrated** to England. There she became a lecturer in sociology at the University of Durham, and she wrote books critical of apartheid. In *One Hundred and Seventeen Days*, she described not only her own experience, but the physical and psychological tortures inflicted upon the black political prisoners, many of whom died in prison. The book was turned into a movie for television, in which she played herself. Also in 1965, First directed the world's attention to the plight of Nelson Mandela, the ANC leader who was serving a life sentence in South Africa. She edited a collection of his speeches, articles, and the statements he made at his trial. They were smuggled out of South Africa and published as *No Easy Walk to Freedom*. She also wrote The *Barrel of a Gun* (1970), an analysis of the causes of military overthrows of the governments of the African nations of the Sudan, Nigeria, and Ghana. In 1972, she turned her attention to the governments and private companies of the United States and Europe, and she showed how their investments in South Africa helped to keep apartheid strong. Her book, which she wrote with Jonathan Steele and Christabel Gurney, was one of the sparks of the divestment movement, in which many Western companies and governments were forced to take their money and business out of South Africa until free elections were held.

In 1979, First returned to Africa. She worked in Mozambique, at the Center for African Studies at Eduardo Mondlane University. She led a group of professors who were studying the conditions of migrant workers in South Africa. On August 17, 1982, she was killed when a letter bomb exploded as she was opening it. Many people blamed the South African government for killing one of its most courageous and effective foes. Her story was told to the world through the 1988 movie *A World Apart*, written by her daughter Shawn Slovo. *See* SLOVO, JOE

Freire, Paulo

(1921-   )

BRAZILIAN EDUCATOR AND SOCIAL ACTIVIST

> The oppressed, having internalized the image of the oppressor and adopted his guidelines, are fearful of freedom. Freedom would require them to eject this image and replace it with autonomy and responsibility. Freedom is acquired by conquest, not by gift. It must be pursued constantly and responsibly. Freedom is not an ideal located outside of man; nor is it an idea which becomes myth. It is rather the indispensable condition for the quest for human completion.
>
> —from *Pedagogy of the Oppressed*, 1970

Paulo Freire spent twenty years in **exile** from his native land of Brazil for trying to teach the peasants to read. He taught them, not with "See Spot Run" books, but by using texts that explained to them the causes of their poverty and oppression. Literacy, Freire explained, was one tool that was necessary for the oppressed of Brazil to shake off the chains of domination. When a democratically elected government returned to power in Brazil, Freire was named secretary of education for São Paulo, the largest city in Brazil. He has worked tirelessly to put his radical and transformational education philosophy into practice.

Freire grew up in Recife, Brazil, in a middle-class family. All around him were people living in extreme poverty and squalor. In 1929, following the worldwide **depression** brought on by the United States stock market crash, Freire's family lost their money and found themselves living as poor people. He was often hungry, and because of this, he found it difficult to concentrate in school. He fell behind in his schoolwork, and at the age of eleven he vowed to spend his life fighting against hunger. No other child, he vowed, should ever have to experience what he himself went through.

Freire was puzzled by the "culture of silence" of the poor. He did not understand why they did not protest against their poverty, and take steps to end it. Gradually he came to think that the system that kept them poor also took away their awareness of the economic, social, and political crimes that were being committed against them by the wealthy. The poor were taught to see themselves as the rich saw them. He felt that the educational system, which could not even teach the poor to read, was a major tool for keeping them in silence and passiveness. Freire turned to education as the means for teaching the oppressed people of Brazil to fight for their rights. He wrote his doctoral dissertation at the University of Recife in 1959, and put his ideas into practice when he became a professor of history and philosophy of education at that institution. He experimented with teaching **illiterate** adults how to read using material that would increase their awareness of the world, and liberate their thinking. Instead of following the traditional model of education, in which the teacher would choose the material and the student would passively accept the teacher's authority, Freire firmly believed in starting with the student's interests and experiences. Student and teacher were equal partners in the process. In fact, the student-teacher relationship would not work unless both parties were "teacher-learners" and "learner-teachers."

One of Freire's favorite educational techniques, designed to get oppressed people to see the "big picture," was to ask about the "problem behind the problem." In every discussion of oppressed people's lives and places in the world, they were encouraged to ask: Why? Once local problems like inadequate housing were exposed to the problem-posing technique, the peasants quickly learned to see that the entire system was stacked against them. They learned to look at symptoms and find the root causes, and, as Freire showed, this made them revolutionary. They developed what Freire referred to as a "critical consciousness," or sense of dissatisfaction with the way things were, and the will to act to change things.

The success of Freire's adult literacy campaign was made painfully clear when a military **coup** (overthrowing of the government) occurred in Brazil in 1964. Freire was immediately jailed by the coup leaders and spent more than two months in prison. Upon his release, he was exiled from Brazil. He went to Chile, on the west coast of South America, where he spent five years running literacy programs for the United Nations Educational, Scientific, and Cultural Organization (UNESCO) and the Chilean Institute for Agrarian Reform. He set up literacy programs in the Central American country of Nicaragua under the Sandinistas, and in former Portuguese colonies in Africa. He became a visiting professor of education at Harvard University and spread his ideas about education throughout the world—everywhere, that is, except in Brazil, where his teaching methods were banned.

In 1988, members of Freire's **socialist** Workers' Party were elected mayors of three Brazilian state capitals, including São Paulo, which has a population of more than twelve million people. Freire was invited back to Brazil, to reform the São Paulo school system. He immediately found huge problems. The military government had mistreated the public schools. Before implementing a new curriculum, Freire had to find the money to repair buildings, facilities, and desks. More than a quarter of a million children in São Paulo did not attend school at all. Freire starting running classes for them in community centers and churches. He has worked to make schools more democratic; places where teachers, parents, and children all have a voice in making schools "happier, more open places."

Gandhi, Mohandas

(1869–1948)

LEADER OF NONVIOLENT INDIAN INDEPENDENCE MOVEMENT

My personal faith is absolutely clear. I cannot intentionally hurt anything that lives, much less fellow human beings, even though they may do the greatest wrong to me and mine. Whilst, therefore, I hold the British rule to be a curse, I do not intend harm to a single Englishman or to any legitimate interest he may have in India. . . . I know that in embarking on nonviolence I shall be running what might be termed a mad risk. But the victories of truth have never been won without risks, often of the gravest character. Conversion of a nation that has consciously or unconsciously preyed upon another, far more numerous, far more ancient and no less cultured than itself, is worth any amount of risk.

—Mohandas Gandhi, on achieving goals through nonviolent means

Mohandas Karamchand Gandhi, known to the people of India as Mahatma ("great soul"), led the Indian people in a nonviolent struggle to gain independence from Great Britain. Much of what is known about his early life comes from his autobiography, *My Experiments with Truth*. He was born on October 2, 1869, in Porbandar, India, into a Vaisya (merchant) **caste** family of grocers and moneylenders. He was influenced deeply by his mother, a follower of a religion called Jainism, which preached nonviolence to all living things, as well as strict vegetarianism. Gandhi, a shy and serious boy, was married at the age of thirteen (a common occurrence at the time in India; less so in the twentieth century) to a girl named Kasturba, according to their parents' plans. In time they had four children of their own.

During Gandhi's childhood, the British ruled over a vast foreign empire, including India and South Africa. As a subject of the British crown, Gandhi was allowed to study law in London, and then he later returned to India to practice law in 1891. He was not very successful, however, and in 1893 he jumped at the chance to work for an Indian law firm in South Africa for a year. He immediately felt the prejudice of that society toward Indians (for more than a century, South Africa, especially the east coast city of Durban, has been home to a large Indian population), and he remained there for twenty-one years, editing a newspaper called *Indian Opinion*, and leading the campaign for Indian rights in South Africa.

It was during this time that Gandhi developed his method of nonviolent struggle, which he called *satyagraha* ("steadfastness in truth"). The truth that he proclaimed was that all people, even violent oppressors, could become just and loving if their violence was met by love, rather than by more violence. He organized campaigns of **civil disobedience**, in which many people broke laws they considered unfair and peacefully accepted the consequences. He organized strikes by Indian mine workers, and was himself arrested by the British many times. The effectiveness of his efforts convinced many people that nonviolent struggle could be an effective tool in winning India's independence from Great Britain.

In 1915, Gandhi returned to India and organized workers who were angry at the unfair treatment they received at the hands of the British rulers of India. He used *satyagraha* to successfully oppose British laws that made it illegal to organize opposition to the government. At one point, his followers became so frustrated that they began to riot. Gandhi immediately called off the protests, and he began a fast (refusal to eat or drink anything) to impress upon his followers that their behavior was more important than the immediate results of their movement. On April 13, 1919, in the northeast Indian city of Amritsar, British troops opened fire on a crowd of unarmed Indians demonstrating for independence, killing hundreds of them. Gandhi turned to direct political protest, leading the Indian National Congress in a three-year policy of noncooperation with the government. In 1930, he led hundreds of people on a two-hundred-mile march to the sea, where they made salt from sea water to protest the Salt Acts, which forced people to buy salt only from the British government. He led boycotts of British goods, and encouraged Indians to learn how to weave, to foster economic self-sufficiency, the dignity of labor, and independence from the British textile industry.

Gandhi led a life of total simplicity. He gave up the Western suits that he had worn as a young lawyer, and instead wore *dhotis*, traditional Indian garments of white cloth that were wrapped around the body, rather than tailored. Many Indians had been ashamed of wearing their traditional clothes, and Gandhi restored their pride. He wove all his own clothes, often spending several hours a day at the loom.

In his life he spent a total of seven years in jail. In addition to fighting the policies of the British government, he also worked for changes in Indian society. He tried to raise the status of the Untouchables, the lowest caste in India, whom he called Harijans ("children of God"). He worked to bring about peace between the **Hindus** and Muslims who shared the vast Indian subcontinent. When India finally achieved independence in 1947, Gandhi fought against its partition into a Hindu state (India) and a Muslim state (Pakistan). He began a hunger strike on January 13, 1948, at the age of seventy-eight, to protest the terrible violence that was occurring among Hindus, Muslims, and others. So great was his moral influence that five days later the leaders of the warring groups agreed to stop the fighting. On January 30, 1948, on his way to a prayer meeting in Delhi, Gandhi was assassinated by a Hindu fanatic who opposed his tolerance of Muslims.

People from all over the world mourned Gandhi's death. He showed that great love, great courage, and great strength could combine to change the world. He spoke of his whole life as an experiment with truth, and never claimed to have discovered all of it. His methods and philosophy have formed the basis of many other social justice movements around the world, including the civil rights campaign of Dr. Martin Luther King, Jr., in the United States in the 1950s and 1960s. Many of the **activists** whose biographies appear in this volume were inspired by Gandhi's example.

Garrett, Peter

(1954–   )

AUSTRALIAN ROCK MUSICIAN, POLITICIAN,
AND ENVIRONMENTALIST

> [The labels "rock musician" and "politician"] are highly mislead-
> ing. Rock singer I can live with. But I can't stand being in the com-
> pany of most politicians, and I don't count myself as one. I am an
> activist, a direct, political activist. Not in the sense of waving the
> left-wing newspaper, but in the sense of wanting to involve myself
> in my community. When I jump up on stage, I let that all go and
> just sing and dance. But there is no difference in the man. I am not
> schizophrenic.
>
> —Peter Garrett, on his philosophy of life

Peter Garrett, the lead singer for the Australian hard-rock band
Midnight Oil, doesn't just sing about environmental politics. He
makes them, as a member of the Australian Senate and as a leader of
the Australian environmental and antinuclear movements. On stage,
the six-foot-three, shaved-head rock star leaps across the set, shouts
out lyrics that often refer to the plight of the Aborigines, the original
inhabitants of Australia, and dances until sweat covers his body. Off
stage, he is a serious and effective social **activist** who has brought the
message of environmental protection to millions.

Garrett was a law student in the mid-1970s, planning a career as a
"socially responsible lawyer," when he answered a local paper's ad
placed by a band looking for a singer. The group, Midnight Oil, was
at that point a surfers' band that played Beach Boys songs in small
clubs that overlooked the Pacific Ocean. A surfer himself, Garrett au-
ditioned for the job, and soon found himself in show business. He
quickly brought his social conscience into the work the band was
doing, and they transformed themselves into a hard-rock group that
sang about the degradation of the environment and the mistreatment
of the Aboriginal people. The band quickly decided that it would be
hypocritical of them to sing about social problems and not do anything about them, so in 1977 they launched their "new" band with a
benefit concert for the international **environmental** group Green-
peace. As their popularity grew, Garrett and the others made sure that

the money they made was used to further the causes they were singing about. They met with Aboriginal groups to discuss music and politics, and performed with Aboriginal musicians in the Outback (the vast, dry desert of Australia's interior) and on concert stages.

Garrett decided to use his fame and commitment to energize the Australian environmental and antinuclear movements. In 1984, he ran for a seat in the Australian Senate as a candidate for the Nuclear Disarmament Party. In 1989, he was appointed head of the Australian Conservation Foundation. He gave speeches to the Australian Senate, and became an environmental advisor to the prime minister. In 1990, he was elected to the Australian Senate.

Garrett, who is married and has three children, splits his time between politics and music. Garrett and Midnight Oil are still producing albums and touring the world. They gave a protest concert in front of Exxon headquarters in New York City to protest the oil company's failure to clean up the oil spill from one of its tankers, the *Exxon Valdez*, in Prince William Sound, in Valdez, Alaska. They continue to sing about the destruction of the environment, as well as the beauty of the earth that is still left.

Geldof, Bob

(1952–   )

IRISH MUSICIAN, HUMANITARIAN

Old people still die of cold every winter in houses beside ours. Children still get abused. People still go hungry. It must be our responsibility. We can't simply blame governments. These are our own neighbors. We must rediscover a sense of individual responsibility for each other.

—Bob Geldof, on caring for others

Bob Geldof organized Band Aid and Live Aid, rock-and-roll events dedicated to feeding the people suffering through a famine in the

African nation of Ethiopia. He convinced some of the most famous musicians in the world to participate, and raised more than $200 million in famine relief. In 1986, he was honored for his efforts and was made a knight by Queen Elizabeth II of England.

Geldof was born in Dublin in 1952. He was a rebellious son and student. He sent false grade reports home so his father would think he was studying hard at school. He loved the new musical style, rock and roll, and saw The Rolling Stones' lead singer, Mick Jagger as a role model. Geldof taught himself to play guitar. He also got involved with a group that helped Dublin's homeless.

When Geldof graduated from college, he drifted from one job to another. He worked in Ireland and in England, and finally got a good job writing for a newspaper in Canada. He never received a work permit there, and after a year he was forced to return to England. Eventually he made friends with other young musicians, and he formed a band, the Boomtown Rats. In the late 1970s and early 1980s they were very successful. Geldof wrote the group's most famous song, "I Don't Like Mondays," to protest the United States's laws that made handguns easily available. In 1984, when the Boomtown Rats were no longer on the charts, Geldof was struggling to promote the band. One evening on television he saw a news story about the famine in Ethiopia. Suddenly his own troubles seemed very small. He got the idea of putting on a rock concert and selling a record to raise money for relief aid to Ethiopia. The problem was that the Boomtown Rats were not popular enough to raise much money.

Geldof's solution was to invite some of the most famous musicians in the world to participate in the project, which he called Band Aid. Sting, Phil Collins, Pete Townshend, Bono, and many others performed Geldof's song, "Do They Know It's Christmas?" as well as their own songs. Geldof also traveled to Ethiopia, and he became personally involved in deciding how the money would be spent. A group of American musicians, including Bruce Springsteen, Stevie Wonder, Tina Turner, and many others, produced a recording called "We Are the World," written by Michael Jackson. Geldof then organized Live Aid, an internationally televised rock concert held in England and the United States. After this, he created Self Aid, a project of Irish musicians helping the poor of Ireland.

After the tremendous success of these projects, Geldof, with his long hair, casual clothing, and unshaved face, met with politicians and world leaders in his crusade to end hunger. When he told British Prime Minister Margaret Thatcher that African countries paid more to the West in interest than they received in aid, she told him that the world hunger situation was not that simple. He replied, "Nothing is as simple as dying, Prime Minister." He was knighted in 1986. He also received many peace awards. Perhaps the greatest monument to his work has been the many benefit concerts and performances given around the world by entertainers, who, like Geldof, want to make a difference.

Gonne, Maude

(1866–1953)

IRISH ACTRESS AND REVOLUTIONARY

Maude Gonne was known as the "Mother of Ireland." She was a well-known actress with whom many men fell in love. She organized women's revolutionary movements to win Irish independence from the British, and undertook relief work to help the Irish people during their conflicts with the British.

Gonne's mother died when she was very young. Her father was a British army officer who had his daughter educated in France until she was sixteen. She returned to Dublin in 1882 to live with her father. She visited France and fell in love with the journalist Lucien Millevoye, who inspired her to fight for the cause of Irish independence. She worked for political prisoners and evicted tenants, and won Millevoye's love. They had two children in the 1890s, but Gonne eventually decided that she had to devote all of her energy to the cause of Irish **nationalism**. She left Millevoye just before the new century began. This provided an opportunity for Ireland's most famous poet, W.B. Yeats, to propose marriage to her, although unsuccessfully. He had met her ten years earlier and was completely swept away by his love for her. He wrote her letters and poems all his life, and implored her to star in his plays. Yeats even proposed to her daughter in 1917. Although he persisted, neither Gonne nor her daughter ever accepted his proposals.

In 1900, Gonne formed a women's group called Daughters of Ireland. The group fought for Irish independence, and Gonne raised money and awareness by lecturing and acting in France, the United States, and England. While in France, she edited a pro-Irish independence newspaper, *The Free Ireland.*

In 1903, after converting to Catholicism, Gonne did accept the proposal of marriage of another Irish revolutionary, John MacBride. Soon after the birth of their son Seán MacBride one year later, the couple separated. Gonne remained in Paris until 1917, the year after the Easter Rising of 1916, in which John MacBride took part. He was executed by the British for his role in the uprising. Gonne returned to Ireland to take part in the struggle against the British. She tended the wounded and the hungry during the Time of Troubles, and opposed the Anglo-Irish Treaty of 1921, which divided Ireland into an independent south, and made the north a part of Great Britain. She continued to work for total independence for Ireland, and founded the Republican Women's Prisoners' Defense League in 1922. This organization was devoted to supporting the Irish Republicans, who continued to fight against the British. Gonne remained devoted to the Republican cause until her death in 1953. An independent, free-spirited, and passionate woman, she was mourned by many Irish Republicans, who saw her as the symbol of their struggle for independence.
See MACBRIDE, SEÁN

Guevara, Ernesto "Che"

(1928–1967)

LATIN AMERICAN REVOLUTIONARY

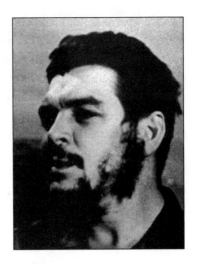

> Guerrilla war is a people's war, a mass struggle. To try to carry out this type of war without the support of the population is to court inevitable disaster.
>
> —Che Guevara, on revolution

Ernesto "Che" Guevara was a revolutionary who worked to overthrow **dictatorships** in Cuba, the Congo, and Bolivia. His **guerrilla** tactics helped Fidel Castro overthrow the dictatorship of Fulgencio Batista in Cuba in the 1950s, and he became a world ambassador for the Cuban revolution and the Cuban minister of industries. He left Cuba after a bitter disagreement with Castro, and was killed in Bolivia in 1967. He remains a symbol of armed struggle against dictatorship to this day.

Guevara was born on June 14, 1928, in Rosario, Argentina. His family was middle class, and both of his parents were politically active when he was growing up. His father fought against **Nazi** propaganda in Argentina, and opposed the dictatorship of Juan Perón. His mother was arrested for her political activity. The two of them supported their son's revolutionary activities all their lives.

Guevara attended medical school in Argentina. He took time out to travel the length of South and Central America by motorcycle, and he eventually reached Miami, in the United States. He was struck by the poverty of the people everywhere. In 1953 he traveled to Bolivia, where he met radical revolutionaries who were trying to overthrow the right-wing governments of Latin America. He trained as a guerrilla fighter, traveling through Costa Rica, Guatemala, and Mexico. He met Fidel Castro in Mexico in 1955, and joined a group of **exiled** Cubans who were plotting to return to Cuba and set up a **socialist** state. They trained outside of Mexico City, led by Alberto Bayo.

Guevara, Castro, and the others were arrested in Mexico in 1956, but were released after a month in prison.

From 1956 to 1959, Castro and Guevara carried out a guerrilla war against the Batista regime. On January 1, 1959, Batista fled Cuba for the Dominican Republic, taking with him more than $300 million that he had stolen from the Cuban people while he was their leader. Guevara helped set up a socialist economy in Cuba, and also established good relations with the Soviet Union, China, and many **Third World** (nations that are socially, economically, and politically underdeveloped) countries. Partly due to a boycott of Cuba and a failed invasion by the United States, the Cuban economy never regained its health. Guevara began criticizing the Soviet Union, Cuba's biggest financial supporter, for abandoning its mission to help the poor of the world. He felt that the Third World needed to develop its own brand of revolution, and not depend on the Soviet Union. Castro needed the Soviet Union too much to risk offending its leaders, so he sent Guevara out of the country on other missions. Guevara disappeared in 1965, and reappeared in the Congo, in Africa, where he joined leftist forces in the civil war there. In 1966, he traveled to Bolivia, where he engaged in jungle warfare against the right-wing government. His idea for freeing the Third World countries from Western **capitalism** was to create many small revolutions all over the world. In Bolivia, he tried to repeat the success of Cuba, in which a small group of fighters won the sympathy of the peasants and overthrew the government. In October 1967, he was captured by the Bolivian government. Deciding that a trial would create too much public sympathy, Bolivian president Barrientos ordered that Guevara be executed on October 9, 1967. Two days later, the Bolivian government released a photo of an air force colonel pointing to a bullet hole in Guevara's chest, to prove to the world that he was really dead. Millions of people around the world honored the life and ideals of the man who had opposed both the capitalism of the West and the orthodox **communism** of the east. Guevara had truly fought for the oppressed peasants of the Third World.

Ham Sok Hon

(1901–   )

KOREAN HUMAN RIGHTS AND PEACE ACTIVIST

> Park Chung Hee-nim, I . . . address you as . . . a man with con-
> science and reasoning . . . You and your military colleagues have
> committed many mistakes. First of all, the military coup was
> wrong. Your intention and goal to correct the national destiny may
> be right, but the means were wrong. When the means are wrong,
> goals lose their meaning . . . You rose with faith only in swords.
> You cannot gain the confidence of people by military power alone.
>
> —Ham Sok Hon, in an open letter to the South Korean people
> during Park Chung Hee's reign of terror in 1961

Ham Sok Hon, or Teacher Ham, has been imprisoned many times
by the Russian, Japanese, and Korean governments for his courageous and peaceful stands against injustice and political division. A
deeply spiritual man, he has inspired millions of Koreans to work toward peace and reconciliation between North and South Korea. He
was nominated for the Nobel Peace Prize in 1985.

Ham was born in 1901 into a peasant family living near Pyongyang, in what is now North Korea. His mother was a silk worker;
and his father, an herbal doctor. During his childhood, Korea was occupied by the Japanese, who oppressed the Korean people and brutally put down attempts by them to win their independence. When
Ham was very young, Japanese soldiers occupied part of his house.
When he was eighteen, he took part in the March First Movement, a
nonviolent Korean protest against Japanese rule. He met Christians
who were involved in the peaceful struggle, and was attracted to their
beliefs. Many of them were involved in the O-san High School, near
Pyongyang, which was created by the poor for the poor, and taught
Korean **nationalism** and spiritual Christianity. Ham received his
teaching certificate at the Tokyo College of Education, where he was
influenced by his teacher Uchimura Kanzo, who was the founder of a
nonchurch Christian movement that Ham brought to Korea. Ham returned to teach at O-san from 1929 to 1939. He was imprisoned in the
1930s for helping Korean independence activists, and again in 1940

and 1942 for supporting free speech and publishing in the Korean language.

After World War II, Korea gained its independence from Japan. The United States and the Soviet Union soon divided Korea in two, with the north coming under **communist** domination, and the south becoming dependent on the United States. Ham commented at the time, "The worst tragedy today is that we have two masters to serve rather than one. Under Japanese slavery at least families could stay together and people could come and go freely. Now parents and children are separated in the divided north and south. Where is the freedom? Where is the liberation? . . . We are a stateless people." Ham traveled to South Korea in 1947, and has not been allowed to cross back into North Korea since.

After the Korean War (1950–1953), in which most of Korea was devastated, the north and south created a demilitarized zone (DMZ) between them that actually contained Korean and American soldiers and more than 150 nuclear weapons. Both the North and South Korean governments became extremely militarized, and they oppressed their own people. Family members separated by the DMZ were not allowed to exchange letters. Ham has spent his life since then trying to reunite Korea, and fighting nonviolently for **human rights** in Korea. When Park Chung Hee took over the government of South Korea in a military **coup**, Ham objected to his reign of terror in a letter to thirty million South Koreans. In 1975, following Park's banning of all political opposition, Ham signed a declaration demanding democratic government. He was sentenced to eight years in prison, but at age seventy-four was considered too old to serve the time. He was arrested two years later for his public statements about democracy on Korean Independence Day. He has supported striking workers, fought for the rights of the poor and oppressed, and continues to remind his fellow Koreans that the two halves of their country must unite.

Ham has written many books on history, religion, and philosophy. He translated a book about Mohandas Gandhi into Korean, and wrote *Korean History from a Biblical Standpoint*, which greatly influenced many young Koreans. He wears traditional white Korean clothes, and has a silvery beard. He is a symbol of hope and courage for the Korean people. He has cautioned the world to find peaceful means to settle disputes between nations: "Which people, which nation, which ideology wins is not the question. All of humankind is in the fight. We have reached the point where there is no hope unless we make a drastic turnabout toward spirituality." *See* GANDHI, MOHANDAS

Hammarskjöld, Dag

(1905–1961)

SWEDISH STATESMAN
AND DIPLOMAT

A mature man is his own judge. In the end, his only form of support is being faithful to his own convictions. The advice of others may be welcome and valuable, but it does not free him from responsibility.

—Dag Hammarskjöld, on human responsibility

Dag Hammarskjöld was a Swedish government minister who became the second secretary-general of the United Nations. He helped resolve many international crises, and he was revered as a man of peace around the world. He died in a plane crash in 1961.

Hammarskjöld was born on July 29, 1905, in Uppsala, Sweden. His father was the prime minister of Sweden, and had also served as a representative to the League of Nations (an international organization that was formed after World War I to prevent future wars. After World War II, it was replaced by a new international organization, the United Nations.). In 1914, his father, then Sweden's prime minister, declared that Sweden would not take part in World War I because international disputes should be settled by law, not war. Hammarskjöld attended Uppsala University, where he received a degree in literature and philosophy by age nineteen. He later studied law and economics. In 1936, he was named Swedish undersecretary of finance. Although Sweden was officially neutral in World War II as well, Hammarskjöld arranged for financial help for the Norwegian government-in-**exile** in London. Norway had been conquered by **Nazi** Germany in 1940.

After World War II ended, Hammarskjöld worked to rebuild the countries of Europe. He worked as an economic advisor in Paris, and got his first taste of international **diplomacy**. In 1952, he worked out a peaceful settlement when the Soviet Union shot down a Swedish plane. Hammarskjöld's efforts may have prevented war.

In 1953, Hammarskjöld was appointed secretary-general of the United Nations. He took an organization that was not thought of seriously by the governments of the world and turned it into a powerful force for peace. He helped avert an international crisis between China and the United States at the end of the Korean War. China had captured some American pilots and refused to release them. Hammarskjöld negotiated with the Chinese for their release. He also tried to bring peace to the Middle East. He secured a ceasefire in the first Arab-Israeli war, in 1948, and another one in the second war in 1956.

Hammarskjöld was killed in a plane crash on September 18, 1961, while he was on his way to the Congo, in Africa, to negotiate a ceasefire in a civil war. After his death, he was awarded the Nobel Peace Prize in 1961 for his life's work to bring international conflicts to peaceful conclusions. He made the United Nations an important international organization, and won the respect and trust of world leaders who did not trust each other. In the speech he gave upon becoming secretary-general of the U.N., he quoted a Swedish poet: "The greatest prayer of man is not for victory, but for peace."

Heinemann, Gustav

(1899-1976)

GERMAN POLITICIAN AND PEACE ACTIVIST

> After God has twice dashed the weapons from the hands of the
> Germans they should not reach for them a third time; . . . one must
> have patience to discern the will of God in the governance of the
> world and await developments peacefully and quietly.
>
> —Konrad Adenauer's recollection of Heinemann's argument
> against German rearmament following World War II

Gustav Heinemann led the movement to prevent Germany from
building up its military in the years following World War II. He put
forward plans for uniting East and West Germany, and inspired an entire generation of peace **activists** with his honesty and courage.

Heinemann was born in Westphalia, in the industrial part of Germany. His father managed a medical fund for workers at Krupp en-
terprises, a company that manufactured weapons for the German
military. After graduating from the Essen gymnasium (high school),
Heinemann fought in World War I as a cannoneer in the German Imperial Army. Following the war, he resumed his studies at many different universities, becoming involved in the student democracy
movement in Berlin. He was arrested for trying to stop **fascists** from
overthrowing the Democratic Weimar government in 1920, and was
released when the overthrow failed. He earned doctorates (Ph.D. degrees) in law and political science, and in 1928 he began working as
a lawyer for the Rhine Steel Works. He worked his way up to director of mines and won a seat on the executive board. He also taught
law and economics at the University of Cologne.

Heinemann had been raised as a devout Protestant. When Adolf
Hitler came to power in 1933, the **Nazis** shut down many church organizations, including Heinemann's People's Christian Social Service. Heinemann saw that Hitler wanted the government to control
religious organizations. Along with Pastor Martin Niemöller, Heinemann founded the Confessing Church, a secret anti-Nazi branch of
the German Protestant Church. After the war, he was a founder of the
Christian Democratic Union (CDU), the party that dominated

German politics for many years. In 1949, German Chancellor Konrad Adenauer, head of the CDU, appointed Heinemann minister of the interior. When Heinemann found out that Adenauer planned to rearm Germany and join the Western European nations and United States in the North Atlantic Treaty Organization (NATO), he resigned in protest. Rearming Germany after what it had done in World War II was like giving a drink to a recently cured alcoholic, Heinemann argued. Rather than joining NATO, an organization he saw as dedicated to hostile relations between **communist** countries and the West, Germany should reunify East and West into a peaceful, democratic nation that could serve as a bridge between the two sides. Germany, Heinemann felt, should be a land of absolute peace, "an extending peace for neighboring peoples."

He became a leading figure in two different organizations dedicated to preventing German rearmament. He joined the Social Democratic Party (SPD) and was elected to Parliament in 1957. In a famous speech on January 23, 1958, Heinemann argued that the world did not have to be divided between Christians (the West) and communists. He could not prevent the German military buildup, but hoped to gain many followers due to his dedication and skill in debate. When his loyalty to Germany was questioned by a reporter who asked if he loved Germany, Heinemann replied, "I love my wife, and that's enough."

In 1966, Heinemann became minister of justice. In that post, he removed the penalties that had been enforced on homosexuality and adultery, and he worked to ensure that the law under which former Nazis could be prosecuted for their war crimes in World War II was never allowed to expire. During student riots following the attempted assassination of a radical student leader, Heinemann calmly told the adults of Germany to try to understand the younger generation and their concerns. From 1969 to 1974, he was president of West Germany. He worked for disarmament of both communist and Western countries, and supported research on the causes of war and ways to achieve peace. By the time of his death in 1976, the German peace movement that he had started was an active force in German politics. His dream of German reunification finally occurred in 1989. *See* NIEMÖLLER, MARTIN

Ibarruri, Dolores

(1895–1989)

SPANISH REVOLUTIONARY POLITICIAN

> It is better to die on your feet than to live on your knees. *¡No pasarán!* [They shall not pass!]
>
> —Dolores Ibarruri, on fighting for one's beliefs

Dolores Ibarruri, known as "La Pasionaria" (The Passionflower), inspired the Loyalist forces in the Spanish Civil War with her rousing speeches. She helped to establish the Popular Front Government that fought the **fascists** during the 1930s. After the fascist leader Francisco Franco died, she returned to Spain from her **exile** in the Soviet Union and was elected to Parliament in 1977, at the age of eighty-one.

Ibarruri was born into a poor family whose members had worked in the mines of Gallarta, Spain, for generations. Both of her parents and all of her brothers worked in the mines in which her father's father had died in an accident. Her father was known as Antonio the Gunner for his service in the Carlist army. From her family, she derived both the will to fight and the urge to correct the terrible conditions of working people. At an early age she recognized a conflict between the Christian idea of brotherhood and the gaps between rich and poor that she saw all around her.

As a teenager, Ibarruri suffered from poor health, and found it difficult to get a job. She did not complete a teacher's course, but found work as a household servant after studying dressmaking for two years. In 1916, she married a miner who was involved in the **socialist** movement. He spent a lot of time in jail for his socialist activities, and Ibarruri took care of her children alone from 1917 to 1931. She herself joined the socialist movement, and was deeply impressed by her first encounters with the writings of the German political philosopher and socialist Karl Marx and the German socialist Friedrich Engels. "The more I learned about socialism," she said later, "the more reconciled I was to life, which I no longer saw as a swamp, but as a battlefield."

In 1917, she organized the collection of weapons for miners who were planning a rebellion, and watched as the government violently suppressed it. She was cheered by the news of the **communist** revolution in Russia that same year. She joined the Communist party and began to write articles for its newspaper under the assumed name La Pasionaria. In the 1920s, Ibarruri organized labor strikes and worked to overthrow the **dictator** Miguel Primo de Rivera. In 1931, elections were held to create the Spanish Republic. Ibarruri rose in prominence in the Communist Party and worked for a communist revolution in Spain.

In 1933, Adolf Hitler was elected chancellor of Germany. Rightwing parties in Spain began to work actively to establish a **fascist** dictatorship modeled after Hitler's. Meanwhile, Ibarruri's communists and the socialists led a miners' revolt in 1934, which was suppressed by the government. Ibarruri traveled to the area of heaviest fighting and helped to evacuate children and aid the families of the miners. Also in 1934, she organized the National Committee of Women Against War and Fascism.

By 1936, the fascist threat to the republic had grown so severe that the left-wing parties in Spain set aside their differences and cooperated to fight the fascists. The Spanish Civil War began on July 18, 1936, when General Francisco Franco's army attacked Spain from Morocco, across the Mediterranean Sea in North Africa. Ibarruri rallied the antifascists with a radio speech in which she declared, "*¡No pasarán!* [They shall not pass.]" She administered army hospitals, organized communist groups into fighting units, evacuated nuns from enemy territory, and set up organizations to help soldiers at the front. When Italy and Germany, both fascist states, began aiding Franco, Ibarruri traveled to France and Belgium to enlist support for the republican side as well. She rallied the Spanish people to fight Franco by comparing him to another invading general, Napoleon, and roused the women to fight with knives and boiling oil. She caused the Spanish defense minister to be fired because she did not like the way he was waging the war.

In March 1939, Franco's forces overthrew the Spanish republic and established Franco as dictator. Ibarruri escaped to France, and from there she moved to the Soviet Union. She was elected secretary-general of the Spanish Communist Party in **exile** in 1942, and was named its president in 1960. She maintained contact with underground communist forces in Spain, and regularly broadcast messages from Moscow asking the Spanish people to overthrow Franco nonviolently. When she returned to Spain following Franco's death in 1977, she received a hero's welcome. Though some criticized her for unthinkingly following orders from Moscow, and putting her own career ahead of the interests of the Spanish people, she nevertheless was elected to Parliament, at the age of eighty-one.

Ichikawa, Fusae

(1893-1981)

JAPANESE FEMINIST
AND POLITICIAN

Fusae Ichikawa grew up on a farm in Japan's Aichi area. She said that watching her father be cruel to her mother inspired her to help Japanese women gain more power in their lives. After graduating from a teacher training school in Nagoya, she worked as a schoolteacher in a small village in the Japanese countryside. After she left teaching, she worked as a clerk in a stockbroker's office. Ichikawa next became the first woman reporter on the staff of the liberal newspaper *Nagoya Shimbun*. She also worked as a labor organizer. In 1918, she moved to Tokyo, where she met Hiratsuka Raicho, a woman who had founded the **feminist** Bluestocking Society seven years earlier. Ichikawa took Raicho on tours of factories in Nagoya, to show her the terrible conditions of the working women. She brought together feminist and labor **activists** in 1919 and 1920 to form the New Women's Association. She felt that Japanese women would not achieve safe and fair working conditions unless they won political power. In Japan at that time, women were not allowed to attend political meetings, and did not have **suffrage** rights (could not vote). The New Women's Organization defied this ban. It fought for the rights of women to take part in Japanese politics. One of the laws that Ichikawa tried to change forbade women from listening to or making political speeches.

In the 1920s, Ichikawa directed the Women's Committee of the International Labor Organization. She traveled to the United States from 1921 to 1924, where she made contact with and was inspired by the National Women's Party. When she returned to Japan, she set up the Women's Suffrage League, which worked for the next sixteen years to convince liberal politicians to grant women the right to vote. She organized housewives to become more active in community affairs. The Women's Suffrage League was dissolved in 1940, when all activity in the country became focused on the efforts of World War II.

Ichikawa opposed the rise of **fascism** and **totalitarianism** in Japan during the 1930s, and argued that a war would be bad for Japanese women. During World War II, she mobilized women around the problems that the war was causing, including food shortages and the lack of male heads of households. When Japan surrendered at the end of World War II, Ichikawa was elected president of the New Japan's Women's League, and she led a successful effort to win the vote for Japanese women in 1945. Once this right was established, the league became the League of Women Voters, and fought to protect the rights of Japanese women voters. Because of fears that this right might be taken away, Ichikawa founded a Fair and Clean Elections association, which kept pressure on politicians to make sure that women would always be allowed to vote in Japan. She also led campaigns against licensed prostitution, to protect the health and status of poor Japanese women.

In 1953, Ichikawa ran for political office as an independent candidate for a seat to the Upper House of Councillors in the Japanese Diet (Parliament). She was one of the only members of the Diet not to belong to a political party. She served in the Diet for eighteen years, winning five out of six elections. She was extremely popular with the Japanese people, and so she did not have to rely on big business or political parties for fund-raising money. As a politician, she fought for equality for women and the poor, and opposed the government corruption that she saw all around her. Ichikawa always opposed the other members of the Upper House when they voted themselves increases in pay. She lived simply, unlike many other politicians, and donated all of her pay raises, plus a portion of her salary, to women's organizations. She was known as a voice of conscience and honesty in Japanese politics. After three years out of office, Ichikawa was re-elected in 1975 with one of the highest number of votes in Japanese history. She won again in 1980 with a similar number. She died in 1981, at the age of eighty-eight.

Jacobs, Aletta

(1851–1929)

DUTCH PHYSICIAN AND BIRTH CONTROL CAMPAIGNER

Aletta Jacobs was the first woman doctor in The Netherlands. She devoted her life to gaining rights and legal protection for women. She fought for better working conditions for women, an end to legalized prostitution, and legalized birth control. She started the world's first birth control clinic in Amsterdam in 1882.

Jacobs was born in the town of Sappemeer, the eighth of eleven children. Her father was a country doctor with ideas that were far ahead of his time. She wanted to follow in her father's footsteps, even though few women had ever attended university in Holland, and none had become a doctor. She was taught at home, and in a local school, and managed to become an assistant pharmacist. Jacobs wrote to the Dutch prime minister and asked to be admitted to the University of Groningen. He wrote back and told Jacobs that she could study there only if her father gave his permission. Her father consented, and she entered the university in 1874. After her graduation, Jacobs visited London and met with famous reformers, including Millicent Fawcett. She joined the **suffragette** movement (to give women the right to vote). She also became convinced that she must do something to help poor people, including fighting social injustice.

She joined her father's medical practice in 1879, facing great opposition from men who felt that she should only practice midwifery (helping women to give birth). She decided to start her own practice, and she specialized in teaching poor people about child care, and how to avoid common diseases by keeping clean. Twice a week for fourteen years, she offered free medical advice and treatment to every woman who needed her help. In 1882, she defied the medical establishment by opening the world's first birth control clinic, in which she helped women prevent unwanted pregnancies.

Jacobs felt that the cause of women's misery was their inferior position under the law. She fought for women's right to vote, and led the international suffragette movement. She formed the Association for Women's Suffrage in 1894 and sparked suffragette movements in Washington, D.C., and in Berlin, Germany. During World War I she led the International Congress of Women's "International League for Permanent Peace" with American Jane Addams. She traveled around the world promoting peace, and met with American President Woodrow Wilson in 1915. Her ideas influenced the creation of the League of Nations, and were remarkably similar to Wilson's "Fourteen Points," his recommendations for treating the defeated countries fairly.

Jacobs fought other laws that hurt women. She campaigned to reduce the number of hours that people were forced to work. She fought to improve safety in the workplace, to prevent the many accidents and diseases caused by miserable, substandard conditions in factories. She tried to make prostitution illegal, to protect society in general and women in particular from sexually transmitted diseases. She felt that women needed to be educated about sexuality so that they could make informed decisions about their bodies. To allow them the right to control their own bodies, she fought for changes in marital laws to make women equal with men.

Jacobs married Carel Gerritsen, a journalist and politician, in 1892. They maintained a "free union," a marriage that was not affected by the laws that practically made women the property of their husbands. Her family life ended in tragedy—her only child died at one day old, and her husband died in 1905. She grieved for the rest of her life.

Her last great struggles came about after World War I, when Jacobs discovered that half a million German prisoners of war were being held in Russian Siberia (an area in far eastern Russian prone to harsh climate extremes). She opposed the heavy punishments for Germany after it surrendered to end the war, and she set up a committee to return the prisoners safely to Germany. This work was later taken up by the International Red Cross. At about this time, when women had finally won the right to vote in The Netherlands, Jacobs became concerned about the lack of rights for Asian women. As part of the International Alliance of Women, she worked to help Asian women gain the same rights won by many European women. Jacobs died in 1929, and her life's achievements became an inspiration to many women who have continued to follow in her footsteps. *See* FAWCETT, MILLICENT

John XXIII

(1881–1963)

ITALIAN RELIGIOUS LEADER (POPE) AND REFORMER

> Our duty is to dedicate ourselves willingly, eagerly, and fearlessly to the work required by our own era, thus proceeding on the way the Church has followed for twenty centuries.
>
> —Pope John XXIII, on the obligations of the Catholic Church

Angelo Roncalli, who took the name John XXIII when he was elected pope in 1958, presided over the most far-reaching reforms in the Roman Catholic Church in four centuries. He made the Church more accessible to common people, worked for world peace, and brought about a mending of relations between Christians and Jews. He became one of the most beloved religious leaders the world had ever known.

Roncalli was born in Sotto il Monte, the village in northern Italy where his family had farmed for five hundred years. The third of thirteen children, he helped his father work the fields and gather wood for fuel. He loved reading, and he walked sixteen miles a day in order to attend school. Later in life, he would maintain close contact with his native village. At the age of eleven, he enrolled in a seminary to become a priest. He studied from 1882 to 1890 in Bergamo, and later at the Pontifical Seminary in Rome. He was ordained as a priest in 1904. From 1905 to 1914, he worked as the secretary to the bishop of Bergamo, Giacomo Radini-Tedeschi, who became a second father to Roncalli. He taught at the seminary where he had studied and began the practice of publishing a newsletter to tell people what the parish was doing. He also started writing a history of the saints.

In 1914, Radini-Tedeschi died, and World War I began. Roncalli was drafted into the Italian army, and served for over two years. After the war he briefly became spiritual director of the Bergamo seminary, but in 1921 Pope Benedict XV appointed him to reorganize the Society for the Propagation of the Faith, an organization that supported Catholic **missionary** activity outside Italy. He did such a good job that in 1925 he was assigned to the Vatican diplomatic corps and was made an archbishop. He succeeded in improving the Vatican's relations with Bulgaria and Turkey. During World War II, when the rest of the world did not want to believe that the **Nazis** were murdering six million Jews, Roncalli passed this information on to the Vatican. Shocked when the pope ordered him to do and say nothing because the Vatican had to remain neutral in the war, Roncalli defied the pope's orders. He used the contacts that he had made in Turkey to help Eastern European Jews escape from the Nazis.

Late in 1944, a coded cable from the Vatican was received in Roncalli's office. His secretary was away, so Roncalli decoded it himself. It was an appointment to become papal ambassador to France, a country that had been terribly divided by the German invasion. Many French people had helped the Nazis, and many had fought against them in the resistance. The Vatican had recognized the German puppet government in France, and many French bishops, including the archbishop of Paris, were being accused of collaborating with the Nazis. Roncalli protested that he could not handle such a difficult assignment. He was told that he was the pope's personal choice.

Once in France, Roncalli performed brilliantly. He persuaded many of the collaborating bishops to resign, promoted bishops who had fought in the resistance, and became one of the most popular men in France. In 1953, at the age of seventy-one, Roncalli was expecting to retire when he was reassigned to be patriarch of Venice. He served in this position for six years, and this time he faced few hard challenges. In 1958, he traveled to Rome to vote for the man who would replace Pope Pius XII, who had just died. On October 28, 1958, he was elected pope, at the age of seventy-seven. He took the name John, to honor his father's name and the name of the church in which he was baptized.

People expected John XXIII to be a quiet pope who would not do anything remarkable. Soon he proved them wrong. He was very uncomfortable with the formalities that separated the pope from other people. Traditionally, the pope ate alone and almost never left the Vatican. John had always wanted to be a priest, to minister to people's souls. He began inviting guests to join him for dinner, and he began traveling through Rome. He visited churches, hospitals, orphanages, prisons, and slums, often unannounced.

John had spent many years in the Vatican's diplomatic service. He knew firsthand how much work needed to be done to bring people of different religions and backgrounds together, to end war and promote love and peace. He created a special department in the Vatican to improve relations with non-Catholics. He sent Vatican representatives as observers to conferences held by other religious groups. He worked to improve relations between the Catholic Church and Eastern European **communist** countries that forbade the practice of religion.

He took stands on important political issues of the day. On Easter Sunday, 1963, he released a papal document that was for the first time addressed to all people of the world. Called *Pacem in Terris* (Peace on Earth), it proclaimed that every person had the right "to worship God in accordance with the right of his own conscience and to profess his religion in public." It pushed for increased participation of women in the modern world, and opposed the building and testing of nuclear weapons. It acknowledged that communist countries had an important role in creating a peaceful and just world. It spoke of conciliation between Catholics and non-Catholics, East and West, and rich and poor.

John's most important act was the convening of a council to change some fundamental Catholic traditions. Opened in October 1962, Vatican II, as it was called, brought about revolutionary changes in the Catholic Church. John died in June 1963, as the council was just getting under way, and so he did not live to see the great changes it brought about. When it ended, the Catholic Church no longer considered Protestants to be heretics, and had apologized to Jews for centuries of Catholic **anti-Semitism**. Jews were no longer to be thought of as "Christ killers," and the Catholic Church would stop trying to convert them. Within the Church itself, big changes were put into place. Priests could celebrate mass in languages other than Latin, so all people could understand the service. Religious freedom of Catholics was expanded, and nonclergy were allowed a greater role in the Church. In a few short years as pope, the humble farmer's son had given to millions of people around the world hope that peace and justice were possible. When he died, he was mourned by Catholics and non-Catholics alike.

Joseph, Helen

(1905–1992)

SOUTH AFRICAN ANTI-APARTHEID ACTIVIST

> I also don't doubt for a moment that the revolution will result in a nonracial society. I have just come from being a patient in Groote Schuur Hospital, where they now have integrated the wards. For the first time in my life, I have seen it working. The patients were mixed, the staff was mixed, and the medical officers were mixed; it was totally integrated. It was beautiful. White and black together. And it works. To me that is terribly exciting.
>
> —Helen Joseph, on racial integration

Helen Joseph, the "mother of the struggle" to create a fair society in South Africa, was the first person placed under **house arrest** in that country. She led a number of women's marches against **apartheid**, and was put on trial for treason (crimes against the state) for four years.

Joseph was born in England in 1905, into what she called an "ordinary, run-of-the-mill, middle-class" family. She was originally going to become a music teacher, since the family could not afford to send both her and her brother to university. When her brother failed his entrance exams, she took advantage of the opportunity to study at King's College in London, where she earned an honors degree in English. Upon graduation, she worked in India as a teacher for three years. She got engaged to a man who worked for the Imperial Tobacco Company, traveling around India teaching villagers how to smoke. Joseph wrote that she saw nothing wrong with this at the time: "I was totally apolitical. I was drunk with the lovely life I was living. We few white teachers were terribly spoilt and absolutely politically unaware." At the end of this time, she fell off a horse and fractured her skull. She was told to take it easy for a while, so she did not accompany her fiancé on his business trip in 1931. Instead, she joined a university friend who had moved to Durban, South Africa, and taught at the friend's father's school. While in Durban, she fell in love with someone else and married him. She never returned to India.

Her life and political outlook did not change, however. Her husband was a dentist, and the couple led a comfortable and nonpolitical life. "I played bridge. I played with my garden," she had said. When World War II came, her husband joined the dental corps, and Joseph volunteered to give current-event lectures to women in the air force. The material she was to teach came from England, and was extremely left-wing. She began to realize that she was living in an unjust and intolerant society.

Joseph was thirty-nine years old when the war ended. She left her husband and became the director of a community center in Johannesburg. After this she worked with Colored people (the name given by the South African government to anyone of mixed racial background) in Cape Town, and began to realize that "all I was doing was giving aspirin for a toothache. It was wonderful to build these community centers, but it didn't do much for people's lives. I began to feel it was the whole system that had to be dealt with, and that means engaging in political action," she recalled.

In 1953, she met a political **activist** named Solly Sachs while working with a clothing industry medical-aid society. He brought her into contact with black workers and set her on a political path that she never left. She helped found the radical Congress of Democrats with Ruth First and others. It became the home of many white **communists** whose party had been banned by the South African government. The Congress of Democrats worked with the African National Congress (ANC), which at that time did not accept whites. While the ANC organized in black townships, the Congress of Democrats worked to change the attitudes of white people.

In 1954, Joseph helped organize the Federation of South African Women, a group of black and white women working together to end apartheid and improve the lot of South African women. As part of the Defend the Constitution Women's League, she organized a protest march of white and black women in 1955. The plan was for women from all over the country to meet in Pretoria (the capital) to protest four apartheid laws. Three days before the protest was to occur, the Pretoria city council turned down the women's request for permission to demonstrate. Joseph hit upon a brilliant solution: "I said to [the lawyers] . . . 'Look, if I want to deliver a letter to the minister in Pretoria, not send it by post, and if Mrs. Van der Merwe down the road also wants to take a letter to the minister, and also doesn't trust the post, and if Mirs Sibeko in Orlando also wants to do it, and if we all go on the same day, is that a gathering?'"

In two days, the Women's League organized every woman who was planning to attend the gathering to write and sign a letter to the government ministers. The gathering turned into a huge demonstration, the first by South African women. In 1956, a demonstration march against the issuing of travel passes for black women included more than twenty thousand women. By the time the passes were instituted, in 1963, most of the women leaders of the anti-apartheid movement had been put in jail.

Joseph herself was the first South African placed under house arrest, in 1962. For nine years she was forbidden from leaving her house on evenings and weekends, and was allowed no visitors. Every day, she had to report to the police station at noon. Once she forgot, and she had to spend a few days in jail. She received threatening phone calls, and shots were fired at her house. A bomb was discovered tied to the gate of her house. In spite of all this, Joseph carried on the struggle. She met with people secretly, and often broke the ban against seeing more than one person at a time. In 1987, she published her autobiography, *Side by Side,* which was banned in South Africa. She described the brave men and women with whom she had fought to bring justice to South Africa. *See* FIRST, RUTH

Kern, Eha

(1947–   )

and

Tiensuu, Roland

(1979–   )

SWEDISH TEACHER AND STUDENT ENVIRONMENTAL ACTIVIST

> [I began to feel] a little hopeless that I was not doing more than teaching my pupils to read, write, and count when there were so many problems in the world that needed to be solved. . . . I decided to start influencing my pupils to work with international understanding. I wanted to let the children know of other cultures and how they worked, so we invited people who had lived in other countries to come to the school. A person came from Bali and told them about the rain forest. And then the children started to ask me questions about the rain forests.
>
> —Eha Kern, on environmental awareness

> I thought, "There must be something we can do." I saw a television program where people planted trees to replace some of those that had been cut down. But, of course, we couldn't do that because we live far away in Sweden. Then I thought that instead we could buy the rain forest.
>
> —Roland Tiensuu, on saving nature's treasures

Eha Kern, a Swedish schoolteacher, began to teach her class about the world's tropical rain forests in 1987. The students were so excited about the plants and animals that they wanted to visit the rain forests when they grew up. When the students found out that the rain forests are being destroyed and may not exist in another thirty years, they decided to do something. Led by student Roland Tiensuu, the seven-, eight-, and nine-year olds began raising money to "buy" acres of the rain forest in Costa Rica. The students would not own the land, but it would be protected from being destroyed. They raised more than $30,000 in Sweden, and inspired children all over the world to help save the rain forests. Eha Kern founded Barnens Regnskog—Children's Rain Forest—and involved schools throughout Europe in raising millions of dollars to preserve the Monteverde rain forest of Costa Rica. In 1990, Kern, Tiensuu, and other students were invited to visit Costa Rica by President Oscar Arias Sanchez.

Kern began teaching about the rain forest because she was concerned that her young students did not know much about the world beyond their small village in Sweden. She invited a speaker who had visited the rain forest, and she found that the students were fascinated by the unusual animals found there: jaguars, spider monkeys, sloths, golden toads, and tropical birds. From television programs, the students had learned that in thirty years, there might not be any rain forests left. Roland Tiensuu, one of Kern's students, suggested buying some rain forest. That way, no company could come, tear down the trees, and use up the soil. The students all liked his idea, but Kern did not know if that was possible. Then, through a friend, she heard about the Monteverde program to buy Costa Rican rain forests. An American biologist, Sharon Kinsman, gave a slide show to the class about the Monteverde Cloud Forest Preserve. She told the class that the best thing they could do was protect small pockets of rain forest, so that in fifty or one hundred years, when people finally realize what they have done to the planet, there will be pockets of rain forest left from which to build.

Tiensuu organized the other students to begin raising money. They put on a performance of songs, poems, and puppets, and educated their parents about the danger to the rain forests. They raised money by selling books and paintings, and they raised enough money to buy twelve acres in Monteverde. They were so excited that the class started thinking even bigger. The students wrote to other schools and television stations, and soon they were getting publicity on Swedish television. Soon, many people wanted to help. The students organized rabbit-jumping contests, pony rides, bake sales, and other fundraisers. They wrote to rich people and asked for donations, and started publishing a rain forest newsletter. Her class raised $30,000, which was sent to Monteverde. Students from different countries began sending money in, and in February 1992, forty-five thousand acres were set aside as the Bosque Eterno de los Niños, Spanish for the Children's Eternal Forest. This area has continued to grow from donations sent by the children of the world.

Back in Sweden, Kern organized Barnens Regnskog to raise funds for the rain forest. Thousands of schools across Europe, the United States, and Japan have joined this or similar organizations, and now work to save rain forests in countries like Guatemala, Belize, and Thailand. To honor their work, the king and queen of Sweden visited Kern and her class in their little red schoolhouse. The president of Costa Rica, Oscar Arias Sanchez, invited Kern, Tiensuu, and other students to visit Costa Rica for three weeks. They visited the rain forest, met with Sanchez, and cried when they had to leave. But thanks to their commitment and ingenuity, when they can come back the beautiful rain forest will still be there.

Khaas, Mary

(1927–1995)

PALESTINIAN PEACE ACTIVIST

Mary Khaas dedicated her life to creating peace between Israelis and Palestinians. She joined the only political party in Israel that consisted of Arabs and Jews, created kindergartens in the Gaza Strip refugee camps, and turned her house into a meeting place for Israeli and Palestinian peace **activists**. Her last project was an education program for Palestinian soldiers released from Israeli jails. Despite all the obstacles to peace, she always believed that understanding and respect could bridge any gaps between the two peoples.

Khaas was born into a Christian Palestinian family in what was then the British mandate of Palestine in the late 1920s. Her family lived in the port city of Haifa, where Jews and Arabs lived together in integrated neighborhoods. She was fascinated by the rituals surrounding the Passover holiday, during which Jews are commanded to get rid of all foods made with flour, except for the unleavened (non-rising) matzoh. Her Jewish neighbors used to sell their food to her family during the week of Passover (eight-day festival commemorating the escape of Jews from Egypt in ancient times). The Arabs and Jews of Haifa put a lot of effort into living and working together, as one mixed community.

Khaas spent much of her childhood in the family olive groves. She recalled with fondness harvesting the olives, carrying them to the presses, or watching her mother and aunts cure the different varieties in brine (a salt solution). There were entire winters when there was little to eat except for olives, olive oil, and bread. Khaas was raised as an Anglican Christian, but at an early age she rebelled against the teachings of the church, and was never confirmed.

When relations between Jews and Arabs worsened and sometimes turned violent, Khaas believed in cooperation and respect. In 1948, after Israel declared its independence and won a war against five of its Arab neighbors, Khaas, unlike many other Palestinians, did not leave. Instead, she joined the Israeli **Communist** Party and worked with both Arabs and Jews to create a second state for Palestinians alongside Israel. She also went against the wishes of her family by marrying a Muslim, Mohammed Khaas. He was in an Egyptian prison in Gaza in 1948, and when Israel captured that region in its war of independence, he was moved to Israel. After the war, Egypt refused to take back its prisoners. Mohammed remained in Israel and became the editor of a communist newspaper. Neither of their families would talk to them for a long time because of the intermarriage.

Mary and Mohammed grew dissatisfied with the Communist Party, and they looked for other things to do. When Israel captured Gaza again during the 1967 war, the Khaases made up with Mohammed's family and moved to Gaza to be with them. Mary was angered by the gulf between the wealthy Palestinians and the Palestinian refugees from Israel, who had been left to live in poverty by their neighbors. In the early 1970s, Mary began running kindergartens in the refugee camps. The schools, funded by American Quakers, taught in a very different way than the traditional Arab school. Khaas believed that learning had to come from within a child, and she opposed lecturing to children and making them learn things by heart, instead of thinking, experiencing, and discussing. She also would not allow children in her schools to be punished by spanking or other types of hitting. Most of her teachers were not used to this way of teaching, and she worked very hard to instill her values in them. She insisted that if the Palestinians wanted to build a society that encouraged citizen participation and democracy, they would have to begin at an early age to encourage each child to think for herself or himself, and not follow the commands of a leader.

Khaas also worked to empower (give strength to) the mothers in the refugee camps. Many of them did not know how to read, and their status in their communities was very low. She created a program called Mothers Understanding Methods of Schooling (MUMS) for four-year-olds and their mothers. Since a child's first teacher is its mother, Khaas and her teachers worked with mothers in their own neighborhoods, bringing in books and games and primers (elementary reading texts), to teach the mothers how to teach the children to read. This responsibility gave status to a mother as child's teacher, and many of them learned how to read through teaching their children.

Khaas also taught the Palestinians to regard the Israelis as neighbors, even if they were also political enemies. During the Palestinian uprising against Israel in 1988, when relations between Palestinians and Israelis were incredibly angry and tense, she bullied a group of her kindergarten teachers into visiting an Israeli **kibbutz** (collective settlement) to talk to Jews and to see them as people. Mary and Mohammed used their house as a meeting place for Israelis and Palestinians who were working for peace. Even though they supported the Palestine Liberation Organization (PLO) and its chairman, Yasir Arafat; when the group was calling for the destruction of Israel and engaging in acts of terrorism, Khaas occasionally sent messages to Arafat urging him to recognize Israel's right to exist. Although she was firmly committed to the Palestinian cause, she did not allow anyone to tell her what to think. She refused to cover her face and head with a scarf, which was the dictated way of dress for Arab women, and was threatened with death by **fundamentalist** (believing that their holy books are the literal word of God) Palestinian preachers.

Mary and Mohammed had two sons, one of whom was electrocuted when he was seventeen, and one daughter. The other son went to Beirut, Lebanon, in the 1970s to fight against Syria, and was not allowed to return to Israel after he was captured and then released by Syria. Thousands of the family's Jewish friends wrote to the Israeli government asking that they allow him to return, and in 1993 the government agreed to let him come back to Gaza.

After the Israeli-Palestinian peace agreement of 1993, Khaas left the Quaker kindergartens for a new challenge—teaching thousands of Palestinians who had been released from Israeli jails. Part of their education involved learning about democracy. She hoped that the former prisoners would influence Arafat, who was ruling in Gaza, to become more democratic. Even when the peace process hit obstacles, Khaas was still hopeful. She never gave up on peace, even when Mohammed was not allowed to travel to Haifa for cancer treatments when Israel sealed off the border with Gaza following terrorist attacks. She died of a heart attack in May 1995, at the age of sixty-eight. Israelis and Palestinians alike mourned her passing. *See* ARAFAT, YASIR

Khan, Abdul Ghaffar

(1890?-1988)

PATHAN NONVIOLENT INDEPENDENCE ACTIVIST

Like his famous contemporary, Mohandas Gandhi, Abdul Ghaffar Khan struggled nonviolently for India's independence from Great Britain. A member of a Muslim minority group called the Pathans, he fought against the partition of India and Pakistan, and tried to win the Pathan people's independence from Pakistan. Known as the "frontier Gandhi," he spent a total of thirty years in prison, and both inspired, and was inspired by, Gandhi's "nonviolence of the strong." He continued his nonviolent actions on behalf of the poor and the suffering until his death at close to one hundred years old.

Khan was born near Peshawar, in modern Pakistan, around 1890. He was a member of the Pathan people, a fiercely independent and violent Muslim group. The British were unable to fully conquer the Pathans, despite mass arrests and killings throughout the nineteenth and twentieth centuries. Khan's father was a wealthy chief of his village, and was unusual for a Pathan in that he forgave his enemies. Pathan culture relied heavily on a strict code of revenge.

Khan was the first of his group to be educated in a British **missionary**-run school. When he was nineteen, he turned down a commission in the Guides cavalry unit because the British officers treated the Pathans without respect. He followed his mother's advice and did not pursue an opportunity to study engineering in England. Instead, he married in 1912, had a son, and became chief of one of his father's villages. He opened Islamic schools and taught his people modern techniques of agriculture and hygiene. A local reformer, Haji Saheb, influenced Khan to think about political freedom from the British. The British government was suspicious of Khan's reforms, and they shut down some of his schools. In 1919, he was arrested for taking part in Gandhi's nonviolent protests. He spent three years in prison, most of it in solitary confinement, and lost fifty pounds.

In 1926, Khan was influenced by the Islamic **nationalism** that he saw on a visit to the Middle East. He started a journal in the Pathan language, which was banned by the British and later by the Pakistani government. In 1930, after getting to know Gandhi personally, Khan formed a Pathan resistance group called the Khudai Khidmatgars. Members of this group had to take an oath of nonviolence. For such a warlike society, this was a true change in thinking. Yet the bravery that the Pathan warriors had always shown in battle did not desert them in their nonviolent efforts. The Khudai Khidmatgars were fired at by British machine-guns, attacked by tanks, jailed, tortured, and massacred. Their numbers grew to fifty thousand, as tales of their bravery and heroism spread. One British rifle platoon was severely disciplined for refusing to fire upon the Pathans.

Khan was again arrested, then **exiled** from the Pathan part of India. He joined Gandhi at his ashram (Hindu religious site), and in 1934 he was offered the presidency of the Indian National Congress. He refused, saying that he only wanted to serve, not to lead. He returned to his village and began teaching the inhabitants when he was again put in prison, this time for two years. Upon his release, Khan continued to turn his fellow Pathans into nonviolent soldiers. Gandhi visited the Pathan territory twice in the 1930s, and he called Khan's efforts "the nonviolence of the strong."

In 1947, the British left India. The country was then partitioned into a Muslim state, Pakistan, and a Hindu state, India. Gandhi and Khan both opposed the partition, and the terrible violence that followed. The Pathan territory came under Pakistani rule, and Khan asked for **autonomy** (limited self-government) for the Pathans. The Pakistani government called him anti-Pakistani, and put him in jail for fifteen years during Pakistan's first eighteen years of independence. The Pakistani government destroyed the Khudai Khidmatgars, killing thousands of them.

In 1962, Khan was named Amnesty International's "Prisoner of the Year." In its statement, the organization declared, "Nonviolence has its martyrs. One of them, Abdul Ghaffar Khan . . . symbolizes the suffering of upwards of a million people all over the world who are in prison for their conscience. Despite appeals, the old man still lies in jail." He was seventy-two at the time. Two years later, he was allowed to leave the country for medical treatment. He went into exile in Afghanistan, and his son led the Pathan party during his absence. Upon his return, father and son were imprisoned by the Pakistani government in 1975 for continuing to demand autonomy for the Pathans. In 1983, many people in Pakistan took to the streets and demonstrated for a return to democracy. Khan, at the age of ninety-three, joined them, and was imprisoned again. After several months, international pressure won his release.

Khan never became embittered by his years in jail. He saw his imprisonment as a willing sacrifice for those of his people who were truly oppressed. He was nominated several times for the Nobel Peace Prize, and in 1985, at the age of ninety-five, was invited to speak at the one-hundredth anniversary meeting of the India Congress Party. *See* GANDHI, MOHANDAS

Khan, Begum Liaquat Ali

(1905–   )

PAKISTANI POLITICIAN AND WOMEN'S LEADER

Begum Liaquat Ali Khan, the widow of assassinated Pakistani Prime Minister Liaquat Ali Khan, organized more than two million Pakistani women into a major political movement. She became the world's first Muslim woman ambassador, and later governed a province of Pakistan.

Khan was born in 1905 into an aristocratic Muslim family in north India. She studied at the universities of Lucknow and Calcutta, and at the age of twenty-six moved to New Delhi to teach economics at the Indraprastha College for Women. She married Liaquat Ali Khan, a politician, in 1939. After the partition of India and Pakistan in 1947, he became prime minister of Pakistan. During the time of great violence and suffering following the partition, Begum Khan organized

Pakistani women into a group two million strong. At first they worked as nurses, teachers, and administrators, helping out wherever they could. The first meetings of this group were at Khan's house. Following her husband's assassination in 1951, Khan turned the All Pakistan Women's Association into a women's movement, concentrating on involving women in the political life of the country. The association founded schools and hospitals, and helped women support themselves by building up a crafts industry.

In 1954, Khan was appointed ambassador to Belgium and The Netherlands, the first Muslim woman to hold such a position. Later she represented Pakistan in Italy and Tunisia. She became an active participant in United Nations activities, and she worked for the International Labor Organization as well. In 1973, she was appointed to govern Sind province, the first Pakistani woman to do so. She also was chancellor of the University of Karachi. In 1978, she was honored by the United Nations with its **Human Rights** Award.

Klarsfeld, Beate

(1 9 3 9 –   )

GERMAN NAZI HUNTER

> It is my moral and historic responsibility to bring Nazi criminals to trial and to support the Jewish people and state. And to stop anti-Semitism . . .I am building a bridge between the German and Jewish people.
>
> —Beate Klarsfeld, on her life's work

Beate Klarsfeld has devoted her life to bringing **Nazi** war criminals to justice. She and her husband, Serge, have documented the war crimes of former Nazi officials, and used legal means and publicity to bring them to trial. In 1974, she was nominated for the Nobel Peace Prize.

Klarsfeld was born in Berlin in 1939, the same year that Adolf Hitler invaded Poland and started World War II. Her father served in the German army, and after the war he never spoke about what had happened. Klarsfeld only learned about the Nazi **Holocaust**, the killing of six million Jews and five million others, when she got a job as a nanny in Paris when she was twenty-one. She met a Jewish graduate student, Serge Klarsfeld, whose father had been killed by the Nazis. They were married in 1963.

Beate got a job as a secretary at the French West German Youth Service in Paris, and in her spare time she researched the Holocaust. When the Klarsfelds learned that the man who had been elected as chancellor of West Germany in 1967, Kurt Georg Kiesinger, had been a high-ranking Nazi, they took action. Beate wrote articles describing Kiesinger's war crimes. She was fired by the Youth Service agency because of these articles. The Klarsfelds decided to devote all their time to defeating Kiesinger in the next election. Beate somehow climbed onto the podium of Berlin's Congress Hall, slapped Kiesinger on the face, and shouted "Nazi! Nazi!" She was arrested and almost shot by security forces. When Kiesinger sued her, she used the publicity surrounding the trial to tell the German people about his Nazi past. Kiesinger lost the 1969 election because of all the negative publicity.

The Klarsfelds continued to research the locations of other former Nazi officials around the world. They traveled to Bolivia, in South America, and chained themselves to a bench outside the office of Klaus Barbie, the notorious Nazi "Butcher of Lyon." The Bolivian government did not want the world to know about all the Nazis that it had allowed in after World War II, and threw the Klarsfelds out of the country. Twelve years later, when a new Bolivian government came to power, Barbie was caught and sent to France to stand trial. He blamed Klarsfeld for his capture.

The Klarsfelds have not always relied on governments to bring Nazis to justice. Kurt Lischka, a former Nazi wanted in France, was found living in Germany. When the French government found it difficult to get Lischka because of delays over paperwork, the Klarsfelds tried to kidnap him and bring him to France themselves. Lischka called the police and the Klarsfelds spent a week in jail. In 1984, they were arrested in Chile while trying to arrange for the deportation of Walter Rauff, the designer of the gas chambers, in which concentration camp captives were killed by the poison gas Zyclon-B. Gas chambers were installed in many of the Nazi death camps in order to kill large numbers of people at once. The Klarsfelds' car was bombed in 1979, and they have received letter bombs and death threats from people who want to revive the Nazi movement. Nevertheless, Beate and Serge Klarsfeld continue to pursue justice, and put an end to **anti-Semitism,** by combining thorough research with the ability to capture the media's attention.

Kouchner, Bernard

(1939–   )

FRENCH DOCTOR AND HUMANITARIAN

> I think a universal consciousness is taking shape. It's beginning to demand a minimal respect for human rights. It is an important advance that people recognize that suffering belongs to everyone, that it is not affected by borders.
>
> —Bernard Kouchner, expressing his humanitarian beliefs

Bernard Kouchner is a French physician who has founded two organizations of doctors who bring medicine, medical care, and food to people who are under attack all over the world. He believes that good doctors not only tend to the wounded, but also must try to stop the bombings. His main idea, that people have a "right to interfere" in another country if that country is hurting its own people, was finally accepted by the United Nations Security Council in 1991.

Kouchner was born on November 1, 1939, in Avignon, France. His father's parents, who were Jewish, were killed by the **Nazis** during the **Holocaust** in World War II. Kouchner grew up in the suburbs of Paris, and he was deeply influenced by the left-wing writings of Jean-Paul Sartre and Louis Aragon. In some respects he was a typical teenager. He liked sports cars. He also threw himself into political causes from an early age. He protested for Algerian independence from France, and in 1963 he worked in agricultural **cooperatives** (business owned collectively by all the workers) in Yugoslavia.

In 1964 he became a doctor, and also received a journalism degree. He traveled to Cuba, where he interviewed dictator Fidel Castro and met revolutionary Che Guevara. In 1968, he volunteered for the Red Cross in the African nation of Nigeria, where the government and a breakaway region called Biafra were engaged in a brutal civil war.

Kouchner witnessed suffering, malnutrition, bombed-out hospitals, severe injuries, and deaths. He determined that what he was witnessing was actually a campaign of mass murder carried out by the Nigerian government. The Red Cross does not get involved in political issues, however. It does not take sides, but ministers to the sick on all sides. Kouchner was frustrated by this position. He felt that he could not stay neutral about **genocide** (the murder of an entire people). Good doctors, he thought, should work to end the cause of the suffering, simply treat its victims. They should speak out against **human rights** abuses.

In 1971, Kouchner founded Médecins sans Frontières (MSF), French for "Doctors Without Borders." Its mission was to tend to victims of war, famine, and disease even in countries whose governments were causing the suffering. He proclaimed all of humanity's "right to interfere": "If a child is being beaten in the apartment next to yours, you can call the cops; but you also have a right to break down the door." MSF doctors worked in Jordan, Nicaragua, Lebanon, Vietnam, and Turkey. They brought international pressure on governments to stop killing their own people, and to end wars in which they were involved. Kouchner recalled that many mainstream international aid organizations saw MSF as "dangerous madmen" who entered countries and worked without the consent of the governments involved. (The Red Cross and most other **humanitarian** organizations rely on the goodwill of governments to allow them to do their work.)

In 1979, Kouchner wanted to rescue thousands of refugees from South Vietnam who were stranded on rickety boats in the South China Sea. These "boat people" became the center of international attention when no country would allow them to land. Kouchner chartered a boat, the *Ile de Lumière*, which he fitted with one hundred hospital beds, and planned to sail into the South China Sea and pick up the boat people. The MSF board of directors refused to go along with the plan, so Kouchner resigned and formed a new organization, Médecins du Monde (MDM), or "Doctors of the World." MDM has provided medical relief in Afghanistan, Armenia, Ethiopia, Brazil, Chile, Colombia, Guatemala, El Salvador, Mexico, Mozambique, Poland, and Burma (Myanmar). It has fought for the right to send its doctors anywhere in the world, a principle that has gained widespread acceptance since Kouchner first stated it in the 1960s.

In 1991, the United Nations Security Council passed Resolution 688, which stated that Iraq had to allow international relief workers to enter Kurdistan, an area where the Iraqi government had been conducting massacres against the Kurdish people, an ethnic minority. This was the first time that the United Nations had accepted Kouchner's "right to interfere" as international law.

Kouchner left MDM and became France's minister of humanitarian policy in 1988. He has received many awards for his life's work, and he continues to be active in French politics and the international effort to protect human rights everywhere.

Kübler-Ross, Elizabeth

(1926–)

SWISS-AMERICAN PSYCHIATRIST AND ADVOCATE FOR THE DYING

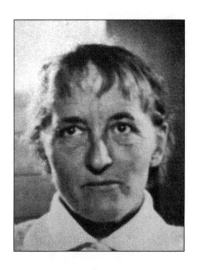

To live on borrowed time, to wait in vain for the doctors to make their rounds, lingering on from visiting hours to visiting hours, looking out of the window, hoping for a nurse with some extra time for a chat, this is the way many terminally ill people pass their time. Is it then surprising when such a patient is intrigued by a visitor who wants to talk to her about her own feelings?

—Elizabeth Kübler-Ross, on the loneliness of dying

When Elizabeth Kübler-Ross was five years old, she almost died of pneumonia. She was kept in a children's hospital isolation ward for weeks, and was allowed to see her parents only through glass walls. She later recollected that the lonely, scary environment was almost as dangerous to her survival as the disease itself. As an adult, Kübler-Ross has devoted her life to helping terminally (deathly) ill patients and their families deal with death in a loving and humane way. Her work was the inspiration for the growth of the hospice movement, which tries to take dying people out of sterile, cold hospitals and let them stay at home or in special hospitals, with loved ones and familiar sights nearby. Thanks to her, many doctors and nurses are now better educated in dealing with the emotional needs of dying patients and their families.

Kübler-Ross was born in Switzerland in 1926, one of a set of triplets. She weighed only two pounds at birth, and was not expected to live. Her mother refused to leave her in the hospital, and instead she took her home and surrounded her with love while she grew strong enough to survive. In her Swiss farming village, she was confronted by death frequently. One of her father's friends fell from a tree, and called all of the neighborhood children into his bedroom to say good-bye before he died. Death was not hidden, but was a natural part of community life. Kübler-Ross drew upon these experiences when she described death as "the final stage of growth" in her 1975 book.

During World War II, Kübler-Ross volunteered at a Swiss hospital to serve the refugees who had fled from the **Nazis**. After the war, she hitchhiked across Europe, lending a hand wherever she could. She worked as a cook, a stone-cutter, and roofer. She also spent some time traveling with a Gypsy caravan, and she helped set up typhoid and first-aid stations. After visiting a Nazi concentration camp, she decided that her goal was to help those who were suffering. She returned to Switzerland and enrolled in the University of Zurich medical school. She married a fellow medical student, then moved to America in 1958. She studied psychiatry and worked with schizophrenics (people who have become mentally detached from reality). She developed a revolutionary treatment technique—she asked her patients what they thought would help them. Later she was to apply this same technique to the dying.

In 1965, Kübler-Ross became an assistant professor at the University of Chicago medical school. Some theology students approached her and asked for her help in studying the dying. She developed a seminar, designed as conversations with people who knew they were soon going to die. Doctors, nurses, social workers, and theology students attended these seminars, and they found that dying people wanted more than anything to tell their stories and describe their feelings. Despite the objections of many doctors who wanted to "protect" their patients from talk about death, the seminar went ahead. Kübler-Ross identified five stages that many terminally ill people experience: denial ("not me!"), anger ("why me?"), bargaining ("why now?"), depression, and acceptance.

Kübler-Ross taught that learning about the stages can help people counsel the dying, and allow them to exit life with wisdom, growth, and dignity. Soon her ideas were being put into place in medical, nursing, social work, and theological school curricula. She traveled around the country giving lectures. Soon colleges, hospitals, and even high schools were offering courses on death and dying. She wrote two books, *On Death and Dying* (1969), and *Questions and Answers on Death and Dying* (1972).

She next turned her attention to terminally ill children, whose deaths were even harder to deal with than the deaths of adults. She argued that children know when they are being lied to, and that they should be allowed to express their feelings about what will happen to them. She also stated that parents of a dying child need to express their anger and grief. Instead of sedating children with drugs, hospitals should provide them with a "screaming room."

Kübler-Ross has worked with nonterminal patients as well. She worked in a children's hospital with the blind and did consulting work for the Peace Corps and a psychiatric institute. She was also medical director of the South Cook County, Chicago, Family Services and Mental Health Center from 1970 to 1973.

Starting in 1968, Kübler-Ross conducted research on life after death. She was intrigued by the possibility that the similarities in experiences of many patients who had been declared dead for a short time meant that life after death was real. She told an audience in 1975 that she was sure that there was life after death and promised the medical data to back it up, but so far has not provided it. Many skeptics claimed that she was guilty of leading patients into denial about death, rather than letting them face it.

Kübler-Ross set up a teaching and healing center in California called Shanti Nilaya, Sanskrit for "Home of Peace." She dedicated the center to the exploration of her beliefs in the survival of the human spirit after death and hoped that it would be the first such center of many all over the world. Whether or not eternal life awaits them, many people have found peace in their final days, thanks to the pioneering and compassionate work of Elizabeth Kübler-Ross.

Laing, R(onald). D(avid).

(1927–1989)

SCOTTISH PSYCHIATRIST

> What I tried to do was to find a theory to fit the facts, rather than the other way around. And I discovered, ultimately, that all I could say was that schizophrenia was one position, one way of seeing things, and that normality was another.
>
> —R.D. Laing, on his feelings about personality variations

R.D. Laing was known as the "antipsychiatry psychiatrist." His most influential book, *The Divided Self* (1960), suggested that the mental illness known as schizophrenia was a sane way of coping with an insane world. Laing wrote that the current treatments for mental illness were more concerned with "controlling" the patient rather than effecting a cure. He founded and directed Kingsley Hall, a therapeutic community in which doctors and patients lived together as equals, and where people were free to go through their insanity without drugs or shock treatment.

Laing was born in Glasgow, Scotland, in 1927. According to Laing, his father was a controlling man who beat him frequently, and his mother was a **fascist anti-Semite**. He originally wanted to study music and become a pianist, but his father would not allow it. Laing read voraciously, and determined that he would not become like his parents. He attended a state secondary school, then enrolled at the University of Glasgow. He studied medicine, specializing in psychiatry. He began to question the psychiatric profession, he recalled later, when he saw one of his professors asking embarrassing personal questions of a teenager in front of a medical class. Laing was horrified at the "brutality and insensitivity" that many psychiatrists showed toward their patients.

After graduation, Laing served in the British army as a psychiatrist. He reported that he enjoyed the company of his "insane" patients more than that of his colleagues. He began to formulate his theories that insane behavior is a defense mechanism against a crazy world, and that mental illness should just be allowed to run its course. He saw the human condition as one where the "Stone Age baby" meets the "twentieth-century mother" and cannot get what it needs in the strange, cold modern world.

Laing taught in the Department of Psychological Medicine at the University of Glasgow until 1956, and then went to London for training in psychoanalysis, the method of treating emotional problems that was pioneered by Sigmund Freud. While in London, Laing completed the book *The Divided Self.* Published in 1960, its stated goal was "to make madness, and the process of going mad, comprehensible." He wrote about schizophrenia in a way to make it understandable to a person who had not experienced it. Laing saw certain family structures, in which a weak personality is in danger of being swallowed up by a stronger personality, as causing schizophrenia. The schizophrenic fights against the "death" of his real personality by developing a series of behaviors that hide the real person away, safe from destruction.

The seemingly crazy and random behavior and speech of many schizophrenics can be decoded, Laing believed. The examples he gave in the book gave voice to many readers' own feelings of alienation in a cold and unnatural world. They interpreted Laing's work as meaning that schizophrenics are the only ones sane enough not to adapt to a crazy world. Laing was hailed as the person who exposed psychiatry as a control mechanism that was more interested in locking people away and drugging and shocking them into conformity than truly dealing with human misery. Many psychiatric professionals were appalled at Laing's conclusions that madness is as "normal" as normalcy.

Laing directed the Langham Clinic in London from 1962 to 1965, but he left because of a dispute with another of the clinic's directors over the use of psychedelic (mind-altering) drugs. Laing had begun experimenting, both on patients and on himself, with LSD, mescaline, and hashish. He felt that these "mind-expanding" substances helped people get in touch with their "inner self." He wrote a long poem, "The Bird of Paradise," in which he described his experiences with psychedelic drugs.

In 1964 Laing founded the Philadelphia Association, which was dedicated to establishing hostels (clinics that had a homelike atmosphere) that provided a humane treatment for schizophrenia. In 1965, the most famous of these hostels, Kingsley Hall, opened in London. In an environment of caring and equality, the mentally ill and their doctors lived together and worked on personal growth and healing. Community outrage over the use of hallucinogenic drugs forced the closure of Kingsley Hall, but other clinics continued doing this work.

Laing expanded his criticism of society as an "unlivable world" in his books *The Politics of the Family* (1969) and *Knots* (1970). He retreated from Western society in the early 1970s, traveling in Ceylon (now Sri Lanka), India, and Japan, meditating with religious teachers and practicing yoga. Upon his return, he lectured across the United States and became a hero of the American counterculture by attacking "state control" of its citizens' minds. Laing continued to work and write until his death, in 1989.

Leach, Penelope

(1 9 3 7 –   )

ENGLISH PSYCHOLOGIST, WRITER, AND EDUCATOR

> What is the use of writing learned articles about the nature and causes of bedwetting if you don't pass it on to the people who are actually having to wash the sheets?
>
> —Penelope Leach, on the importance of getting information about parenting to actual parents

Penelope Leach is an English child psychologist and author. She has written a number of books of advice for parents of babies and young children. She is active in the campaign to stop corporal (physical) punishment of children in schools and homes. She also sits on a social justice committee of the British Labour Party.

Leach was born in London in 1937. Her parents were both writers. She was close to her mother, but feared her father, whom she has said regarded children as "an expensive bore." During World War II, her mother worked for the English government assisting resistance movements in Europe. Her parents separated after the war, but Leach could not live with her mother and her new boyfriend (at the time it was considered a scandal for unmarried couples to live together). Leach attended a boarding school instead, and she hated it. She received a scholarship to the University of Cambridge, where she was more interested in acting than academics. In 1960, she earned a social science degree from the London School of Economics, and she went on to receive a Ph.D. (doctorate) in psychology in 1965. She became interested in child development, and she noticed that most of the research on this topic had been conducted on children whom she did not regard as typical. She was the first researcher to study "normal" children, and their interactions with their parents. She was a lecturer at the University of London from 1965 to 1967.

In her first book, *Babyhood: Infant Development from Birth to Two Years*, published in 1974, Leach made psychological research findings available to parents in language they could understand and apply. In 1977, she wrote *Your Baby and Child*, her most popular book. In it, she tried to present the baby's point of view. She wrote that many parents tell their first child that they are going to have another baby because they love the first child so much, that they want another child like the first. She asked how wives would like it if their husbands decided to marry a second wife because they loved the first wife so much. *Your Baby and Child* has sold three million copies. Part of its success is the simple message that all babies are different, and each one will tell its parents how it wants to be treated. Leach wrote: "Don't do things by the book. Do them by the baby."

Leach has also studied the interactions of babies and their parents, juvenile crime, human personality development, preschool education, and aspects of adolescence. She has written about the difficulties of raising children in Western societies, where the quest for material possessions is so important. She has brought her child care message to cable television and videos.

In 1989, Leach was a cofounder of EPOCH (End Physical Punishment Of Children), an organization dedicated to eliminating corporal punishment from schools and homes. Her **activism** is paying off—England has since banned corporal punishment in schools. She wrote that while discipline is important, children develop best when given the freedom to explore and make mistakes. She called this part of parenting "judicious permissiveness."

Leach serves on the Labour Party commission on social justice. She is working to redesign Great Britain's system of taxes, benefits, and welfare to allow mothers to stay home to care for their babies for longer periods of time. In her opinion, mothers ideally should stay home with their babies for two to three years after birth. Her critics say that this is impossible for 70 percent of British women. Many women feel that she is trying to keep them from having successful careers. She replies that mothers' best interests and children's best interests are not always the same. She feels that mothers should be told that day care is not as good for most children as the care that they themselves can provide.

Lefaucheux, Marie-Hélène

(1904-1964)

FRENCH FEMINIST

Lefaucheux was born with the last name Postel Vinay in Paris in 1904. Her first love was music, which she studied at the Ecole du Louvre. Later she blazed a path for women by becoming one of the first women to study at the French School of Political Science. During World War II, she and her husband, the lawyer and engineer Pierre Lefaucheux, became important members of the resistance to **Nazism**. In 1944, Pierre, who had become the leader of the resistance in Paris, was arrested and taken to Buchenwald concentration camp in Germany. Marie-Hélène somehow convinced his captors to release him. After the war, she received two great honors from the French government: the Cross of War, and the Rose of the Resistance.

While Pierre went into the business world, becoming president of the Renault automobile company, Marie-Hélène entered the political arena. She became a deputy of the French Assembly in 1945, and was vice-president of the Paris Municipal Council. She served in the Senate, and was named vice-president of the Assembly of the French Union in 1959. She worked during these years to better the lives of French women, and students from Africa who were living in France. She represented France in many United Nations (U.N.) conferences on the rights and conditions of women around the world, and served as president of the U.N. Commission on the Status of Women. She was also president of the French National Council of Women and the International Council of Women. She retired from active service in 1963, and died in a plane crash in the United States the following year.

Lefebvre, Marcel

(1905–1991)

FRENCH RELIGIOUS LEADER

> When the pope is in error, he ceases to be pope. . . .It is not us but Rome which is moving toward schism. They are the ones moving toward heresy. I am with twenty centuries of the Church and all the saints in heaven.
>
> —Marcel Lefebvre, on Catholicism

Archbishop Marcel Lefebvre defied the Roman Catholic Church to which he belonged and condemned the reforms made in the Vatican II council of the 1960s. He accused the Church of "paying too much attention to the world and too little to the heavenly city for which we are destined." He denounced the "sin of modernism," and opposed religious and intellectual freedom for Catholics. Pope Paul VI suspended Lefebvre in 1976 after he ordained thirteen priests in his International Society of Priests of Saint Pius X. He continued to build his breakaway church until his death in 1991.

Lefebvre was born in 1905 to a religious, strict Flemish family living on the French border with Belgium. His father supported the right of kings to rule, and he died in a German prisoner-of-war camp during World War II. His mother was jailed by the Germans during World War I. The couple was involved in charity work for war casualties throughout their lives. Lefebvre worked in his family's textile factory during school vacations. He knew from an early age that he wanted to be a priest, and he studied at the French Seminary in Rome, where he was ordained in 1929. After a short stint in a working-class section of the town of Lille, in France, he taught in a seminary in what is now the African nation of Gabon. He became an archbishop, and he remained in Africa until the 1950s. He was influenced by the respect that Islam received in North Africa, and he decided it was because that religion proclaimed itself to be the absolute truth. Catholics, he felt, were becoming too interested in making friends with other religious groups, and were uncomfortable about claiming that Catholicism was the only true path to God.

In the 1960s, Lefebvre worked on Vatican II, a council convened by Pope John XXIII to modernize the Catholic Church. The archbishop was scandalized by what he saw as the "dangerous course" that the Church was taking. Priests were allowed to dress like ordinary people. Prayers could be said in languages other than Latin. More power was given to local church leaders and ordinary Catholics. Lefebvre thundered that this was the work of the Devil, not the Holy Spirit. In 1968, Lefebvre was in Paris during student riots that almost overthrew the government of President Charles de Gaulle. He saw long-haired priests protesting with the students, and he felt that he had to save the Church from what he considered to be terrible changes. He wanted to build a "new Ark," a traditional seminary, that would float above the "modernist flood" that was sweeping away the Catholicism he believed in.

In 1969, Lefebvre formed the International Society of Priests of Saint Pius X, named after the pope who in the early twentieth century had declared modernism to be a "heresy." He founded a seminary in Switzerland to train priests to enter this society. In 1974, in response to Vatican visitors to his seminary who expressed the view that priests would soon be allowed to marry, Lefebvre issued a rebellious declaration. He accused the Vatican of destroying the Catholic Church and the priesthood, and he vowed to ordain (bestow holy orders on) hundreds of priests who would oppose the new laws proclaimed by Vatican II. The pope suspended him in 1976, and forbade him from preaching or carrying out any religious functions. But according to the Church's own rules, an archbishop may not be stopped from exercising his religious duties. Legally, the Church could do nothing to take away Lefebvre's power to teach and to ordain new "traditionalist" priests. He defied the pope by celebrating the mass, his way, before two thousand people in a sports stadium in France in 1976, and he led religious services in private homes throughout Latin America. In 1977, he founded a church in Texas that became his society's international headquarters. His movement attracted an estimated one hundred thousand followers worldwide. Lefebvre never actually formed a rival Catholic Church, but he started a movement that continued to exert a powerful influence on the politics of the Roman Catholic Church worldwide. He died in 1991. *See* JOHN XXIII

Luthuli, Albert John

(1898–1967)

SOUTH AFRICAN ACTIVIST

[The struggle in South Africa is] not for wealth or land or domination, but for the recognition and preservation of the rights of man and the establishment of a truly free world for a free people. . . . In a strife-torn world, tottering on the brink of complete destruction by man-made nuclear weapons, a free and independent Africa is in the making.

—Albert Luthuli, from his speech at the Nobel Prize ceremony

Zulu chief Albert John Luthuli headed the African National Congress (ANC) from 1952 until the organization was banned by the South African government in 1960. He fought, always nonviolently, for the rights of South Africa's black majority, and he spent many years in prison. In 1960, he was awarded the Nobel Peace Prize for his hard work and his courage.

Luthuli was born in 1898, and he spent his childhood in the village of Groutville, in the South African province of Natal. Natal was the homeland of the Zulus, one of the largest black tribes in South Africa. As a young boy he lived with his uncle, who was the chieftain of the village. Luthuli attended a boarding school run by **missionaries**, and he decided to become a teacher. He spent fifteen years at Adams College, first studying and then teaching. He was elected president of the

African Teachers' Association, and he founded the Zulu Language and Cultural Society to keep his culture alive. He married, and gave up teaching when the people of Groutville elected him to be their chief.

As chief, he began to change Zulu society, and he started opposing the laws of the white government of South Africa. He allowed women to join tribal councils and closed down beer halls. He organized the Zulu farmers to fight for more and better land on which to grow their crops. As chief, he traveled around South Africa and met many people involved in the struggle to create a democracy. In 1948, he toured the United States and experienced prejudice because he was black. He said later that this experience helped him understand what was going on in South Africa. In 1949, Luthuli helped organize ANC protests, strikes, and nonviolent demonstrations against the government. In 1952, he was elected ANC president. The government forbade him to remain chief of his village, but his villagers refused to elect a new one. In 1953, he was forbidden to travel more than thirty miles from Groutville. After the ANC passed its Freedom Charter, which Luthuli helped to write, the government arrested him, along with thousands of other protesters. He was released after a number of trials, but was again forbidden to travel after he burned his travel pass, a document that all blacks had to carry with them when they went out. He was also forbidden to see visitors and to take part in political protest.

In October 1960, Luthuli was told that he had won the Nobel Prize. He was deeply moved by the news. He told the Nobel committee, "How great is the paradox and how much greater the honor that an award in support of peace and the brotherhood of man should come to one who is a citizen of a country where the brotherhood of man is an illegal doctrine." Luthuli died in 1967, after being hit by a train. His nonviolent methods strengthened the movement that would bring freedom to South Africa's blacks twenty-seven years after his death.
See BIKO, STEVEN; SLOVO, JOE

Luxemburg, Rosa

(1871–1919)

POLISH-GERMAN REVOLUTIONARY

> The elimination of democracy as such is worse than the disease it is supposed to cure.
>
> —Rosa Luxemburg, on the ills of democracy

Acting in direct contradiction to the quote above, the revolutionary **socialist** Rosa Luxemburg threw herself into the Spartacist uprising that tried to topple the democratic German government in 1919. She was caught and killed by German soldiers, and she became a martyr to many left-wing radicals who had been inspired by her writings and her actions while she was alive.

Luxemburg grew up in a lower-middle-class Jewish household in Warsaw, which was then part of the Polish province of the Russian empire. Her father was a merchant and was involved in intellectual circles in Warsaw. When Luxemburg was eleven, she experienced the terror of a **pogrom**, an organized attack by Russian and Polish soldiers and peasants against Jews. This experience led her to fear all forms of **nationalism**. Although she was very small, very fragile, and lame, she grew up as a self-confident and brilliant student. Her school file mentioned her "rebellious attitude." She was expelled from school for leading an illegal discussion group, and she was helped to escape to Switzerland. In Zurich, she earned her Ph.D. (doctorate degree) in law and political science in 1897, writing her dissertation on the development of **capitalism** in Poland. From an early age she had been attracted to the socialist ideas of Karl Marx, and in Zurich she participated in many socialist activities. She met **exiled** Russian revolutionaries and began a long relationship with a Lithuanian socialist, Leo Jogiches, a wealthy man.

Luxemburg and Jogiches founded the organization that later became the **Communist** Party of Poland, and Luxemburg edited its newspaper. She tried to turn the Polish socialists away from Polish nationalism, and argued that **socialism** would come only when workers from all over the world united against their employers. Nationalism, she felt, was a capitalist trick to keep the workers of one country from recognizing their solidarity with workers from other countries.

Luxemburg moved to Germany in 1898, after marrying an acquaintance in order to get German citizenship. Germany had one of the strongest socialist movements in the world, and Luxemburg quickly became the leader of its left wing when she wrote a powerful book, *Reform or Revolution* (1899), which criticized the idea that socialism could come about through slow, small reforms, instead of a major workers' uprising. In 1905, she moved to Warsaw to take part in the workers' rebellion. She hoped that this event would be the first step toward an international socialist revolution. Her experiences in Warsaw led her to write an influential pamphlet, "The Mass Strike," in 1906. Luxemburg argued that if large groups of workers all refused to work at the same time, they could destroy the capitalist system and bring about revolution.

The leader of the Russian socialist movement, Vladimir Lenin, disagreed with Luxemburg. He felt that the revolution would be led by a small group of intellectuals, who would at first tell the workers what to do. Luxemburg told Lenin that this would simply lead to another form of dictatorship (absolute rule) over the workers. She put forth her ideas as a teacher at the German Social Democratic Party School in Berlin, where she worked from 1907 to 1914. While she taught and wrote, she also agitated for militant action that would lead to the international socialist revolution. She was opposed by the leader of the Social Democrats, Karl Kautsky, who pushed instead for legal reforms. Her attacks on Kautsky caused deep splits in the party.

During World War I, Luxemburg was imprisoned by the German government for her opposition to the war. She criticized the Social Democrats for supporting it, and while in jail she inspired the founders of the Spartacist League, which later became the German Communist Party. After the war, a democratic government was established in Germany. The Communist Party boycotted the elections, against Luxemburg's advice, and the Social Democrats became the leaders of Germany. Despite her belief in democracy, Luxemburg took part in the communist Spartacus uprising of January 1919. The German government crushed the rebellion, and captured its leaders. Luxemburg was arrested and murdered on January 15. Soldiers who could not wait until she was brought to trial killed her and dumped her body into the Landwehr Canal. Those responsible for her death were let off with almost no punishment.

Luxemburg became an inspiration to radicals all over the world. Although she did not always live by her own principles, she expressed a distaste for violence, and favored freedom of thought. A Jew by birth, she spoke of her solidarity with oppressed people everywhere. An ardent **feminist** (activist for women's rights), she fought for men as well as women.

Maathai, Wangari

(1940–   )

KENYAN ENVIRONMENTALIST AND HUMAN RIGHTS ACTIVIST

> Poverty and need have a very close relationship with a degraded environment. It's a vicious circle. Land is one of the most important resources in Kenya and all of Africa. Its fertile topsoil ought to be considered a valuable resource—especially since it is so difficult to create. However, . . .thousands of tons of topsoil leave Kenya's countryside every year. During the rainy seasons, it flows in red streams down the slopes, into muddy rivers, and finally to the Indian Ocean—where it can never be retrieved. Yet we seem unconcerned.
>
> Losing topsoil should be compared to losing territories to an invading enemy. And indeed, if African countries were so threatened, they would mobilize their armies, the police, the reserves—even citizens would be called in to fight.
>
> —Wangari Maathai, on environmental destruction

Wangari Maathai coordinated the Green Belt Movement (GBM), through which tens of thousands of African women have planted millions of trees to combat soil erosion and deforestation. She has fought for **human rights**, and women's rights, and has convinced many Kenyans that the environment and politics are linked together. She has been arrested and beaten numerous times by the Kenyan government for her opposition to government policy. In 1991 she received the Goldman **Environmental** Prize.

Maathai was born on April 1, 1940, in Nyeri, Kenya, into the Kikuyu tribe. She grew up surrounded by nature, and she learned from her mother to treat living things with love and respect. One of her favorite living things was a giant wild fig tree. Her mother would not even allow her to gather its dead twigs. Maathai vividly recalls the experience of drawing water from a spring near the tree. Her parents were very modern in their beliefs, and they did an unusual thing—they let their daughter go to school. Maathai attended Loreto Limuru Girls' High School, where she was encouraged to apply for a scholarship to go to college in the United States. She attended Mount Saint Scholastica College, Kansas, where she received her B.A. (bachelor's degree) in 1964. She continued her studies at the University of Pittsburgh, earning an M.A. (master's degree) in 1966. She returned to Kenya that same year. She was saddened to see the changes that were being made to Kenya's environment; her fig tree and thousands like it had been chopped down, and the spring had dried up. In their place were tea plantations.

Maathai became a research assistant in the University of Nairobi's school of veterinary medicine. Very few women in Kenya received even a high school education. Maathai was treated badly by most of the men with whom she worked. Nevertheless, she overcame many obstacles to become the first woman to receive a Ph.D. (doctorate degree) from the University of Nairobi, and later the first female department chair. In the early 1970s, her husband ran for the Kenyan Parliament, and Maathai traveled around the country with him, learning about the poverty of the Kenyan people who lived in cities and rural areas. She vowed to help these people, and she set up an employment agency. In her university studies, she learned of a link between **malnutrition** (diseases caused by a lack of healthy food) and a lack of wood for fuel. She learned that half of Africa's trees had been cut down in the twentieth century, and that fifty-five million Africans did not have enough wood fuel to cook their food. She realized that the health of the people and the health of the land were closely related, and she organized her first tree-planting campaign to fight malnutrition.

In 1977, Maathai coordinated the Green Belt Movement, which

taught women how to plant trees, and provided them with seedlings, shovels, and political and environmental education. She felt that women, who make up 70 percent of Africa's farmers, could gain power through seeing that they could make a difference. Once women organized around tree planting, they could fight for many other issues as well. Maathai began the campaign in schools, where children first got involved, and then they "took the message home to their parents and eventually got women's groups interested," Maathai remembered.

Maathai made sure that poor, unemployed, and handicapped people got jobs at the GBM. Anyone who kept a tree alive for three months outside a nursery received a small amount of money. The project was originally funded by corporate donations and checks from women around the world. Seeing its success, the Kenyan government began spending large amounts of money on tree planting, and more than thirty other African nations have done the same. Tens of millions of trees have been planted in Africa, thanks to Maathai's vision and commitment.

Maathai has also been one of the government's loudest critics. When she divorced her husband in the early 1980s, she lost the divorce settlement and was actually thrown in jail by the divorce judges. She has fought to gain equal rights for women, who in Kenyan society are expected to be submissive to men, and dependent on them. In 1989, she organized protests over the government's plans to build a sixty-six story skyscraper and government complex in Uhuru Park, in downtown Nairobi. Members of Kenya's Parliament demanded that the GBM be declared illegal, and they dismissed Maathai and her group as "a bunch of divorcées." Human rights organizations around the world took note of the "climate of fear" that gripped the Kenyan government. Daniel Arap Moi, the president, took a number of steps that virtually ended democracy in Kenya. He ended free elections, outlawed opposition parties, and banned journals critical of the government. When Maathai protested against these changes, Moi said that it was "un-African and unimaginable for a woman to challenge or oppose men." Foreign investors in the skyscraper were convinced by the GBM protest, and they took away funding for the building.

Following her success, Maathai was harassed even more by the government, and she was beaten unconscious during a women's demonstration protesting the illegal imprisonment of their sons. Her work was drawing international attention and support. She received the Right Livelihood Award in 1984 and the Goldman Environmental Prize in 1991, along with many others. In 1993, she heard about ethnic fighting in the Rift Valley region of Kenya, and she went there to help the victims of government troops. The army had been driving opponents of Moi from their homes. Maathai is still in and out of prison, and hospitals, for her actions opposing the government. She said recently of the army actions in the Rift Valley, "This is wrong. And the politicians must be stopped. . . . I'll stop them. If nobody's stopping them, I'll stop them."

MacBride, Seán

(1904–1988)

IRISH ACTIVIST AND HUMAN RIGHTS ACTIVIST

> The growth of torture has been described as epidemic. To control dissent and maintain power, governments have submitted torture to intellectual analysis and produced progressively more sophisticated methods of cowing, punishing, and eliminating real or imagined opponents of their regimes.
> —Seán MacBride, on human rights violations worldwide.

Seán MacBride, an Irish patriot and political leader, was a cofounder and chairman of **Amnesty** International, an organization that works for the release of political prisoners around the world. MacBride worked for many years to make **human rights** issues part of international trade and diplomatic agreements. He received the Nobel Peace Prize in 1974, and the Lenin Peace Prize in 1977.

MacBride was born in South Africa in 1904. His parents were involved in the Irish struggle against British domination of Ireland. His father, John MacBride, was executed by the British for his part in the 1916 Easter Rebellion; and his mother, Maude Gonne, an actress and Irish **nationalist**, was imprisoned in London. MacBride was educated in schools in Paris and Dublin, and as soon as he turned thirteen he joined the Irish Republican Army (IRA) as a youth volunteer. He worked in the Irish political underground for the next twenty years, spending some time in prison. In 1936, MacBride rose to commander-in-chief. Gradually, however, he reached the conclusion that war would not solve people's problems. He went to law school, graduated in 1937, and was elected to the Irish Parliament. After World War II, he formed a new political party in Ireland that was dedicated to re-uniting the north with the Republic of Ireland, in the south. In 1948, his party won the election, and he became foreign minister. He played a large role in the creation of the office for European Economic Cooperation.

In 1961, MacBride met Peter Benenson, a British lawyer who defended political prisoners around the world. Together they founded Amnesty International, an organization dedicated to ending torture and imprisonment of political prisoners all over the world. MacBride was chairman of Amnesty International from 1961–1975, and he also served as a trustee of the International Prisoners of Conscience Fund. In 1972, he led Amnesty International in an international "Campaign for the Abolition of Torture." In 1973, the United Nations appointed MacBride its commissioner for South-West Africa (now the independent country of Namibia). He worked to convince South Africa, which controlled South-West Africa, to grant it independence. (This finally happened in 1990.) He also labored to provide blacks in South-West Africa with education to prepare them to govern themselves. After a long and varied career in the service of world peace and human rights, MacBride died at the age of eighty-four in 1988.
See BENENSON, PETER; GONNE, MAUDE

Makarios III

(1913–1977)

CYPRIOT GREEK ORTHODOX
ARCHBISHOP AND
POLITICAL LEADER

> We believe one ideology can be fought only by another . . . not by force.
>
> —Archbishop Makarios, on solving disputes peacefully

Archbishop Makarios III, ethnarch of the Orthodox Church of Cyprus, was both the religious and political leader of that island's four hundred thousand ethnic Greeks from 1950 until his death in 1977. He fought for independence from Great Britain and enosis (union) with Greece. He became president of the independent Republic of Cyprus in 1960, and he was briefly deposed in a revolution in 1974. He publicly condemned violence by his followers, but he blamed the British for making bloodshed necessary.

Makarios III was born Michael Christedoulos Mouskos in 1913 in Ano Panayia, Paphos, Cyprus. Cyprus, a small island in the Mediterranean Sea forty miles from Turkey, was populated with a mixture of ethnic Greeks and Turks, with the Greeks making up 80 percent of the population. His family were poor Greek peasants. He attended the local village school, and attended the Abbey of Kykkos, hoping to become a Greek Orthodox priest. He excelled in his studies and received an abbey scholarship to attend the Pan Cypriot High School in the capital city of Nicosia, where he graduated in 1936. In 1938, he was ordained a deacon of the Greek Orthodox Church, and he traveled to Greece to study at the Theological College of the University of Athens. In 1943, he graduated, and then returned to Kykkos as a teacher. Three years later he was ordained a priest, and he went to the United States to study at the School for Theology at Boston University. While he was in the United States, he was elected metropolitan (bishop) of Kition, and he returned to Cyprus before finishing his studies. In 1950, he was elected archbishop and ethnarch of Cyprus, after the old Archbishop Makarios II died.

Makarios III soon embroiled himself in political controversy. Cyprus had been ruled by Great Britain since 1925, after Greece refused to accept the island following World War I. Within the Greek community on Cyprus, there was strong sentiment for a movement called enosis, which desired that Cyprus become part of Greece. Many in the Turkish minority feared that they would lose their rights if Cyprus left the British Commonwealth. In January 1950, shortly before Makarios III took office, the Greek Orthodox Church held a citizens' plebiscite (vote) on the question of union with Greece. Ninety percent of the Greek Cypriots voted in favor of it. Makarios took these results to the British governor of Cyprus and demanded that Great Britain give up control of the island. The governor refused to consider the matter, so Makarios III took his people's case to the world. He traveled to many different countries, including England, France, the United States, and Indonesia, and he worked within the United Nations to bring about an end to British rule in Cyprus. Turkey, however, fearing for Turkish nationals in Cyprus, said that it would claim Cyprus for itself before it ceded it to Greece. Greek Cypriots began resorting to violence, and the riots soon spread to the countries of Greece and Turkey as well.

In 1955, the British governor was replaced by a field marshal, who began holding talks with Makarios III that would lead to limited self-rule by the Greeks on Cyprus. When the talks broke down, violence broke out all across the island. Greek leaders of the Cypriot Communist Party urged a full-scale revolt. British troops occupied the island and arrested 150 **communist** leaders and outlawed the party. Makarios III was caught in the middle—uncomfortable with the violent tactics of the communists, but basically supporting their cause. The British were angered that Makarios III opposed the arrests, and the outlawed communists warned him that violent struggle would continue until the British were forced off the island. Meanwhile, the Athens radio broadcast messages to Cyprus encouraging **terrorism**. The British government held Makarios III responsible for not taking a firmer stand against terrorism, and was angered by his uncompromising position in the negotiations. On March 9, 1956, the British deported (sent away) Makarios III. The Greek government protested, and the terrorism on Cyprus intensified.

Fighting continued until 1960, when Great Britain agreed to leave Cyprus. Makarios III returned, and he was elected president of the Independent Republic of Cyprus. Makarios III was reelected in 1968 and 1973, but he was deposed in a military **coup** in July 1974. The coup leaders were Greek Cypriots who still wanted the island to become part of Greece. Turkey invaded Cyprus to prevent this union, and Makarios was reinstated five months later. Despite his efforts to hold the country together, Cyprus was partitioned in 1975 into a Greek state, the Republic of Cyprus; and a Turkish state, the Turkish Republic of North Cyprus. Makarios III ruled in the Greek area for two more years, and died in 1977.

Mandela, Winnie

(1934–   )

SOUTH AFRICAN ACTIVIST

> I would gladly go and water that tree of liberation with my blood, if it meant that the children I am bringing up under [present] conditions will not lead my kind of life . . . I find myself strength from the knowledge that each step I take the nation is behind me.
>
> —Winnie Mandela, on the fight to end apartheid

Nkosikazi Nobandle Nomzamo Winifred Mandela, known to the world as Winnie, was for many years her husband Nelson Mandela's only contact with the outside world. While he spent twenty-seven years in prison, Winnie was herself under constant surveillance and restriction by the South African security forces. She was "banned" for twenty-seven years, a state of virtual **house arrest**, and spent two years in prison, most of that time in solitary confinement. She has been hailed as the fearless leader of the black **liberation** (freedom from rule by others) movement, and criticized as being too violent and power-hungry to lead the struggle. When Nelson Mandela was released from prison in 1990, he soon distanced himself and the African National Congress (ANC) from the woman who had been his tireless supporter for almost three decades.

Winnie Mandela was born in 1934, in a rural village in Pondoland. By the time her mother died, when Winnie was nine years old, there were nine children in the family. Her father, a history teacher and later Transkei (a black homeland within South Africa's borders) minister of agriculture, raised the family after his wife's death. Winnie attended elementary schools in the Transkei, and then moved to Johannesburg, the largest city in South Africa, to study at the Jan Hofmeyer School of Social Work in 1953. When she graduated two years later, at the age of twenty-one, she was the first black medical social worker in the country. She soon made friends with young blacks who were organizing against the **racist** laws of **apartheid**, which made blacks second-class citizens in South Africa. She met Nelson Mandela, one of the ANC leaders, in 1957. Even though he was eighteen years older than she, and about to stand trial for treason (crimes against the government), the couple was wed in June 1958. She said later that she knew when she married Mandela, she married the anti-apartheid struggle as well. Winnie was arrested for the first time in September 1958 for her part in a mass women's demonstration. She joined the ANC women's league and the Federation of South African Women, and she soon rose to leadership roles in both organizations. She was fired from her job as a medical social worker after her arrest, and she threw herself into the struggle full-time.

Meanwhile, Nelson was sentenced to life in prison in 1964, while in the middle of a five-year sentence he was already serving. The couple had spent only a few months together as a family with their two daughters. Winnie took on the additional role of Nelson's advocate (spokesperson) on the outside. She found herself at the center of media attention. She began defying the South African government by wearing the outlawed black, green, and gold colors of the ANC. In 1962, Winnie was "banned" by the government. This meant that she could not be quoted in the press, could not enter schools, universities, publishing houses or courts, could not leave a certain area, could not meet with more than one person at a time, and could not meet with any other banned person.

Mandela disobeyed the ban many times over the years. In 1970, she spent seventeen months in solitary confinement. Because of her situation, she was unable to raise her daughters. She sent them to schools in Swaziland (an independent kingdom bordering on South Africa), where they were forced to leave by South African security officers.

In 1975, her banning orders expired, and they were not renewed for ten months. During this time she organized the Black Women's Federation. In 1976, following the Soweto (a large, all-black township outside Johannesburg) riots in which police fired on crowds of black children, Mandela organized the Black Parents' Association to help blacks with medical and legal expenses. She was banned again, and in 1977 she was sent to live in a black township on the outskirts of an extremely conservative white town, Brandfort. She immediately organized the black community there, setting up a nursery school, a soup kitchen, a mobile health unit, and self-help projects. In 1985, her house was firebombed. She accused the government of planting the bomb, and she vowed to ignore any restrictions put on her. She made her first public speech in twenty-five years at a funeral in 1986. She said that the blacks would liberate the country "together, hand in hand with our boxes of matches and our necklaces," a reference to a method of mob execution where a car tire filled with gasoline is placed around the victim's neck, and set on fire. At a time when other ANC leaders had begun to call for negotiations and peaceful protest to end apartheid, Winnie Mandela seemed to be growing more impatient and militant.

She became an extremely controversial figure in the ANC in the years just before Nelson's release from prison in 1990. She moved into a new, elaborate home in a very fancy part of Soweto, and she surrounded herself with a group of black men called the Mandela United Football Club. They were accused of terrorizing the neighborhood, and of robbing, beating, and killing many blacks. In 1988, the group was accused by South African police of killing a fourteen-year-old black leader, Stompie Moeketsi, who had led a 1,500-member "children's army" in making the streets of Soweto safe. Winnie Mandela said that the police were lying, but her Football Club was soon blamed for other murders as well. The Congress of South African Trade Unions and the United Democratic Front, the two largest organizations in South Africa, both condemned Winnie

Mandela and her group. Nelson, about to be released from prison, persuaded Winnie to remove the bodyguards from her home.

When Nelson was released in 1990, it soon became clear that he and Winnie no longer saw eye to eye. While trying to keep their disagreements private, their different political strategies soon brought them into conflict. When Nelson Mandela was elected South Africa's president in free elections in 1994, many people saw that as the triumph of his nonviolent approach to change. Winnie's violent tactics, including the murder of a young boy, had only hurt the anti-apartheid movement. With some historical perspective, it may soon be said that Winnie Mandela's greatest contribution to the end of apartheid was the encouragement she provided to her imprisoned husband.

Masih, Iqbal

(1982–1995)

PAKISTANI ACTIVIST AGAINST CHILD LABOR

Iqbal Masih was born in the village of Muridke, Pakistan, into an extremely poor family. When he was four years old, he was sold into slavery by his father because his family was in debt, and they had no other way of raising money. The carpet factory owner who bought Iqbal purchased him for 600 rupees ($12), and Iqbal's family used the money to pay for his brother's wedding. Iqbal worked more than twelve hours a day, seven days a week, for six years. He was beaten, verbally abused, and chained to the loom by the factory owner. His physical growth was severely stunted because he was not given enough food to eat. Despite all of his hard work, his family's debt increased to 13,000 rupees ($250).

Iqbal's case was not unusual. The International Labor Organization estimates that twenty million people in Pakistan are enslaved. They are called bonded laborers, because they can be bought out of slavery when they or their family raise the money. But in almost all cases, like Iqbal's, the family's debt just gets bigger, so the workers are slaves for life. Seven and a half million of the Pakistani bonded laborers are children, and five hundred thousand of them work in the carpet industry. To combat this, a Pakistani man named Ehsan Ulah Khan founded the Bonded Labour Liberation Front (BLLF). This organization fought for the passage in 1992 of the Abolition of Bonded Labour Act in the Pakistani Parliament, which made bonded labor illegal. Very little changed for Iqbal and other children, however, because the carpet factory owners are rich and powerful men who often control the local police forces. The BLLF began holding rallies and celebrations to inform bonded children of their rights under the new law.

In 1992, Iqbal and some other enslaved children in the carpet factory heard about a freedom day celebration given by the BLLF. Iqbal and some other child slaves defied the order of the factory owner and attended the celebration. They learned that they could not be forced to work, and that they were free to attend one of the 240 village "freedom schools" that the BLLF had established. Iqbal was so moved by what he heard that he stood up at the celebration and gave a speech, which was printed in the local papers the next day. He refused to go back to the factory. Instead, he contacted a BLLF lawyer and got a letter of freedom. He showed it to the factory owner, and left to attend school.

Iqbal did very well in school. He skipped two grades in two years. He did not forget the other children in Pakistan and other countries who were still enslaved, however. He traveled around Pakistan, encouraging children to free themselves, giving talks to children all over the country, informing them of their rights. In December 1994, Masih toured Sweden, talking to hundreds of schoolchildren in that country. Swedish schoolteacher and activist Britt-Marie Klang, who opened a BLLF school in Sweden, convinced a Swedish drug company to give Iqbal $14,000 worth of Human Growth Hormone, to try to repair the years of **malnutrition** and abuse. He then visited the United States to receive a Reebok Youth in Action award. He spoke to many children about the system of child labor that oppresses millions in Pakistan, India, and Nepal. At Cambridge Friends School, in Cambridge, Massachusetts, he learned how to use computers. For the first time in his life, he played games. The students taught him how to thumb wrestle, and he was given a Nintendo Game Boy to take home with him. He met the president of Brandeis University, in Massachusetts, who was so impressed that he offered Masih a four-year scholarship. Also in the United States, Masih received medical attention. It was discovered that he had tuberculosis (a disease that affects the lungs), and he was given medicine for it. With his health improving, Iqbal looked forward to the future, and to his dreams of becoming a lawyer so that he could fight for the rights of the other enslaved children of the world. One of his heroes was American President Abraham Lincoln. Masih spoke of one day freeing the children of the world from slavery.

Tragically, his life was cut short before his thirteenth birthday. He returned to his village for a visit to his family in April 1995, and he was shot and killed while riding his bicycle. It was Easter Sunday. At first it was believed that factory owners had killed him, but it later appeared that he was murdered in a senseless, random crime. Eight hundred people attended his funeral, and his body was wrapped in the BLLF flag as he was laid in the ground. His brave life and tragic death have strengthened the commitment of people around the world to abolish child labor permanently.

Menchú, Rigoberta

(1959–   )

GUATEMALAN HUMAN RIGHTS ACTIVIST

> My country has two faces. There is the ugly face of blood and violence, and there is another face which is silent now, silent and unseen.
>
> —Rigoberta Menchú, on the mass killings
> of Guatemala's native peoples

Rigoberta Menchú was awarded the 1992 Nobel Peace Prize for bringing to the attention of the world the terrible plight of the **indigenous** (original native) peoples of Guatemala. The Maya and other indigenous groups have been persecuted by wealthy landowners and the Guatemalan military during a civil war that has gone on for over thirty years. During this time, according to **human rights** groups, one hundred fifty thousand people have been killed, fifty thousand have "disappeared" and are thought to be dead, one hundred thousand have been widowed, two hundred fifty thousand children have been orphaned, and more than one million have lost their homes. Menchú has organized the Guatemalan peasants to fight the oppression and the killing. Fearing for her life, she escaped to Mexico in 1981, and she often travels around the world telling people what is happening in her country.

Menchú was born in 1959, the sixth of nine children of Vincente Menchú, a community leader, and his wife, a midwife and healer. The Menchús were Quiché Maya; the Mayan Indians make up about 75 percent of the population of Guatemala. Even though they are the majority, they have virtually no power in society. Guatemala is ruled by a military government that has massacred entire villages of peasants, and often targets human rights activists and organizers for execution. Menchú's family worked for subsistence wages (just enough to live on) picking coffee beans, often from three in the morning until dusk. Menchú herself followed this schedule when she was eight years old. One of her brothers died from inhaling pesticide fumes, and another died of **malnutrition** while working in the coffee field. Menchú's family were forbidden by the landowner to stop work and bury him, and at the end of that day, they were sent away without pay for the two weeks they had just worked.

When she was twelve, Menchú traveled to Guatemala City to become a maid for a wealthy family. She was forced to sleep next to the family dog, which was treated better than she was. She returned to her village and discovered that her father had been imprisoned. He had organized his village to resist the taking of Mayan farms by wealthy landowners. Menchú and her mother fought for his release, which came one year later. After this, Vincente and Rigoberta continued organizing the peasants to fight for their rights. When he was imprisoned for life in 1977, Rigoberta joined the Committee of Peasant Unity, known by its Spanish initials as CUC. She learned Spanish, as well as three Indian dialects, to help her organize people.

In 1979 and 1980, her father, mother, and a brother were killed by the government in separate incidents. At the time Menchú was leading labor strikes by cotton and sugar workers. When she learned that her own life was in danger, she fled to Mexico. There she worked with other Guatemalan refugees and heard many stories of suffering. She vowed to continue to fight for the Mayan cultural heritage, and for the basic human rights of indigenous peoples throughout Latin America. She began giving speeches around the world. In Paris in

1982, she dictated her story to Venezuelan anthropologist Elisabeth Burgos-Debray, who published it as *I, Rigoberta*. The book has been translated into twelve languages, and it inspires **activists** around the world.

In 1992, the same year as the five hundredth anniversary of Columbus's voyage to the Americas, the Nobel Committee awarded Menchú the Peace Prize. Some criticized the decision because Menchú seemed to support violent resistance to the Guatemalan government. Menchú noted: "The only road open to me is our struggle, the just war. The Bible taught me that . . .We have to defend ourselves against our enemy, but, as Christians, we must also defend our faith within the revolutionary process." Menchú took the $1.2 million prize money that she received for winning the Nobel Prize and set up the Vincente Menchú Foundation, which aids Guatemalan refugees and fights for the cultural survival and human rights of indigenous peoples throughout Latin America.

Mother Teresa

(1910–   )

YUGOSLAVIAN HUMANITARIAN
IN INDIA

We try to pray through our work by doing it with Jesus, for Jesus, to Jesus. That helps us put our whole heart and soul into doing it. The dying, the crippled, the mentally ill, the unwanted, the unloved—they are all Jesus in disguise. We have very little, so we have nothing to be preoccupied with. The more you have, the more you are occupied, the less you give. But the less you have, the more free you are. Poverty for us is a freedom. . . . I find the rich much poorer. Sometimes they are more lonely inside. They are never satisfied. They always need something more. . . . I find that poverty is hard to remove. The hunger for love is much more difficult to remove than the hunger for bread.

—Mother Teresa, on caring for society's poorest people

Agnes Gonxha Bojaxhiu, now called Mother Teresa, was born in Skopje, in what was then Macedonia, in 1910. Her family were Albanian Christians who lived in harmony with their Christian and Muslim neighbors. Her father was the town's grocer. She decided to become a nun at the age of twelve, and she took her vows in a Irish order of nuns, the Sisters of Loretto, when she was eighteen. The Sisters of Loretto ran a mission in Calcutta, India, where she went after completing her training in Darjeeling, India. She worked at St. Mary's School, for wealthy girls, first as a teacher, and later as principal.

Just outside the walls of the school were the slums of Calcutta. Mother Teresa saw thousands of homeless children, poor orphans, sick adults, and people suffering from leprosy (a medical condition that eats away at a victim's flesh and limbs). Because it was (incorrectly) believed that leprosy was extremely contagious, no one would help, or even go near the lepers. In 1946, Mother Teresa heard a "call within a call," and she decided to leave the convent and live among the poor. It took two years to get the permission of the Catholic Church to do so, and in 1948 she left the convent and received medical training from American nuns in India. The outdoor classes attracted other volunteers, who later formed the **Missionaries** of Charity. They believed that by serving the poorest people on earth, they were serving God directly. In 1957, the Missionaries of Charity opened a treatment center for lepers in a home for dying poor people in Calcutta. In the next few years, with increased support from the Roman Catholic Church in India, they opened leper treatment centers in other Indian cities.

In 1965, Mother Teresa received permission from the Vatican to open Missionaries of Charity centers outside India. She sent nuns to Venezuela, Ceylon (now Sri Lanka), Tanzania, Australia, Italy, Jordan, London's East End, and New York's South Bronx. More than 12,000 coworkers minister with Mother Teresa to the poor of the world. In 1979, she received the Nobel Peace Prize. In her acceptance speech, she told the world of her love and respect for the people she serves. She spoke of the beautiful things the poor have taught her. She explained that the person who gives help is really the recipient of much more than the one who receives the help. The helper must be completely humble. Mother Teresa continues to show the world that simple service can provide the richest life of all.

Myers, Norman

(1934–   )

ENGLISH-BORN ENVIRONMENTALIST AND WRITER

> We are witnessing one of the most remarkable biological phenom-
> ena ever to overtake life on the earth. A single species, our own, is
> eliminating the planet's genetic stock more rapidly than at any time
> in the past . . . We still have time—though only just time—to slow
> and even stem the tide of extinctions.
>
> —Norman Myers, in a plea to stop man's destruction
> of the environment

When Norman Myers was thirty-six years old, he already had had
careers as a **colonial** administrator for the British empire in the East
African nation of Kenya, a high school teacher, a wildlife photographer, and a writer. Nevertheless, he began his fifth career by getting a
Ph.D. (doctorate degree) in wildlife biology and becoming the
world's leading authority on **environmental** conservation. He has
helped governments, companies, and other organizations design eco-
logically sound policies in more than ninety countries. He has popu-
larized the "Gaia Hypothesis," which states that the entire earth is one
living organism of which all living things are a part, and he has
alerted the world to the destruction of the tropical rain forests.

Myers was born in Whitewell, England, a small village near Manchester. His father was a sheep herder who taught his four children
about conservation by not wasting anything. He "would use a nail
time after time, until it rusted away," Myers recalled. The family of
six lived in a house with no electricity and no indoor toilet. His
mother had been a schoolteacher before she got married, and she saw
to it that her children got an education. Sometimes the four of them
made up half of the total number of students at their local primary
school. Myers excelled there, as well as in his high school, but he
failed to be admitted to Oxford, one of England's finest universities.
His mother insisted that he try again. The second time he impressed
his interviewer by admitting that he didn't care about getting in to
Oxford, but he had reapplied only to please his mother.

After five years at Oxford, Myers left in 1958 with a degree in modern languages and a diploma in overseas administration. He got a job in Kenya because he had heard it was "a nice spot to live." At the age of twenty-four, he was put in charge of thirty thousand acres of land on which lived fifty thousand Masai tribespeople. His supervisor told him to report back in six months, and not to bother him in the meantime. Myers soon won the respect of the Masai by surviving a thirty-mile hike on a blazing-hot day. He joined a game of placing stones on a rhinoceros's back until it woke up. The trust that he established with the Masai enabled him to work well with them. He was later made an honorary elder (similiar to a chief).

During his three years as an administrator, Myers for the first time became interested in wild animals. It started with his seeing an ordinary giraffe. Soon he began wandering in the savanna (a tropical grassland) looking for birds, cheetahs, lions, elephants, zebras, and many other animal species. When Kenya pressured Great Britain for independence in 1961, Myers left the foreign service and looked for a reason to stay in Kenya. He found a job teaching in Kenya's capital, Nairobi, in the first school in Africa that accepted both black and white students. On his vacations, he traveled to game reserves and photographed animals. To pay for these trips, he started sending his photos in to competitions, and he won many prizes.

In 1965, he married Dorothy Halliwell. After becoming tired of teaching Latin and Shakespeare to teenage boys, in 1966 Myers became a full-time nature photographer. He got involved with film as well, making television movies about African wildlife. In 1966, while on a lecture tour of the United States, Myers read Fairfield Osborne's book, *The Plundered Planet* (1948). The basic idea of the book was that human beings were overusing the earth, which did not have enough resources to continue to be used this way. This book turned Myers into an environmentalist. He published his first statement of his environmental philosophy, along with many of his nature photographs, in his first book, *The Long African Day* (1972).

When sales of his photographs slowed, Myers enrolled in a Ph.D. program in wildlife biology at the University of California at Berkeley. He earned his doctorate by 1973, then returned to Kenya, where he became a citizen. He became a consultant in land-use planning for scores of different clients. Using his knowledge of Swahili (the local language), research skills, and political and scientific background, he was able to negotiate land deals that preserved ecosystems and saved wildlife, such as the building of a game reserve at the base of Mount Kilimanjaro, the highest mountain in Africa. He has advised the United Nations, the World Bank, the World Wildlife Federation, the Smithsonian Institution, and many other organizations.

Myers soon mastered many different areas of specialization, including tropical forests and other bioregions, the greenhouse effect, population growth, economics, "gene revolution" agriculture, and threatened species and genetic resources, among many others. Because of his wide knowledge, he was able to make connections that few others could. He became very concerned about the destruction of tropical rain forests. He found that the rate of destruction of the forests was far greater than anyone had expected. When he began his research, it was assumed that approximately one species of plant and animal per year was becoming extinct. His early figures led him to change that to one per day, and now Myers is convinced that between twenty and fifty species are becoming extinct every day. The effects of this mass extinction are being felt all over the world. Deserts are growing larger, the quality of the earth's environment is deteriorating, and humans are destroying thousands of species that may turn out to be critical to our own survival.

Myers drew international attention to the environmental crisis by publishing a list of eighteen "hot spots" where the most species lived and where the habitat was being destroyed at the greatest rate. International conservation efforts have focused on these "hot spots" to do the most with a small amount of money. Myers has changed many people's thinking about what sort of development is appropriate in an area: It must preserve the soil, water, air, and plants and animals that now live in it. Myers has written many books and more than two hundred scientific papers to get his points across. He is not afraid of taking controversial stands in public, or in debate with fellow scientists. He is a leading scientific advocate of the Gaia Hypothesis, and in 1984 he produced a book titled *Gaia: An Atlas of Planet Management*, which has been called "so accurate that it cannot be faulted and so attractive that it cannot be put down." The book has been translated into eleven languages, and has sold close to one million copies. Myers is currently writing about the effects of national security policy on the environment.

In the mid-1980s Myers and his family moved from Kenya to England so that his two daughters could go to school there. As a professor at Oxford and Cornell University in New York State, he continues to research and publicize the environmental challenges that humans face. He still finds time to travel and photograph wildlife, in between running marathons and setting the world record for running up Mount Kilimanjaro (thirteen and a half hours roundtrip). He remains hopeful about the future: "We have the chance . . . to be the first to live in final accord with our Spaceship Earth—and hence in final harmony with each other. The ancient Greeks, the Renaissance communities, the founders of America, the Victorians, enjoyed no such challenge as this. What a time to be alive!"

Nasrin, Taslima

(1962–   )

BANGLADESHI WRITER AND FEMINIST

> I strongly believe that the fundamentalists are using religion to promote their own businesses and self-interests, both financial and sexual, and I have exposed them through my writing. They had made an issue out of me, but this is intended to intimidate writers and poets and others from taking a stand against fundamentalism.
>
> —Taslima Nasrin, on being persecuted for her feminist beliefs

Taslima Nasrin is a Bangladeshi doctor and writer whose attacks on religious **fundamentalism** and the oppression of women in her country led to a death sentence being imposed on her by Muslim extremists. In a country where many women are not allowed to sit at the dinner table with the men, and many eat only leftovers, Nasrin has shocked many and delighted many more with her sexually explicit novels and her antireligious statements. In 1994, the threats against her life became so serious that she was forced to go into **exile** in Sweden. She lives there now, surrounded by bodyguards trying to protect her from Muslim fanatics or others trying to claim the $1,250 reward for her death.

Nasrin first rebelled against religion in her own family, becoming an atheist (one who rejects all belief in God) because of the discrimination she felt from her religious parents. Her first husband died, and she divorced her second husband, an almost unthinkable act in

Bangladesh. She shocked her society even further by living with a man without getting married. Nasrin began her professional career as a doctor, and she was shocked at the terrible health problems that women suffered in Bangladesh. She saw that many of the crises were caused by the strict interpretation of sharia, or Muslim law, that kept women powerless and inferior to men.

Nasrin took up the battle with her pen, arguing in newspaper columns, poems, and novels that women should be given equality under Islamic law. Noting that the Koran (the Islamic holy scriptures) allows Muslim men to have up to four wives, Nasrin suggested that women be allowed to have up to four husbands. The more she wrote, the more radical she became. Her novels were filled with sexually explicit scenes. In a country as repressed as Bangladesh, they sold like wildfire, especially among the young. She advocated sex outside of marriage, and she argued that married women could have sex with other men if they so desired. She saw the oppression of women centering around men's control of women's sexuality. If women regained that control, then they would no longer be second-class citizens in their own families.

The Bangladeshi government caved in to pressure from the mullahs (high leaders in the Muslim faith), and banned her novels in 1993. They also seized her passport, so that she would not be able to travel around the world criticizing the treatment of women in the Muslim world. Her novels topped the best-seller lists in India, however, and her case has been taken up by international **human rights** organizations such as **Amnesty** International and International PEN (Poets, Playwrights, Essayists, and Novelists) Women Writers Association. Her story has been reported in newspapers in the United States and all around the world.

Nasrin said that she deliberately tried to provoke the fundamentalists with her statements. Responding to criticism by some moderates in Bangladesh that they basically agreed with her but felt that she was moving too fast, she replied, "Unless I shock them, they will not react, and that's the reason the fundamentalists and male chauvinists are against me." True to her word, she called for even wider and more basic social and religious reform. At the same time, atrocities committed against women increased, and Nasrin brought many of these to the world's attention. She wrote about a woman who was burned at the stake for having sex with a man who was not her husband, and about a teenage Muslim girl who was whipped 101 times for allegedly having a **Hindu** boyfriend.

In September 1993, a group calling itself the Council of Soldiers for Islam offered to pay a reward of $1,250 to anyone who would kill her. They called Nasrin the "Salman Rushdie of Bangladesh," a reference to the author of a book called *The Satanic Verses* who is under a death threat by Ayatollah Khomeini of Iran, because the book allegedly insulted the Muslim faith. Mobs began to demonstrate outside Nasrin's ninth-floor apartment, which she hired guards to protect. The government of Bangladesh did not come to her aid, and even Bangladeshi women's groups did not try to help her. One leader of the Bangladesh Women's Council said that she did not think that the death threats were serious. "If these fundamentalists kill her, then we will protest it," she explained. Bangladeshi government officials even hinted that Nasrin had slowly killed her first husband with her **feminist** (in favor of women's rights) views. Even the female prime minister of Bangladesh refused to support her. Nasrin's 1993 book *Shame* was banned by the government. Finally, on June 4, 1994, the government issued a warrant for her arrest.

Nasrin went into hiding. In the middle of August she escaped to Sweden, where she continues to write and speak out against the oppression of women in Bangladesh and in other Muslim countries. She still lives in fear of losing her life, and has hired bodyguards to follow her everywhere. She writes about the atrocities committed against women, and has inspired many people in the Muslim world to question the beliefs and the actions of the fundamentalists. Her goal, as she explained in an interview nine days after coming to Sweden, is simply "to wake women up." *See* BENENSON, PETER; EL SAAWADI, NAWAL

Neill, A(lexander). S(utherland).

(1883–1973)

SCOTTISH EDUCATOR AND WRITER

> In my school a child is free to go to lessons, or stay away from
> lessons because that is his own affair, but he is not free to play a
> trumpet when others want to study or sleep. . . . We do not teach
> etiquette. If a child licks his plate, no one cares—indeed, no one
> notices. We never groom a child to say "Thank You" or "Good
> Morning." But when a boy mocked a new lad who was lame, the
> other children called a special meeting and the offender was told
> that the community, and in no uncertain terms, that the school, did
> not relish bad manners.
>
> —A.S. Neill, on his philosophy of educating young people

A.S. Neill was the founder and director of the radical Summerhill
school in England. He put into practice his philosophy that children
are naturally good, that they instinctively know what is best for them,
and they become "problem children" only when adults try to force
them to do things. At Summerhill, all classes were optional, and all
school decisions were made by a meeting in which Neill, the teachers, and the students got an equal vote. Neill was criticized by many
for insisting on freedom for children when the educational philosophy of the time was to control and shape children into productive
adults. Neill insisted that rules and discipline would not teach children how to govern themselves, which was the most important skill
they needed to learn. He once remarked that he would rather have
graduated from Summerhill a "happy street cleaner" than a "neurotic
scholar."

Neill himself knew about rigid education firsthand. He was the
only one of the eight children of a poor Scottish schoolmaster and his
wife who did not go to the local academy. He recalled being fascinated by engineering and inventing, but he was one of his father's
slowest students. He dropped out of school at the age of fourteen, and
he was forced by his father to work in the office of an Edinburgh gas
meter factory. He held other odd jobs, and eventually he returned to
his hometown of Forfar to become a student teacher in his father's
one-room school. He spent four years there, and then he moved on to

a school in Fife, where he spent three miserable years in a school that disciplined children severely. He left and spent two years in a better school in Newport-on-Tay.

At the age of twenty-five, Neill entered Edinburgh University to study agriculture. He found that he could pass his classes even though he did not understand the lectures. Switching to English, he received his master's degree (M.A.) in 1912. Instead of becoming a teacher, Neill moved to London and went into publishing, where he wrote and edited educational encyclopedias, and he became the art editor of a new London magazine. The magazine never published a single issue, since World War I broke out just as the publication was going to press. Neill returned to Scotland and to teaching. He became the headmaster of Gretna Green School. He wrote four books about his experiences, and about his growing conviction that education that was forced upon children was doing something harmful to them. He left the school to fight in World War I, and during the war he met Homer Lane, an educator who convinced Neill that the best treatment for children who were behaving badly was to teach them how to control themselves, rather than controlling their behavior for them. Lane also explained to Neill how the psychological theories of the psychoanalyst Sigmund Freud were important in working with children.

After the war, Neill eagerly tried to apply his new theories of education to the King Alfred School in Hampstead, London. The school was not ready for his unusual methods, and he was forced to leave in 1920. He contacted other educators who shared some of his views, and he set up an international school in Dresden, Germany. Fighting broke out in Dresden, so Neill moved the school to Austria, where its curriculum and methods of operation angered local peasants and government officials. In 1924, the school relocated in England, in Leiston, a town in Suffolk. Set up as a coeducational (boys and girls together) boarding school, it was named Summerhill.

From the beginning, Summerhill was set up as a radical experiment in education. In the early years of the school, most of the students went there because no other school would take them, or because they had behavioral and learning problems that were so severe that their parents were willing to try almost anything. Students were as young as five, and as old as sixteen. All of them were treated as equals by Neill and the other teachers, and none of them were forced to do anything that they did not want to do, so long as they were not harming others. All classes were optional. Some students did not attend a single class for years, but instead followed other interests, or simply played. Neill thought that play was one of the most important tasks of childhood, and he trusted that children, when left to their own decisions, would do precisely what they needed to do in order to grow up into responsible and happy adults.

Unlike most other educators, who measured their students' success in terms of grades, later jobs, or wealth, Neill valued happiness, sincerity, balance, and flexibility. Many students and visitors at Summerhill wrote amazed descriptions of how well the system seemed to work. English government inspectors wrote in 1949, "The children are full of life and zest. An atmosphere of contentment and tolerance pervades the school. . . . The children's manners are delightful. . . . Initiative, responsibility, and integrity are all encouraged." In spite of Neill's statement that he would be proud to produce happy street cleaners, most of Summerhill's students did very well at some of the best colleges in England and around the world. Additionally, Neill noted, there was very little homesickness at Summerhill, and very little illness among the students. Neill felt that this was because "we are on the side of the living process—for we approve of the flesh." He was referring to the open and relaxed atmosphere at Summerhill about teenage sexuality. Neill felt that the constant moral judgments that adults taught to children about sex made the children feel "dirty" or "naughty" when they had natural sexual feelings. These bad feelings created hostility in children, even if the children were not aware of it, and led to bad behavior. The adults would punish the supposedly bad behavior and tell the children that they were "bad," and the vicious cycle of punishment and misbehavior would grow stronger still. The solution, according to Neill, was to "break down the child's superimposed conscience, his self-hatred."

Neill did this through "private lessons" with troubled children, as well as through the school as a whole. His private lessons were like therapy sessions. He wrote about many of them in his books. Once, a student lied to him about getting an uncle's permission to leave Summerhill by train and meet the uncle somewhere. Neill discovered the lie, but he did not criticize the student. Instead, Neill drove him to the train station and gave him some spending money, which he said the uncle had sent to him. Ashamed and caught in his lie, the student admitted it, apologized, and the pair returned to school. Another student who had recently transferred from a strict school was invited to see Neill in his office soon after he arrived. He sat, distrustful of Neill and his kindness, when Neill suddenly reached across his desk and offered the student a cigarette. The student was shocked—he would have been expelled for smoking in his old school. Neill was trying to break down the student's distrust, as well as his hatred and fear of rules.

Many critics of Summerhill saw it as a place without rules, where all behaviors were acceptable, no matter how bad or destructive. Neill answered these criticisms in two popular books, *Summerhill*, written in 1960, and *Freedom—Not License!*, published in 1966. He explained that no one was allowed to step on the rights of anyone else, and that the community always acted to keep people from acting selfishly. Many of Neill's ideas have become accepted parts of progressive educational philosophy and practice. Although the Summerhill model was not put into practice in other places, many aspects of it have influenced education in the twentieth century. The importance of listening to and respecting the child is accepted by many educators today. Neill died in 1973, at the age of ninety. His influence is still being felt today, and many consider him to be an educational prophet ahead of his time, and ours.

Ngau, Harrison

(1959–   )

MALAYSIAN ENVIRONMENTAL ACTIVIST

> In the village, minus the timber companies, life is peaceful. No one says he owns this or that . . . I guess that is very different from life in the city, where everyone is for himself . . . "You mind your business, I'll mind mine" is the norm. I don't know if that is civilization.
>
> —Harrison Ngau, on the destruction of the rain forest

Born on July 15, 1959, Harrison Ngau, a member of the Kayan tribe of Borneo, has worked to stop logging companies from cutting down the trees of his tribal land, the rain forest of Sarawak province. Since the 1970s, Ngau (pronounced "now") has organized local and international groups to force the Malaysian government to negotiate with the rain forest tribes.

Ngau's Kayan tribe, as well as the Penan and Kenyah tribes of Sarawak, have been decreasing in number for many years. Originally hunter-gatherers who lived off the renewable produce of the forest and the wild boar that lived there, the tribes have seen the trees cut down, the soil eroded, and the pollution from the logging operations kill the remaining plants and animals. Ngau began his activities by organizing petitions and letter-writing campaigns. He led tribespeople on marches to the Malaysian capital city of Kuala Lumpur, and began blocking the roads so that loggers could not get to their camps.

Ngau combined this local **activism** with international media attention. He has worked with the Malaysian chapter of Friends of the Earth, Shahabat Alam Malaysia (SAM), to drum up international pressure on the government to stop the loggers. The government officials had many reasons not to want to listen. In addition to the fact that Malaysia exports 50 percent of the world's hardwood, one of the largest logging companies is owned by the Malaysian minister for environment and tourism. Other large logging interests are owned by corporations in Japan. Ngau set out to create enough publicity to embarrass the Malaysian government. He and twelve other tribesmen met with the government in 1987 to complain about deforestation. When the talks proved useless, Ngau and members of several tribes began invading logging camps and blocking roads. The attention that these protests generated shamed the government, which responded by throwing Ngau and many other protesters in jail. He was locked up for sixty days in solitary confinement, without any charges, and interrogated twice a day. After his release, he was forbidden to leave his house at night without permission for two more years. Ngau and SAM received international attention and support in 1988 when they won the $100,000 Right Livelihood Award, known as the "Alternative Nobel Prize." In 1990, Ngau won the Goldman **Environmental** Prize. He used the $60,000 award to get a loan to finance his campaign to win a seat in the Malaysian Federal Parliament. He won in 1990, beating the deputy minister of public works. In Parliament, Ngau works to protect the rights of the rain forest tribes, and is studying for a law degree in order to better serve his people. He has forced the government of Sarawak to begin serious negotiations over logging practices that are destroying tribal homelands, but he still faces an uphill battle.

Niemöller, Martin

(1892–1984)

GERMAN PASTOR, RESISTOR TO NAZISM, AND PACIFIST

Martin Niemöller commanded a submarine for the German navy during World War I, and he supported a 1920 attempt by Adolf Hitler to seize power in Germany. He voted for Hitler from 1924 until his election in 1933. This was an unlikely beginning for the man who organized Protestant opposition to Hitler's policies, spent eight years in prison and concentration camps, and led post-Germany's peace and disarmament movement after World War II.

Niemöller was born into a Lutheran Protestant family in Lippstadt, a town in the Westphalia region of Germany. His father was a Lutheran minister at a time when to be a good Christian meant being a good soldier as well. As a result, Niemöller, who excelled in academics and athletics, chose to begin his career by serving in the imperial Germany navy. When World War I broke out, Niemöller commanded a U-boat (submarine) in the Mediterranean Sea, and won an Iron Cross for his attacks on British ships. When Germany lost the war, a shocked Niemöller refused to turn over his submarine to the English. He resigned from the navy, and returned to Germany horrified at what he saw. The new Weimar government, a democracy, was hateful to him. He considered **emigrating** to Argentina, and he worked as a farm laborer so that he would be able to own a farm there one day. Niemöller supported Hitler and the **Nazi** Party, believing that their brand of "positive Christianity" was what Germany needed to become strong after its defeat. He fiercely opposed the **communists**, and he joined a right-wing student army called the Academic Defense Corps. He commanded a battalion of this organization in a battle against communist rebels in Westphalia. During this time he got married, to Else Brenner, and eventually had five children. One of them was later killed on the Russian front in World War II.

Niemöller was attracted to the church following the war, and he became an ordained minister in 1924. He worked in various parishes, becoming pastor of a church in an upper-class Berlin neighborhood. When Hitler was elected Germany's chancellor in 1933, Niemöller felt that the Nazis and the church could work together to solve Germany's problems. But it soon became obvious that Hitler intended to rule over the church. He appointed a state bishop and tried to prevent clergy from speaking in opposition to any state policy. Niemöller spoke out against Hitler's policies as early as 1933, and he organized the Pastors' Emergency League to protect the independence of the church. More than four thousand pastors joined with him, and they formed what became known as the "Confessing Church." This organization, within the official Protestant church in Germany, proclaimed that Hitler, far from being a true Christian, was actually a pagan (one who has little or no religion) masquerading as a Christian. In 1934, Niemöller demanded that the church be independent from the state, and he stated his opposition to the Nazi policies against Jews and other minorities.

Niemöller spoke out against Hitler and his policies from his pulpit and in newspapers. The Nazi secret police, the Gestapo, questioned and harassed him frequently, and in 1937 he was arrested and put in prison for seven months. At his trial, he was found not guilty of high treason (crime against the state), and was set free. Soon afterward, he was arrested again and sent to a concentration camp as Hitler's personal prisoner. Hitler offered to release him if Niemöller would stop criticizing him, but the pastor refused. He remained in concentration camps until the end of the war.

Niemöller became even more controversial after the war. He criticized the Protestant church in Germany for not opposing the Nazis, and he said that he and other church leaders were cowards. They and the German people had failed to resist Hitler and Nazism, and so were partly responsible for the 35 million lives lost in both the **Holocaust** and the overall fighting in World War II. Niemöller was elected president of the Evangelical Church of Germany in 1945, a position he held for eleven years. He was a leader of many other Protestant organizations as well.

Niemöller broke with church tradition by becoming deeply involved in the politics of postwar Germany. He criticized German society, and opposed efforts by Germany to make itself a militarily strong country again. He thundered, "God has destroyed our weapons," meaning that the German defeat in World War II was a divine punishment for the sins of the German people. He also insisted that rearming would divide German society. Germany had been divided into a **capitalist** West and a communist East after the war, and Niemöller insisted that the two sides had to live together in peace. He was called a communist by other pastors, but he increasingly felt that any sort of warfare was wrong. He called upon Christians to imitate the life of Jesus, and live according to the Bible both in public and private.

In 1954, he decided that it was immoral for Christians to serve in the armed forces. This was a long way from his experiences as a U-boat captain. He joined the War Resistors' League and became president of the German chapter, and he joined the Fellowship of Reconciliation. He criticized the German military so severely that in 1959, the West German defense minister sued him for slandering the army. In 1964, he embarked on a campaign against the development of nuclear weapons, which he called "a blasphemy of the living God." He felt that the strategy of deterrence, in which enemies build up large nuclear arsenals to prevent the other one from attacking, showed a distrust of Jesus Christ. Niemöller's willingness to attack public policy from a religious position angered many who felt that politics and religion had nothing to do with each other. But it also inspired many religious people around the world to act out their religious faith in their everyday lives, and to take moral stands against immoral governments and policies. Niemöller died in 1984, at the age of ninety-two. *See* BONHOEFFER, DIETRICH

Noel-Baker, Philip John

(1889–1982)

ENGLISH PEACE ACTIVIST AND POLITICIAN

> While I have health and strength, I shall give all my time to the work of breaking the dogmatic sleep of those who allow the nuclear, chemical, biological, and conventional arms race to go on.
>
> —Philip Noel-Baker, upon his retirement from the House of Commons, 1970

Philip Noel-Baker spent his life working for peace, and against weapons of all kinds. He wrote influential books about the international arms race, served in many positions in the English government, and was awarded the 1959 Nobel Peace Prize. When he died in 1982, at age ninety-two, he was hailed as "the conscience of the House of Commons."

Born Philip Baker (he added his wife's last name to his own when he was forty years old), he was the son of a prominent Quaker businessman who served on the London County Council and in the House of Commons. Noel-Baker attended the University of Cambridge, where he was a brilliant student, speaker, and athlete. He ran in three Olympic Games, and he won a silver medal in the 1,500-meter run in 1920, the year he captained the British team. At Cambridge, he was president of the Debating Society. During World War I, he refused to fight because of his Quaker belief in nonviolence. Instead, he volunteered for the Friends' Ambulance Service, and he won medals for bravery during the war. He married Irene Noel, of Greece, in 1915.

Following the war, Noel-Baker found his life's purpose as part of the international movement to end war and get rid of the world's weapons. He became an assistant to the secretary-general of the League of Nations (an international organization dedicated to peace), and was involved in the Paris Peace Conference. He went to Russia in the early 1920s to do relief work during the famine that followed the civil war there. In 1924, he became a professor at the University of London, and he wrote three books in the next three years that established him as an expert on international affairs. In 1929, he was elected to Parliament, and he served as the private secretary to Foreign Secretary Arthur Henderson. Although Henderson was a conservative and Noel-Baker was a **socialist**, the two were united in their attempts to rid the world of weapons of war. In 1931, both men were defeated in Parliamentary races, and Henderson took Noel-Baker with him when he became the president of the World Disarmament Conference in Geneva, Switzerland. In this role, Noel-Baker began studying the arms industry, and he produced a giant work, *The Private Manufacture of Armaments*, in 1937. He concluded that the arms race continued so strongly because the arms industry manipulated the news media, politicians, and public opinion.

Although Noel-Baker was a **pacifist** (one opposed to all violence), he opposed the English government's policy of not fighting against the **fascists** in the Spanish Civil War in the 1930s. When he was returned to Parliament in 1936, his debating skills caught the attention of Winston Churchill, who made him secretary to the Ministry of War Transport in 1942. After World War II, Noel-Baker represented Great Britain at the United Nations, and he led the Labour Party in 1946–1947. In a variety of government positions, he served in the House of Commons from 1950 to 1970. His only child, Francis Noel-Baker, was elected to Parliament at age twenty-five in 1945.

Noel-Baker worked hard for multilateral arms reductions, which meant that both sides in the Cold War, the **communists** (supporters of an economic system in which private property is outlawed) and the Western countries, would agree at the same time to give up their weapons. He opposed those pacifists in the West who believed that their countries should disarm without worrying about the Soviet Union. He was awarded the 1959 Nobel Peace Prize for his efforts to make the world a safer place. In the early 1970s, following his retirement from the House of Commons, he became president of the British Vietnam Association, which opposed the American involvement in the Vietnam War. In 1977, he was made a member of the House of Lords, and he continued to counsel younger members of the Labour Party until his death.

PANKHURST FAMILY

Pankhurst, Emmeline

(1858–1928)

ENGLISH SUFFRAGETTE

Pankhurst, Christabel

(1880–1958)

ENGLISH SUFFRAGETTE AND LESBIAN ACTIVIST

Pankhurst, Sylvia

(1882–1960)

ENGLISH SUFFRAGETTE, PACIFIST, AND SOCIALIST

Pankhurst, Adela

(1885–1961)

ENGLISH-AUSTRALIAN SUFFRAGETTE AND SOCIALIST

> Deeds not Words.
> —motto of the Women's Social and Political Union

> We have tried meetings and processions, we have tried demonstrations, all to no avail, and now at last we have to break windows. I wish I had broken more.
> —Emmeline Pankhurst, on fighting for women's voting rights.

Emmeline Pankhurst and her three daughters began their **activist** careers as the "wild women" of the English movement to win women the right to vote (suffrage). Known as "**suffragettes**," the women who campaigned for the vote had written petitions, marched in demonstrations, and campaigned legally for changes. Emmeline and her daughters decided that these "gentle" tactics would get them nowhere; since women could not vote, they could not influence the political process through normal means. The Pankhursts organized women to badger politicians in public, storm Parliament, throw stones at the prime minister's house, and refuse to pay fines to avoid jail sentences. Their militant tactics made them legends all over the world. Emmeline died soon after women were granted the vote in England, but her three daughters continued their activism for many years. They went in very different directions, but they all had in common their mother's fearless attitude and militant tactics.

Emmeline was born in Manchester in 1858. Her father was a calico printer, and his family of ten children was quite well off. Both of Emmeline's parents were radical reformers who supported the brand-new movement to give women the right to vote. At the age of fourteen, she attended her first suffragette meeting. She went to school at first in Manchester, and then to a boarding school in Paris, France. At the age of twenty-one, she married a radical lawyer, Dr. Richard Pankhurst, and both of them became active in the women's rights movement. They had three daughters, in 1880, 1882, and 1885, after which they moved to London. Richard was unable to find work in the field of law because of his radical views, so Emmeline became a shopkeeper. When he died in 1898, she and her daughters moved back to Manchester, where Emmeline became a registrar (record keeper) of births and deaths in a working-class district. Her daughter Christabel, age eighteen, became her assistant.

In 1903, Emmeline, Christabel, and Sylvia formed the Women's Social and Political Union (WSPU), an organization dedicated to fighting for women's rights. Christabel had been educated in Switzerland after finishing with Manchester High School, and she had studied for a law degree at Victoria University in Manchester. Sylvia had studied art in Manchester, and had won scholarships to the art Accademia of Venice and the Royal Academy of Art. The three woman brought their different talents to the job of winning "Votes for Women." Emmeline's strategy was to force the Liberal Party, which was on the verge of ruling England, to allow women to vote. In 1905, the Parliament debated a suffrage bill for just a few minutes before moving on to a question about requiring front and back lights on carts. Emmeline and a group of women began a protest on Parliament Square. She stood on a box and spoke until the police took her away. The English public was scandalized at seeing such behavior by women. But it was just the beginning. Christabel and some friends interrupted a meeting of the Liberal Party by standing in the audience and demanding to know whether the Liberal government would give votes to women. The women were told to sit down, and when they refused, they were thrown out of the hall. They tried to reenter and ask the question again, when they were arrested. Emmeline offered to pay Christabel's fine, but Christabel refused to let her. She went to jail, and all England was talking about her. Even the wife of the speaker that she had interrupted said that the Pankhursts were right.

The suffragettes showed up at most Liberal Party meetings all over England. Even when no females were allowed in the meetings, young women would lower themselves from the rafters and display the banners that Sylvia had designed. Women disguised themselves as men to gain admittance to the meetings, where they would heckle the speakers. After the Liberal Party won the election, it still did not grant women the vote. The Pankhursts organized a group of women to follow the new prime minister wherever he went. He had to be protected by the police. Emmeline organized fifty-seven women, including Christabel, to storm Parliament. They were arrested, and they promised to continue breaking the law until they could influence politics by being allowed to vote.

The Pankhursts organized suffrage parades, and they were pelted with rotten fruit and snowballs, but more and more women were joining the movement. When Emmeline called a protest meeting in London's Hyde Park in 1908, more than 250,000 people showed up. The prime minister was advised by his cabinet to "pay no attention to these cats mewing." To force him to pay attention, Emmeline and three other women took a taxi to his house, threw one stone each, and broke four windows. They were immediately arrested. Soon thereafter, another group of women came and broke windows. By the end of the day, two hundred women were arrested. They were sentenced to nine months in prison. Emmeline somehow communicated with all of the prisoners, who went on a mass hunger strike. Whenever a woman would become gravely ill as a result of not eating, she would be taken from the jail and force-fed. When she regained her health, she would be put in jail again. Emmeline called this a "cat and mouse" game. She made public appearances on a stretcher during this time. When she was released for medical reasons for the twelfth time, she left England and went on a lecture tour of the United States, raising money for the suffragettes. During World War I, she gave up her work for women to help with recruitment. She adopted four orphans after the war, and she resumed her work for women. In 1920, women over the age of thirty were granted the vote. Emmeline joined the Conservative Party in 1926 and ran for a seat in Parliament. She died in 1928, shortly after women were granted the same voting rights as men.

In 1912, Emmeline and Christabel were charged with conspiracy. Emmeline went to jail, and Christabel escaped to France, where she joined a **lesbian feminist** group. While in France, Christabel continued to work for women's rights in England. In addition to fighting for voting rights, Christabel attempted to secure women's sexual rights as well. She campaigned to make prostitution illegal, and she worked to protect women from falling victim to sexually transmitted diseases. In 1914, both she and Emmeline worked full-time to recruit for World War I. After the war, she ran for Parliament and was defeated, and she turned to religion. She preached about the Second Coming of Christ, wrote Christian books, and settled in California in 1940.

It was World War I that caused a break between Emmeline and

Christabel on the one hand, and Sylvia and Adela Constantia on the other. Both Sylvia and Adela Constantia were opposed to the war. After being arrested thirteen times and going on hunger strikes as part of the suffragettes, Sylvia turned to **socialism** and **pacifism** in 1914. She founded the socialist pacifist magazine, *Worker's Dreadnought*, in 1914, and ran it for ten years. She headed health clinics for women, a Montessori school (a type of school that uses specially prepared teaching materials and games, and stresses freedom for the child), cheap restaurants where the poor could eat nutritious food, and a toy factory where the workers were also the owners. The English government fined her for what it saw as antiwar propaganda. In 1920, after the Russian Revolution that toppled the czar (the royal ruler), Sylvia hid on a Finnish ship that traveled from Finland to the Soviet Union. She met Vladimir Lenin (the Russian **communist** leader), and wrote a book about her experiences. She returned to England and became a leader of the British Communist Party, but she was expelled when she refused to give up control of the *Worker's Dreadnought*. In 1928, she refused to say who was the father of her child, in order to protest society's prejudice against unwed mothers. In the 1930s, she protested against the policies of Italian **fascist** dictator Benito Mussolini, and she helped the Abyssinian people of Ethiopia in their struggle to be free of Italian colonial rule. She moved to Ethiopia in 1956, and edited a newspaper there until her death.

Adela took part in the suffrage movement with her mother and sisters until she moved to Australia after a disagreement with Emmeline. Adela joined a group that became the Women's Peace Army in 1914, and she protested against World War I. She became an organizer with the Victoria Socialist Party, and was fined and put in jail repeatedly. She wrote a play, edited a newspaper, and traveled across Western Australia. She married Tom Walsh, a socialist with three daughters from a previous relationship. The couple had a son together. They worked in the early 1920s to organize the Seaman's Union, and helped to form the Australian Communist Party. Later they opposed the communist (communism: an economic system in which private property is outlawed) tactics and goals, and moved on to other projects. Adela started the Australian Women's Guild of Empire in 1929. In 1939, she worked to ally Australia with another Pacific Rim nation, Japan, instead of with the other members of the British Commonwealth, but she gave up that idea after Japan bombed

Pearl Harbor, Hawaii. When her husband died in 1943, Adela became a nurse, and she worked with retarded children. Like her mother and sisters, she pursued many different causes and many different careers with energy and a fighting spirit.

Pérez Esquivel, Adolfo

(1931–   )

ARGENTINIAN HUMAN RIGHTS ACTIVIST

> You cannot talk solely of human rights in terms of torture and imprisonment and killing. True, this is the gravest aspect. But we must also look at the case of the peasant who has no land and is dying of hunger.
>
> —Adolfo Pérez Esquivel, on human suffering

Adolfo Pérez Esquivel was awarded the 1980 Nobel Peace Prize for his work to help the peasants of his native Argentina. He was secretary-general of Servico Paz y Justicia, or Service for Peace and Justice (SPJ), an organization that works nonviolently for social change in Latin America. He was imprisoned a number of times, and was tortured by the Argentinian government. Due to the tireless efforts of Pérez Esquivel and others, in 1983 the repressive Argentinian government was replaced by a parliamentary democracy.

Pérez Esquivel was born in Buenos Aires, the capital, in 1931. He studied art in college and graduate school, and spent fifteen years as a successful artist and professor of art. Many of his sculptures are still in public places all over Argentina. In 1974, he retired from college teaching and plunged himself into a second career: secretary-general of SPJ. He traveled all over Latin America, documenting abuses of **human rights**, helping those fighting against political repression and injustice, and bringing world attention to the lack of political freedom in much of Latin America. He was arrested in Brazil in 1975, and in Ecuador in 1976. He tried to convince the United Nations to set up a Human Rights Commission that would protest against the types of abuses of human rights that were occurring in his native Argentina.

Thousands of Argentinians who had dared to speak out against the government had "disappeared," and most were feared dead. These *desaparecidos* included labor leaders, local **activists**, and journalists. In his book *Prisoner Without a Name, Cell Without a Number*, Argentinian writer Jacobo Timerman described the torture that he received in an Argentinian prison. In spite of what Pérez Esquivel knew about what happened to critics of the government, he continued to call for nonviolent protest. In 1977, he was arrested when he entered a police station to renew his passport. He was immediately thrown in prison, without a trial or an interrogation, and was held and tortured for fourteen months. He refused to speak of the tortures once he was released. Yoga exercises and prayer helped him survive the ordeal. He later spoke about his torturers: "When you experience this extreme situation of being between life and death, you try to understand what Christ said on the cross: 'Father, forgive them, for they don't know what they are doing.' But I thought that, yes, these people *did* know what they were doing. . . . What I discovered little by little was that what the torturers did not know was that they were persons, and that we were persons. They had lost their identities." Following his release from prison, Pérez Esquivel was placed under **house arrest**, but he was allowed to travel once again beginning in 1980.

Pérez Esquivel has derived much strength from his Roman Catholic faith. His vision for the Church in Latin America is an institution that does much more for the people than perform and officiate at baptisms, weddings, mass, and funerals. It stands with them and fights for their right to live free from fear and hunger. However, the official churches in Argentina, both Catholic and Protestant, did little to help Pérez Esquivel and SPJ. When he was awarded the Nobel Peace Prize in 1980, the religious leaders in Argentina remained silent. His calls for social and economic reform are too radical for many mainstream church leaders. Yet Pérez Esquivel sees poverty at the root of all the misery and repression in Latin America. In a vicious cycle, the repression in turns leads to greater poverty. Pérez Esquivel has been a leader in helping peasants get land of their own and organizing workers to achieve better working and living conditions. His efforts contributed to the establishment of democratic government in Argentina in 1983, and the prosecution of those government officials guilty of torturing and killing the *desaparecidos*. *See* TIMERMAN, JACOBO

Pethick-Lawrence, Emmeline

(1867-1954)

ENGLISH SUFFRAGETTE AND SOCIAL WORKER

Emmeline Pethick-Lawrence was a leader of the movement to give women the right to vote in England. She was arrested many times for her militant tactics, which included breaking windows at the prime minister's house. In 1912, following a bitter fight between her and other militant **suffragettes**, Emmeline and Christabel Pankhurst, she joined the international women's peace movement.

Born in Bristol, England, Emmeline Pethick was given a proper education for an upper-class girl of her time. She studied in private schools in England, France, and Germany, and returned to England to work as a social worker in a west London mission, from 1890 to 1905. She became interested in the problems of young working women, especially the hardships of poor working conditions, long hours, and no vacation. She helped to found an organization to help these young women, called the Esperance Club. She fought to win annual vacations for the female workers, and she started a dress-making business that was a model of good working conditions. The women who worked there shared in the profits, worked only eight hours a day, earned a decent wage, and received vacation time each year.

Pethick married Frederick Lawrence in 1901, and in an unusual gesture for the time, each of them changed their last name to Pethick-Lawrence. Both were active in the women's suffrage (right to vote) movement. Emmeline Pethick-Lawrence became a leading figure in the struggle after meeting Emmeline Pankhurst in 1906. Pethick-Lawrence agreed to become the treasurer of the Women's Social and Political Union (WSPU), and she raised a great deal of money for the organization. The following year the Pethick-Lawrences started the group Votes for Women, which brought the message of the suffragettes to the public with creative tactics and dramatic success. The sight of upper-class women being arrested and carried away by policemen inspired many English women to support the movement, and it made many men nervous about the political power that angry women could use, even without having the right to vote.

In 1912, Emmeline Pethick-Lawrence and Emmeline and Christabel Pankhurst were arrested for breaking windows. After their release, the Pankhursts unexpectedly criticized Pethick-Lawrence's views and tactics, and they forced her out of her leadership position in the WSPU. She and her husband joined the United Suffragists. She represented the British branch of the Women's International League for Peace in the United States in 1912, and she became increasingly active in international peace efforts following the outbreak of World War I in 1914. She attended the Women's Peace Conference at The Hague, The Netherlands, in 1914. Once women won a limited right to vote and were allowed to run for Parliament in 1920, Pethick-Lawrence ran as a Labour Party candidate for a section of Manchester. She later served as president of the Women's Freedom League for many years. She died in 1954. *See* PANKHURST, CHRISTABEL AND EMMELINE

Rama Rau, Dhanvanthi

(1893-1987)

INDIAN SOCIAL WORKER

Dhanvanthi Rama Rau was born in Hubli, India, to a wealthy, aristocratic family. She attended St. Mary's High School, in Hubli, and then became one of the first Indian women to attend college. She earned a master's degree (M.A.) from the University of Madras, an amazing accomplishment for a woman at that time. Rama Rau then became an assistant professor of English at Queen Mary's College, Madras, from 1917 to 1921. She married a prominent diplomat and politician, Sir Bengal Rama Rau, and began to work for social reform in India. She was especially concerned about the rights of girls and women to choose whether and when to become pregnant and have children. In 1927, she became a leader of the All-India Child Marriage Abolition League, an organization dedicated to ending the practice of forcing young girls to marry much older men. In the 1930s, she worked for the International Alliance for Suffrage and Equal Citizenship, a group that fought for women's **suffrage** (right to vote) and their right to take part in Indian government. When India won its independence from the British in 1947, Rama Rau was president of the All-India Women's Conference, which she had founded a year earlier.

Rama Rau became concerned about the connection between India's exploding population and the lack of control women had over their bodies and reproduction. She became involved in an international movement to provide **contraception** (methods of preventing pregnancy) and information about sex and pregnancy to girls and women. She founded the Family Planning Association of India in 1949, and she led the organization until 1963. In 1950, she helped to found Planned Parenthood International, and was that group's president from 1963 to 1971.

She remained active in Indian politics as well. She was the chairperson of the Indian government's Social and Moral Hygiene Enquiry Committee and a member of the Central Social Welfare Board. In these roles she put pressure on the Indian government and people to take care of the poorest and neediest of India not just with charity, but with jobs and education as well.

Rama Rau had two daughters, both of whom achieved notable success. Her older daughter, Premila Wagle, born in 1920, became a successful Indian businesswoman. Her younger daughter, Santha Rama Rau, born in 1923, became a well-known novelist, and helped her mother write her memoirs in 1977. Dhanvanthi Rama Rau died in 1987.

Reich, Wilhelm

(1897–1957)

AUSTRIAN PSYCHOANALYST, SCIENTIST, AND SEXOLOGIST

> When sexuality is prevented from attaining natural gratification, owing to the processes of sexual repression, what happens is that it seeks various kinds of substitute gratifications. Thus, for example, natural aggression is distorted into brutal sadism . . . [The average person] reacts to the imposed severe compulsion [of sexually repressive morality] with promiscuous impulses; he defends himself against both. Morality is a burden, and instinct appears as a tremendous danger. The man reared under and bound by authority has no knowledge of the natural law of sex-regulation; he has no confidence in himself. He is afraid of his sexuality because he never learns to live it naturally. Thus, he declines all responsibility for his acts and decisions, and he demands direction and guidance.
>
> —Wilhelm Reich, from *The Mass Psychology of Fascism*, 1933

Wilhelm Reich began his medical career as a brilliant assistant to Sigmund Freud, the founder of psychoanalysis. Within a few years, Reich was expelled from the German Psychoanalytic Society because of his radical politics and disagreements with Freud. He was hounded out of Berlin by the **Nazis**, who confiscated and burned his books. He created the sexual political movement within the German and Austrian **Communist** parties, and was later thrown out of the party because his sex-counseling clinics were attracting non-**Marxists** to the communist cause. He spent the last years of his life in the United States, where the Food and Drug Administration (FDA) jailed him for refusing to answer a complaint against him, and burned his books. So far as is known, Reich was the only person ever to have his books burned both by the Nazis and the United States government. He died in a federal prison in 1957.

Reich was born in the town of Dobrzcynica, in Galicia. His father, who once had been an orthodox Jew, had given up his Jewish culture, and refused to teach his children anything about the Jewish religion or the culture. When Reich was a young boy, the family moved to the Ukraine, Russia, where they lived on a large farm and raised beef cattle. He was a solitary boy, although not by choice. His family would not let him associate with either the Ukrainian peasant children or the

Yiddish-speaking Jewish ones. He took an early interest in biology, collecting and breeding butterflies, insects, and plants in a small lab of his own making. His parents both died when he was young: his mother of suicide, and his father from tuberculosis (a disease that destroys the lungs). From the age of seventeen, Reich attended school and ran the family farm simultaneously. He joined the Austrian army when World War I broke out, and by 1916 he had been made an officer. He enjoyed and excelled at sports, riding horses, and shooting. He served on the Italian front three separate times.

In 1918, he studied at the Vienna University law school, but he grew bored and switched to medicine. He was extremely poor in those days. Lacking money to buy clothes for school, he often appeared in class in his military uniform. He was a brilliant student, and he graduated from the six-year medical program in only four years. During his undergraduate years, he came under the influence of Freud, who was giving seminars on sexology (the study of sex). Reich and some other Freudians protested the university's unwillingness to study sex as a serious subject. As soon as he graduated, Reich began practicing psychoanalysis, as taught by Freud, and he also practiced psychiatry. He soon found that his own opinions on the causes of neuroses and psychoses (types of psychological disturbances) and on their treatment differed significantly from Freud's. Reich found that almost all his patients experienced sexual problems, and when these were cleared up, the emotional problems solved themselves. He gradually came to view all forms of psychological illness as symptoms of dammed-up sexual energy, which was not allowed to express itself because human culture would not allow it. Sex was seen as something dirty and shameful, rather than an important and natural bodily function. Reich felt that society took perfectly healthy infants and killed their ability to feel and express pleasure. Those infants in turn grew into warped adults, who did the same to their children. It was impossible, Reich felt, for a sexually healthy person to exist in a sexually repressive society.

In the 1920s, as he was working out his sexual theories, Reich discovered the writings of the political and social philosopher Karl Marx. He joined the Austrian Socialist Party in 1924, and he threw himself into party politics. He agreed that the **capitalist** system (in which companies, factories, and lands are privately owned) oppressed the workers. His important question was: Why do the workers stand for it? His answer was a combining of the work of Freud and Marx—sexually repressed people had lost touch with the ability to regulate, or control, their own behavior. They feared their "naughty" or "evil" impulses, and therefore they looked to an external authority to control them, to tell them what to do. In his book *The Mass Psychology of Fascism*, written during Adolf Hitler's rise to power in Germany, Reich identified what he called the "authoritarian character structure." This type of person was created by a family in which the father was the ruler, and in which God was called upon to punish people for their sins. Reich suggested that it was a simple step to desire a dictator, a national father figure who would tell the whole nation what to do.

To fight against **fascism** (following a **dictator**), Reich worked within the **Socialist** and Communist parties to create a network of sexual education and counseling clinics for poor people who could not afford a private psychoanalyst. Reich was unprepared for the level of sexual ignorance and fear that he encountered. He became convinced that sexual repression of adolescents was causing untold suffering among them. Teen suicide, pregnancies, depression, and other mental illnesses were but a few of the consequences of a strict sexual morality that told sexually mature adolescents that their thoughts, desires, and actions were sinful. Many teenagers believed that they would be punished, either by disease or damnation, if they masturbated. Reich organized the sex political movement of the Communist Party, both in Berlin and Vienna. He was successful in attracting close to fifty thousand new members to the German Communist Party, because nowhere else in Germany could such information about sex, birth control, and abortion be obtained. Reich created the German Association for **Proletarian** Sex Politics, an organization that made demands that sound radical even today: free birth control advice and **contraceptives** to all who desire them, nurseries in factories and other large places of employment, abolition of laws against abortion and homosexuality, and home leave for prisoners, among others. Communist Party officials decided that Reich was a threat to the party's ideology, and that he was trying to become the leader. He was expelled from the party in 1934, one year after it had been made illegal by Hitler. At the same time, Reich was expelled from Freud's Psychoanalytic Society for his political views.

After traveling and trying to settle down in Denmark, England, and Sweden, and being forced to leave each country because he was considered a bad influence on youth, Reich settled in Norway in late 1934. He lived in Oslo, the capital, for five years, and developed his theories on an organic life energy which he called "orgone" energy, that he believed filled the universe. He published some of his theories in 1937, and was attacked relentlessly by the Norwegian press for more than a year. His most controversial statement was that inorganic (lifeless) particles could become transformed into living matter if orgone energy were present. Newspapers ridiculed the possibility of life being created out of nonlife, with headlines like "God Reich Creates Life." Rumors were spread that he had gone mad.

Reich moved to New York in 1939, one month before World War II broke out. He worked as a professor of medical psychology at the New School for Social Research in Manhattan. After a camping trip in Maine, he decided that the pure natural surroundings of Rangeley, Maine, were the perfect location for his science lab and institute, which he named Orgonon. He continued to pursue the study of orgone energy, and he performed experiments on fighting cancer with the use of orgone energy accumulators, or specially constructed boxes that he believed concentrated the orgone and fought cancer. He tried to control vast amounts of orgone energy in his experiments to manipulate the weather. Many people thought of him as a madman, because he engaged in so much research that contradicted everything scientists believed about the world. In the early 1950s, at the height of the "Red Scare," when U.S. Senator Joseph McCarthy ruined the careers of thousands of prominent people by accusing them of being communists, rumors reached the Food and Drug Administration (FDA) that Reich was using the orgone energy accumulators as an unproven cancer therapy. The FDA filed a complaint against Reich, ordering him to appear in court to defend himself and his science. Reich refused to go to court, writing by way of explanation that he did not recognize the ability of the legal system to make judgments about science. He was sentenced to prison for contempt of court, and he died in Lewisburg Penitentiary in Pennsylvania in 1957. He succeeded in making himself, and not his work, the legal issue, so that once he died, the FDA's case against him, the orgone accumulators, and the rest of his experiments died with him. After his death, the

FDA raided publishers' warehouses, seized copies of his books, and carted them off to incinerators, claiming that they were false advertising for his orgone accumulators.

His influence is felt today in many aspects of life. He changed psychology forever with his ground-breaking book, *Character Analysis*, and he inspired the entire field of body-mind medicine with his insight that our bodies contain all of our memories and thoughts and experiences locked within them, unless we consciously allow them to flow out. He linked the psychological and the political in a way that had never been done before. He insisted that any true revolution would have to simultaneously change both the external system and the character of the people. The fear and hatred that his work inspired during his lifetime perhaps points to some uncomfortable truths that he discovered about the deepest secrets of human beings.

Robles, Alfonso García

(1911-1991)

MEXICAN DIPLOMAT

Alfonso García Robles was a Mexican diplomat and foreign minister who worked for more than twenty years to bring about nuclear disarmament in Latin America. He won the Nobel Peace Prize in 1982.

Robles was born in Zamora, Mexico, in 1911. He originally wanted to become a priest, but he ended up studying law in Mexico City, Paris, and The Netherlands. He worked for the Mexican embassy in Sweden for two years, and in 1945 he attended the conference that formed the United Nations (U.N.). The following year he joined the United Nations secretariat. From 1962 to 1964, he was the Mexican ambassador to Brazil. In October 1962, the Cuban missile crisis (the Soviet Union sent huge numbers of nuclear missiles to Cuba, and the U.S. insisted that they be dismantled and removed, or war could follow) threatened to turn into nuclear war. Robles felt that he had to try to eliminate all nuclear weapons from Latin America. He began negotiating with neighboring countries to stop trying to develop nuclear weapons, and to give up any that they had. He was not discouraged by the slow progress he made. When some reporters covering his efforts began to become impatient for a treaty, he warned them, "You must realize that foreign policy is an extremely delicate thing and there is nothing worse than adoption of precipitous [overly quick] decisions." In 1967, twenty-two Latin American countries signed the treaty of Tlatelolco. Robles also wrote the Nuclear **Nonproliferation** (not spreading) Treaty that was signed one year later.

In 1982, the world community recognized Robles's vision and patience by awarding him the Nobel Peace Prize. He lent his support to the controversial Nobel Prize nomination of Guatemalan **activist** Rigoberta Menchú, who won the prize in 1992. He spoke up for **human rights** and nuclear nonproliferation until his death, in 1991. *See* MENCHÚ, RIGOBERTA

Romero, Oscar

(1917–1980)

EL SALVADORAN PRIEST AND HUMAN RIGHTS ACTIVIST

> He who wants to withdraw from danger will lose his life. But the person who gives himself to the service of others will be like a grain of wheat that falls to the ground and dies—but only apparently dies, for by its death, its wasting away on the ground, a new harvest is made.
>
> —Oscar Romero, on the importance of serving others

Oscar Romero was a Catholic priest who opposed the murderous military **dictatorship** of his native country, El Salvador. He evolved from a "churchy" religious leader who argued that priests should stay out of politics to one of the government's fiercest opponents. After being nominated for the Nobel Peace Prize, Romero was killed during a church service by a government assassin in 1980.

Romero was born in a village in a mountainous region of El Salvador that could be reached only by foot or horse. His father was a telegraph operator, and he provided for his family a lower-middle-class existence. Romero was a devout member of the Roman Catholic Church from his youth, and when he was old enough he attended religious seminaries in San Miguel and San Salvador, both in El Salvador, and in Rome, Italy. He returned to San Miguel to serve as a parish priest, and he gained a reputation for being rather ordinary. He slowly worked his way up in the Salvadoran church, edited the San Salvadoran archdiocese newspaper, and ministered in a rigid and disciplined way to his flock. Romero recalled, "In those days I lived a very private life, anonymous, you might say."

In the mid-1970s, the military government of El Salvador began killing its opponents among the lower classes. Death squads caused the "disappearances" of people who criticized the government or fought for the rights of the peasants. A number of Catholic clergy joined the **liberation theology** movement, which saw Jesus as a revolutionary fighter for the rights of the poor and oppressed, and organized these groups to liberate themselves from oppression by the government and the wealthy landowners. Romero wrote a number of editorials criticizing priests who became involved in politics, and he became known as a conservative.

Because of his refusal to criticize the government, Romero moved up rapidly in the Catholic Church hierarchy. In 1975, he was appointed auxiliary bishop in the town of Santiago de Maria, and he was for the first time made aware of the suffering of the peasants at the hands of the government. Working closely with the people, Romero gradually changed his views on what a priest should do for his congregation. "I would say I evolved rather than changed. The circumstances of the country led me to overcome my timidity and come closer to the people," Romero remembered.

The archbishop of San Salvador, the capital of El Salvador, was an opponent of the government. The military dictator Arturo Molino pressured the Vatican in Rome to force the archbishop, Luis Chavez y Gonzalez, to retire, and to replace him with someone who could be counted on to support the government. In 1976, the Church appointed Romero, who had not publicly voiced his new feelings. The government knew only that Romero would be likely to go along with what they said, and they gave him a fancy ordination ceremony. Three weeks later, the Jesuit priest Rutilio Grande was murdered for organizing a strike at a sugar mill north of San Salvador. Surprising everyone, Romero closed all Church schools for three days, and he declared that the Church would boycott all government functions until the government got to the bottom of Grande's murder. More priests were murdered, and the military attacked the town where Grande had been organizing. In July 1977, a new president was inaugurated, and Romero refused to attend the ceremony. The government's death squads made it known that all Jesuit priests would be killed if they remained in El Salvador.

Romero fought back. He listed the names of the *desaparacidos* ("disappeared" persons) in the archdiocese newspaper. He gave weekly sermons attacking the military government and the terror it inflicted on its own population. Many opponents of the government gathered at his Sunday masses, including the poor workers and peasants who were trying to organize for better living and working conditions. The Vatican became nervous at Romero's behavior, after priests who supported the El Salvadoran government denounced him as a **communist**. Romero was told to tone down his attacks on the government, and when he did not, he was ordered to go to Rome for "consultations."

Romero attended the funeral of the priest Ernesto Barrero in 1978. Barrero had joined with the **guerrilla** group Popular Forces of Liberation, and was killed during fighting with the government. At the funeral, Romero justified the use of violence by a priest "when a dictatorship seriously violates **human rights** and attacks the common good of the nation . . ." One year later, the president was overthrown, and the government that replaced him contained some nonmilitary people. Romero was still suspicious of the new government, and he refused to give it his total support until he had some proof of its goodwill. When he was nominated in 1979 for the Nobel Peace Prize, his influence became even greater. Threats were made against his life, and he began to realize that he was in grave danger. He continued to read out the names of those "disappeared" by the new government, and on March 23, 1980, Romero gave a sermon telling soldiers to follow their conscience rather than the "sinful commands" of a brutal government. The next day, Romero led mass in the chapel of a hospital that served people dying of cancer. During the service, he was shot and killed by a single assassin. At his funeral, government hit men opened fire on the crowd of more than fifty thousand, and they killed close to one hundred people. The world mourned the violent death of the timid priest who had found his courage, and was shocked at the violence against his mourners. Shortly before his death, Romero said in an interview, "I do not believe in death without resurrection. If they kill me, I will arise in the Salvadoran people."

Russell, Dora

(1894–1986)

ENGLISH FEMINIST AND EDUCATOR

Dora Russell was the daughter of a well-known British government official, Sir Frederick Black. She attended Sutton High School and Girton College, Cambridge. In 1917, she accompanied her father to New York and worked as his secretary when he was chairman of the British mission to the United States. When she returned to England, she found her way into a circle of radical **feminists** and **socialists**. In this group she met the philosopher and mathematician Bertrand Russell. They traveled to the Soviet Union and China in 1920–1921. He was already married, but Dora Russell became his mistress, and she was already pregnant with his child when he divorced his wife and married Dora. The couple believed in open marriage, which meant that each of them was free to have romantic and sexual relationships with others.

Russell found that society frowned especially on sexually free women. Its laws made it difficult for a woman to decide whether to have children or not once she became sexually active. In 1924, at the same time that she was running unsuccessfully for a seat in Parliament, she founded the Women's Birth Control Group with Margaret Sanger and Marie Stopes. She also fought for women to be able to take paid time off from work if they had babies. In 1925, she published a book, *Hypatia: or Women and Knowledge,* which challenged the way women were controlled by men. She saw the institution of marriage as one that made women the property of their husbands. She argued that women should be allowed, as owners of their own bodies, to have sex with whomever they wanted. The book became a bestseller once the newspaper *The Sunday Express* wrote that it should be banned.

In 1927, Dora and Bertrand Russell started a school near Petersfield, England. Called Beacon Hill School, it taught children without trying to force them to do anything. This "permissive" education had as its main philosophy that children were naturally curious, and they would learn what interested them without having tests, grades, and punishments. Beacon Hill School was famous for its decision not to impose adult authority on the students. The teachers did not make rules, nor were any punishments given. All decisions were made by a school council in which each teacher and each student had one vote. The curriculum included Russell's views on sex, as well as factual sex education, and an emphasis on thinking skills rather than the accumulation of knowledge. Russell did insist on daily showers, and she made her students brush their teeth. One student forced to brush his teeth snarled at her, "Call this a free school?" Dora remained at the school until 1939, four years after Bertrand ended the relationship. While they were together, Dora had had many other relationships, as well as a son and a daughter by an American, Griffin Barry. In 1940, Dora married Pat Grace.

During World War II, Russell worked for the British government, in the Soviet Relations Bureau of the Ministry of Information. When the war ended, she returned to her **activism**. She helped to found the National Council for Civil Liberties, an organization that fought to protect the rights of citizens to speak, worship, and gather without interference from the government. She also became concerned about the Cold War between the West and the **communist** (economic system in which private property is outlawed) world, and the danger of the buildup of nuclear weapons and the possibility of war. She became active in the Campaign for Nuclear Disarmament (CND) in the 1950s, and she led to the formation of the Women's Caravan of Peace, which traveled from Great Britain across Europe in 1958. She also maintained her interest in education throughout her life. In 1983, at the age of eighty-nine, Russell published a book about the bad effects of technology titled *The Religion of the Machine Age*. She had begun the book fifty years earlier, after her trips to the Soviet Union and the United States. Also in 1983, she led a CND rally while in a wheelchair. She died in 1986, shortly after participating in an antiwar rally at an air force base in Cornwall, England. *See* STOPES, MARIE

Sadat, Jihan

(1934?-)

EGYPTIAN SOCIAL ACTIVIST

It is a fact that I have enemies.
But I believe also that the majority of women are with me.
The old ways will never
return. . . .The wheel never
turns back.

—Jihan Sadat, on modernizing
Egyptian society

Jihan Sadat, widow of assassinated Egyptian president Anwar El Sadat, has worked for change in Egyptian society both as the country's "first lady," and as a private citizen following her husband's death. She encouraged her husband to make peace with its neighbor Israel, for which he received the Nobel Peace Prize in 1978. She also inspired "Jihan's law," which gave women rights in divorce cases, and a decree that reserved a number of seats in Egypt's Parliament for women.

Sadat was born sometime around 1934, to an Egyptian father and British mother. Her father was a doctor, and her mother a school-teacher. Her mother, who was not a Muslim, nevertheless took part in Muslim ceremonies and was devoted to her husband and family. Her father treated his two daughters as the equals of his sons, and he encouraged them all to become independent. This independence had its limits. While in high school in Cairo, Jihan met the unemployed revolutionary, Anwar elSadat, who was twenty-nine years old. They met in 1948, possibly when she brought cookies to a relative who was imprisoned next to Sadat (both for anti-British activities), and they were married the following year. Jihan's parents opposed the marriage for a number of reasons: Sadat was too dark-skinned, too old, a revolutionary, and too poor. Unlike most Egyptian women of the day, Jihan chose her own husband.

Anwar Sadat began his rise to power after the overthrow of King Farouk in 1952. While he worked his way up the power structure,

Jihan Sadat was busy raising her four children. She volunteered, against her husband's will, as a Red Cross nurse during the 1967 war with Israel. He felt that she should have devoted all her energy to their children. In 1970, Sadat was named president of Egypt. Jihan immediately took on a high public profile and a leadership role. She became the president of the Monufiya People's Council, and campaigned vigorously for women's rights. She fought for the right of women to receive birth control and sex education, and she was criticized by many in the Arab world, who were not used to women getting involved in politics. Libyan **dictator** Muammar el-Qaddafi sent top-level aides to Anwar Sadat to protest the fact that his wife appeared in public, and did not wear a veil.

Jihan Sadat founded the S.O.S. Children's Villages, which provided a home and an education to Egyptian orphans. She founded and raised money for a rehabilitation home for Egyptian war veterans, and got Frank Sinatra to sing at the opening. In 1974, she went to college for the first time, obtaining a bachelor's degree (B.A.) from the University of Cairo, and getting a master's (M.A.) in Arabic literature in 1980. She began to view Israel not as an enemy, but as a possible friend. Although she refused to meet Israeli Prime Minister Yitzhak Rabin's wife, Leah, at an International Women's Year Conference in 1975, she did try to help an Israeli mother find her son, who had disappeared in the 1973 war. Anwar found out about this and criticized her for her actions.

She also had an influence on him. She helped convince him to take the bold and unexpected step of traveling to Israel and beginning the process that led to a peace treaty between Israel and Egypt. She helped the Egyptian Jewish community transfer holy books from Egypt to Israel. Jihan persuaded her husband to enact two laws that helped Egyptian women. One of them allowed women to receive a divorce if their husband took a second wife. The women could keep their house, and have custody of the children. The second law set aside thirty seats in the Egyptian Parliament and 20 percent of all local council seats for women. Jihan's prominence in the country led to a great deal of criticism by many Egyptians, who felt that she was not acting like a proper Muslim wife. **Fundamentalist** Arab women protested and then walked out of a talk that she gave at the United Nations Decade for Women conference in 1980.

In 1981, Anwar Sadat was assassinated by Egyptian fundamentalists. Jihan went into mourning for more than a year and did not appear in public in Egypt. In 1983, she traveled to the United States to continue her studies in literature, and to teach about the role and history of women in the Islamic world. She continues her role as someone who is walking a middle path between being a traditional Muslim woman and a **feminist** (for women's rights) revolutionary. She receives criticism from both sides, but remains as independent of spirit as the high school student who married an impoverished revolutionary who became a world leader and peacemaker.

Sakharov, Andrei D.

(1921–1989)

RUSSIAN NUCLEAR PHYSICIST, PEACE ACTIVIST, AND DISCOVERER OF PEACEFUL USES FOR NUCLEAR POWER

Although Andrei Sakharov is best known as a **human rights activist** and campaigner for nuclear disarmament, activities that earned him the Nobel Peace Prize in 1975, he was also a nuclear physicist. Sakharov was born on May 21, 1921, in Moscow. His father was a physics teacher. From a very early age, young Andrei demonstrated an exceptional interest and ability in science.

Sakharov graduated from Moscow State University in 1942. Sakharov's excellence as a student earned him an exemption from military service, and he did not fight in the Soviet army during World War II, although he was of draft age. Instead, he continued his studies. In 1945, Sakharov began work at the P.N. Lebedev Institute of Physics in Moscow. In 1947, he received his doctorate in physical and mathematical sciences. This was considered an important achievement, because doctorates in what was then the Soviet Union were usually awarded only to older, more experienced scientists.

From 1945 to 1948, Sakharov studied thermonuclear reactions. From 1948 to 1956, he took part in nuclear-weapons research for the Soviet government. This top-secret research is believed to have led to the detonation of the first Soviet hydrogen bomb in 1953. At the same time, however, Sakharov was also working on peaceful uses for nuclear energy. With Igor Tamm, his teacher and research partner, Sakharov proposed that controlled thermonuclear fusion—the basis for harnessing nuclear power for electricity—was possible. In 1953, in recognition of his contribution to Soviet science, Sakharov became the youngest member ever elected to the Soviet Academy of Scientists.

In addition to doing his scientific research, Sakharov was interested in political issues. In the late 1950s, he argued against government plans to make job training a part of all high-school course requirements. He argued that students gifted in math and science were at their most creative when they were young and that they required advanced classes that would allow them to enter the university early. The debate went on for several years, but eventually Sakharov's ideas were accepted.

In the 1960s, Sakharov and other Soviet intellectuals became dissatisfied with the government's control over their research and writing. In July 1968, *The New York Times* published "Progress, Coexistence, and Intellectual Freedom," an article written by Sakharov that had been read by many intellectuals in the Soviet Union, but could not be printed in Soviet newspapers because of government **censorship**. In that article, Sakharov warned against the dangers of war, hunger, and environmental pollution. He argued for a reduction in the number of nuclear weapons, for an increase in cooperation between countries with different political beliefs, and for intellectual freedom and the elimination of censorship in the Soviet Union.

Sakharov continued to speak out against his government and to lobby for international human rights. His books and letters earned him an international reputation, and the Nobel Peace Prize in 1975. The Soviet government, however, was less pleased with his public statements. Sakharov was denied permission to travel to Stockholm, Sweden, to receive the prize, and in 1980 he was banished to Gorky, a remote Soviet military city that he was not allowed to leave.

In 1986, Mikhail Gorbachev, the new Soviet leader, ordered that Sakharov be released from Gorky. Changes in the Soviet Union were so great that Sakharov, who was once publicly condemned for his political opinions, was elected to the Congress of People's Deputies in 1989. Sakharov died in Moscow on December 14, 1989. *See* BONNER, YELENA

Schindler, Oskar

(1908–1974)

GERMAN INDUSTRIALIST AND RESCUER OF JEWS
FROM THE NAZIS

> Beyond this day [the Nazi liquidation of the Cracow ghetto, which
> Schindler witnessed from a hilltop above the ghetto], no thinking
> person could fail to see what would happen. I was now resolved to
> do everything in my power to defeat the system.
>
> —Oskar Schindler, on his determination to rescue Jews
> from Hitler's ovens

Oskar Schindler was known before World War II as a fun-loving,
irresponsible gambler, drinker, and ladies' man. When he offered to
run an enamelware factory in Poland during the war, all who knew
him assumed that he saw it as a selfish opportunity to make some
easy money. They would have been surprised to learn that he spent
most of the war years risking his reputation, his fortune, and his life
to save Jews from extermination by the **Nazis**. The story of his life
was told in filmmaker Steven Spielberg's 1993 Academy Award–
winning movie, *Schindler's List*, based on Thomas Keneally's book
of the same name.

Schindler was born in the industrial city of Zwittau, in the Austrian
empire. The city came under Czech rule at the end of World War I.
His father owned a farm machinery plant, and Schindler took engineering classes at the local German-speaking grammar school as he
prepared to inherit his father's business. He had Jewish friends, and
his next-door neighbors were a rabbi and his family. Schindler was a
wild youth. He owned one of the finest motorcycles in Czechoslovakia, and he loved racing more than anything. In 1929, he married Em-
ilie, a quiet woman who adored her charming, boisterous husband,
and in spite of the economic hard times he managed to get a good job
as a sales manager at the Moravian Electrotechnic Company. He traveled a great deal for his jobs, and he had a great many girlfriends in
different European cities. In 1937, Schindler began wearing the
swastika, the emblem of the German Nazi party. Once the German
army invaded Czechoslovakia in 1938, however, Schindler was ap-

palled at its bullying of the Czech population, and its illegal seizures of private property. As war approached, he sought out business possibilities with the German military. When he heard that the army needed enamel cookware, he offered to furnish and run a factory to produce it. His factory, the Deutsche Email Fabrik (DEF), was located in Cracow, Poland, a town that before the war had had a Jewish population of fifty thousand. He hired as his business manager a Jewish accountant named Itzhak Stern. At first distrustful of Schindler and seeing him as a Nazi war profiteer who would use Jewish slave labor to make a fortune, Stern soon came to see that Schindler was essentially a just man who found the Nazis to be barbaric. The Jews who worked at DEF were treated with decency and respect, even though officially they were virtually slaves. Schindler found himself acting more and more to help Jews. He gave jobs to hundreds of Jews at his factory, and when the Nazis tried to mistreat them, he complained that he could not produce the necessary equipment for the German army if his workers were being interfered with. He soon began bribing Nazi officials with fancy dinner parties, fine wine, and expensive gifts. Believing that his only interest was making money, the Nazis accepted his "soft spot" for Jews as a smart business decision.

The Nazis worked out their "final solution" to the Jewish problem in the early 1940s. The solution became known as the **Holocaust**, and consisted of the murder of six million Jews and five million others considered not fit to live. Schindler learned about these plans, and eventually he came to believe them, after witnessing the first step in the liquidation of the Cracow Jewish Ghetto in March 1943. From that point forward, Schindler's entire life was devoted to saving as many Jews as he could. He had to play a dangerous and difficult game, pretending to be a greedy businessman to the Nazis, while at the same time spending a fortune to bribe Nazi officials to let him add names to his list of protected workers. He also spent a fortune buying black-market (purchased illegally) food and medicine for his Jewish workers.

Stern got Schindler in touch with young **Zionist** Jews from Palestine who were working to save Jews from Hitler. As a high-ranking member of the Nazi Party, Schindler was able to confirm the terrible and incomprehensible rumors that Germany, supposedly one of the most civilized nations on earth, was murdering millions of people solely because of their Jewishness. The information that Schindler provided was passed on, eventually reaching President Franklin Roosevelt and British Prime Minister Winston Churchill. Schindler also gave huge sums of money to the Zionists to help them in their task. He was arrested by the Nazis a number of times, but he managed to get released each time. Once, he was jailed for kissing a Jewish maid at his birthday party. As the destruction of the Jewish communities of Europe continued, Schindler began taking bigger and bigger risks, and he became obsessed with the idea of helping Jews. Once in 1944, a trainload of Jews was waiting in the blistering midday heat to be carted away to a concentration camp. Schindler, who was driving by the train yard with the head of the Nazi government of Cracow, suggested to the Nazi that the people in the train might be thirsty. He pretended to joke about how funny it would be to call out the fire brigade and hose down the train. Enjoying Schindler's "humor," the Nazi agreed. Schindler himself turned the hose on the train, making sure that all the passengers got a chance to drink. He also quietly told his assistant to pack food supplies for the journey.

DEF remained operating in Cracow even after all the Jews who had not gotten on to Schindler's list had been deported (sent away). But in the fall of 1944, the Nazis ordered that the factory be shut down. Germany was losing the war, and the army had no more need of pots and pans. The first priority was the extermination (death) of the Jews. Schindler was frightened that his safe haven for Jews had reached its end. He managed, somehow, to convince the Nazis that he needed his 1,100 loyal and skilled workers for his next factory, an ammunition-making plant in Brinnlitz, Czechoslovakia. The men were shipped to Brinnlitz on one train, and the women—Schindler thought—on another. He was horrified to learn that the women's train had been diverted to Auschwitz, the Nazis' largest death camp. He promised the Jewish men that he would rescue their mothers, wives, and daughters. He first tried offering the Auschwitz officials a very unusual bribe. He sent one of his secretaries, a pretty young woman, to Auschwitz with a list of the women's names, a suitcase filled with the best food and alcohol, and her body to offer to the officials. When this did not work, he went to Auschwitz himself. The officials understood his need to have workers at his ammunition factory, but they wondered why it had to be these particular women. Schindler explained that it had taken years to train them. One of the officials wondered whether the nine- and eleven-year old girls were also "skilled munitions workers." Schindler, lying, told them that he needed small hands to polish the insides of the shell casings. He got the women back.

Schindler's Jews, as they now called themselves, worked at Brinnlitz until the end of the war. Schindler was very concerned that they not produce any ammunition that might actually hurt anyone. He stalled production for months, and when the Nazi officials began to get suspicious, he turned out one truckload of antitank shells. He received a telegram on his thirty-seventh birthday from the angry manager of a nearby armaments assembly plant. Somehow, every single one of Schindler's shells had failed quality-control tests. Schindler was overjoyed.

During the winter of 1944–1945, it became clear that Germany was going to lose the war. Right under the noses of the Nazi SS (Gestapo) guards, Schindler smuggled small weapons into his factory, and he secretly distributed them among the workers. He arranged for Zionist **activists** to give them military training. A few hours before the Allied armies entered Brinnlitz, Schindler gave a speech to his workers and the SS guards on the floor of his factory. For the first time, he admitted publicly what he had been doing all these years. He told his workers to restrain themselves once they were freed, and not take revenge against all the German people. He told the SS guards that they were free to go, and that the Jews would let them go peacefully if they left without using violence. At five minutes after midnight, Schindler left the factory. As a Nazi Party member and owner of a work camp, he was in danger of being arrested for war crimes. His Jews wrote long letters of explanation, which they gave to Schindler as he started his journey.

After the war, Schindler returned to Germany and tried to start a business. He could not seem to make a success of anything he tried. Many of the Jews whom he had saved stayed in touch with him, and they helped him out however they could. The state of Israel honored him many times. When he died in 1974, his body was buried in a Catholic cemetery in Jerusalem, according to his wishes.

Seed, John

(1950–   )

AUSTRALIAN ENVIRONMENTALIST AND PHILOSOPHER

> One of the reasons that we live lives of quiet desperation is because miracles are somehow opaque to us. What if every human being in the world woke up tomorrow realizing that they are cells in a larger body rather than being self-interested something-or-others? . . You can't see any happy people out there based upon how much stuff they fill their lives with . . .When we behave in a righteous way on the earth, such innocent joy is possible to us that other consumerist things fall away.
>
> —John Seed, on the relationship between humans
> and their environment

When John Seed and his neighbors watched bulldozers approach the rain forest next to their farms in New South Wales, Australia, they knew that they had to do something. Following his neighbors, Seed threw himself in front of the heavy machinery and prevented the bulldozers from destroying the forest—for the time being. From that moment on, Seed became a defender of forests all over the earth. He has been arrested for engaging in **civil disobedience** (a strategy of social protest by refusing to obey unjust laws) to save trees, traveled hundreds of thousands of miles to spread his message, and taught many native peoples how to harvest and sell rain forest products without destroying the forest itself.

Seed studied psychology and philosophy at Sydney University, in Australia, and worked in London in the early 1970s as a systems analyst for International Business Machines (IBM). After an experience with a psychedelic (mind-altering) drug, he changed his view of life. He began to regard the path his life was taking as "nonsense." He became attracted to **Buddhism**, and became a sculptor. Later he returned to New South Wales, where he became a farmer of avocados and macadamia nuts. He joined a community of people who meditated, and, as he put it, "loved each other, delivered our own babies, and grew clean food." He still regarded the rain forests that grew next to his farm as "scrub," or useless land, until the day the bulldozers came to clear a portion of it for human use. His neighbors asked him to join in the protest, and he agreed "just out of neighborliness." When they threw themselves in front of the bulldozers, Seed found himself joining them. He recalled saying to himself, "What is this? None of the Buddhist teachings said anything about this."

Seed quickly decided that Australia's rain forests were doomed unless action were taken quickly. He became a leader of the rain forest campaign in New South Wales, leading protest camps and blockades to prevent crews from destroying trees. He organized the first Australian reforestation conference in New South Wales. Although not a biologist by training, he read everything he could find about the state of the world's forests. He discovered that one of the reasons the rain forests were being destroyed so quickly was that most of the nutrients were located in the plants themselves, not in the soil. When the trees were cut down for farming, the land would only grow crops for two or three years. After that, cattle could graze on the grasses that would grow for a few years more. After five or six years, the old rain forest would become a desert, and the humans trying to make a living as farmers and ranchers would move on, cut down the next stretch of rain forest, and start all over again. Seed studied ways of using the rain forest to prevent logging of the trees, and to provide a steady, permanent source of money from the rain forest. In 1982, he worked with members of the Koroga tribe on the Solomon Islands, in the South Pacific Ocean, to develop a plan for conserving the rain forests, and to fight the large international companies that were cutting down rain forest trees for wood. In the following year he led a blockade of the Franklin River in the Australian state of Tasmania, to save the rain forest there.

Seed saw the need to inform the rest of the world about the danger to all existence on earth if the rain forests continued to be lost. He organized "rain forest roadshows," in which he traveled around the United States, talking and showing slides of the harm done to the rain forests. Everywhere he went, he tried to start a Rain Forest Action Group. As of the mid-1990s, there were two hundred of these groups around the world. He lectured wherever he could: Ivy League universities, small colleges, secondary schools, conversations, meetings, and bars. To keep people informed, he founded and edited a magazine called *World Rain Forest Report*.

In 1984, he traveled to Papua New Guinea, an island just north of Australia, where he became involved in a movement known as eco-forestry, in which local villages harvested rain forest products slowly, so that the forest would survive and the trees would grow back. He saw this as an alternative to the clear-cutting (total clearing of rain forest land) of the forests done by big industrial corporations. He continued to travel around the world, participating in demonstrations, facing attack dogs, getting arrested for civil disobedience, and producing television documentaries about the rain forests of Australia.

During all of this **activism**, Seed was reconnecting his goals of saving the planet to his training in philosophy. He knew that the rate of destruction of the rain forests was still increasing, and that much of it was caused by the materialist lifestyles of people who live in the "developed" countries in the world. He began to think about ways to get people to change their lifestyles so that humans would live in harmony with the earth, rather than using it up. He thought about the tactics that he was using to educate people, telling them about the danger to themselves and to the earth if the deforestation continued. He decided that this message was not enough. "The activities that can really fulfill and uplift a human being have been lost in this culture or even deliberately killed, perhaps. . . . I don't believe that people are capable of sacrificing what they believe to be their well-being or self-interest. But when their conception of self grows . . . then it's very easy."

Seed explained that he had learned to desire a lifestyle in harmony with the earth the way some other people desire an expensive BMW automobile. "If five billion people wanted it, the earth could thrive." When people become aware of how to achieve true happiness, rather than trying to own as many things as possible, then the damaging lifestyles will just "fall away." Seed felt that laws would not solve the problem, "because people can get around laws." Using guilt would not work either, and fear would work only "for a little while. It's really only ecstasy that's going to help us."

To change the way people tried to be happy, Seed and Professor Joanna Macy designed a workshop called "The Council of All Beings," in which people were helped to identify with all the creatures on the planet Earth, and not just the humans. Participants would make and wear masks that expressed the spirits of animals. They would learn how to come into close, loving contact with trees, animals, mountains, and the earth itself. The "Deep Ecology" movement, as its founders referred to it, represented a religious, social, and philosophical commitment to living in harmony with all life on Earth. In 1988, Seed and Macy, along with Arne Naess and Pat Fleming, wrote *Thinking Like a Mountain: Towards a Council of All Beings,* which was published in seven languages, and which formed the basis for "Council of All Beings" workshops all over the world.

Seed continued his direct political activism at the same time that he was connecting it to spiritual growth. In 1989, he helped get funding for **Third World** (countries that are underdeveloped socially, economically, and politically) development and rain forest conservation projects. He also traveled to and helped villages and nonprofit organizations in India, the Solomon Islands, and Ecuador. With the money that he has raised from the sale of his book and from his lectures and workshops, Seed has funded many projects himself. In 1991, he was arrested for trying to protect old-growth forests in New South Wales.

Seed has continued to work full-time to save the rain forests of the planet Earth. He has supported the development of small, portable sawmills run by local villagers, and helped to provide a forty-foot boat to carry the timber from the forest to local markets. If the "eco-timber" is cheaper to buy than the lumber gotten from clearcutting, Seed hopes that the destruction of the rain forests will slow down. In spite of all the damage that has been done, and the fact that Seed believes that a miracle is needed to save the earth, he remains optimistic. He said, in a moment of reflection, "If I'm descended from a fish that learned to walk the land, then with a pedigree like that, I can't give up the possibility that such a miracle might take place again, and the question is: What are the conditions for such a miracle, and is there anything that we can do to help bring it about?"

Senesh, Hannah

(1921–1944)

HUNGARIAN POET AND RESISTANCE FIGHTER

> My God, my God,
> that these things should never end:
> the sand and the sea, the rustling of the water
> the lightening of the heavens, the prayer of man.
>
> Blessed is the match consumed in kindling flame.
> Blessed is the heart with strength to stop its beating for honor's sake.
>
> —Hannah Senesh, from her collected poetry

Hannah Senesh, a young Jewish girl, left Hungary for Palestine in 1939, just after **Nazi** armies swept across Europe and sent millions of Jews to their deaths in concentration camps. In Palestine, she farmed, wrote poetry, helped build the Jewish homeland, and looked forward to a long and happy life. But when she heard that Jewish units were being formed to parachute into Hungary to try to rescue Jews who had not escaped, she volunteered immediately. She led a small group into enemy territory, but they were captured by Hungarian policemen. When the Nazis interrogated and tortured her, she refused to tell them the radio code that she used to communicate with the Allied armies. She was killed after being put on trial for treason.

Senesh was born into a warm and happy Jewish family in Budapest, the capital of Hungary. Her father, Bela, was a playwright, and he spent much of his time entertaining Hannah and her older brother, George, with stories, trips to the zoo, and outings to amusement parks. After Bela died of a heart attack when Hannah was only six, her mother took the children to his plays so that they would not forget him. Hannah excelled at school, winning prizes for her writing. She also enjoyed studying about Judaism, and took pride in her heritage even though her family felt more Hungarian than Jewish. She attended a Protestant high school that allowed Jews in as long as they paid three times the normal tuition. Hannah's performance in school was so good that she only had to pay double. She kept a diary during those years, and she wrote of her intentions to become a writer. When she was elected to her school's literary society, she was thrilled. She soon learned, however, that only Protestants could be members. This brush with discrimination made her realize that her future in Hungary would be limited by **anti-Semitism** (hatred of Jews simply because of their religion). She began thinking about moving to Palestine and helping to build a Jewish homeland.

After Adolf Hitler conquered Austria, and appeared to be preparing for an all-out war, Senesh decided to move to Palestine. She studied Hebrew, joined a **Zionist** (Nationalist Jewish) youth group, and applied for an exit visa to leave Hungary. By March 1939, she applied for admission to an agricultural girls' school in Palestine. She was accepted, and left for Palestine shortly after World War II broke out. She spent two years at Nahalal Girls' Farm, learning how to grow food and take care of animals. After graduating, she chose to live on a **kibbutz**, or collective farm, near the Mediterranean Sea port of Caesarea. From 1941 on, as news of the murder of Jews by the Nazis spread, Senesh wrote in her diary about her conflicting feelings. On the one hand, she was happy in Palestine, doing exactly what she wanted to do. On the other hand, she saw that most other Jews in the world were not so lucky, and she felt that she must do something to help them. Her mother's letters told her how bad the situation was in Europe, and how close the Nazis were to conquering Hungary. Hannah was overtaken by the idea of returning to Hungary to get her mother out and to help rescue other Jews from the Nazis.

Many other Jews in Palestine felt as she did. A Jewish fighting brigade, the Palmach, formed a special unit that was to work with the Allied armies in the fight against Hitler. Senesh joined this unit after she heard about it in February 1943. She and the other volunteers were going to try something new—they were going to parachute into the Balkans and Hungary, and try to make contact with Jews and others who were fighting against the Nazis. They had to be able to speak the local languages fluently, understand the local people, and be familiar with the geography of the region. Senesh and the other volunteers had all left those areas recently, and were perfect choices for the mission. They also knew that they would face many hardships, and were prepared to die for their cause.

Senesh and the other thirty-one volunteers joined the English military and were trained and tested by rescuing Allied pilots shot down behind enemy lines. Once there, they set up resistance units to the

Nazis. After this "training," the Palmach volunteers were free to try to rescue Jews. In January 1944, Senesh and the others left for Egypt. She received a one-day delay so that she could see her brother, George, who had arrived in Palestine on the day before she was supposed to leave. The group spent two months in Cairo, waiting for English instructions. Others described Senesh as fearless, excited, and alert. She was always optimistic and encouraging to others. Finally, on March 13, 1944, Senesh and four others were flown to Italy. The English and American military personnel were dumbfounded at the presence of a female paratrooper in the group.

Senesh and the others were flown over Yugoslavia, where they jumped. They spent the next few months living in forests, enduring forty-eight hour marches without food and rest through swamps, and coming under enemy fire. Senesh was the group's leader, and she impressed everyone who met her. The partisans (fighters against the Nazis) were amazed at her strength and courage. Senesh insisted that they had to cross into Hungary, but she was repeatedly told by partisans that it was impossible to cross the border. At one partisan headquarters, news came over the radio that the Nazis had invaded Hungary. Senesh wept, and she announced that she could wait no longer. She would not listen to the partisans or to her own unit; she ordered her troops to follow her into Hungary. When the partisans refused to help them, they set on by themselves in June 1944. On the way, the five fighters met three others, a Frenchman and two Jewish boys trying to get to Palestine, who agreed to join them.

Despite heavy German patrols, the group managed to sneak into Hungary using a compass and a map. When they came to a Hungarian village, Senesh and the Frenchman waited in the bushes, while the others tried to make friendly contacts. They were approached and questioned by the Hungarian police, and one of the boys panicked. He drew his gun and killed himself, and soon the whole group, including Senesh, was captured. Nazi authorities discovered her radio, and they demanded to know the code that she used to send information to the English. With this code, the Nazis could have sent bomber planes to the wrong targets. Even under extreme torture, Senesh refused to reveal the code. She was put on a train to Budapest. She tried to kill herself by jumping out of the train window, but she was caught. In jail in Budapest, the Nazis once again tortured and threatened to kill her if she did not reveal the code. When she refused, they found her mother, and brought her before Senesh, threatening to torture and kill her, too, if Senesh would not cooperate. She somehow found the strength to refuse again. She and her mother were put in separate cells, and occasionally found ways to be together.

At the end of October 1944, Senesh was brought to trial before a military court in Budapest. She made long speeches attacking the moral and political cowardice of the Hungarian state. The judge ordered all visitors out of the courtroom so that they would not hear what Senesh was saying. She continued to criticize the judges, and to threaten them. Because the American and Russian troops were closing in on Hungary, the judges were frightened about what would be done to them if they sentenced Senesh to death. They postponed her sentence for a few days. On the November 7, however, the sentence of death was passed anyway. Senesh wrote her last few poems during this time. She felt sad that she had not accomplished her mission, but she also understood that she had sacrificed her own life to a noble cause. In one of her last poems, she reflected on personal sacrifice for a cause in the line: "Blessed is the match consumed in kindling flame." The match of Hannah Senesh's life went out with three rifle shots in the courtyard of a Budapest prison, but the flame she kindled still burns in the hearts of those with the courage to fight against injustice.

Sharansky, Natan (Anatoly Shcharansky)

(1948–)

SOVIET-JEWISH DISSIDENT AND ACTIVIST

> I hope that the absurd accusation against me and the entire Jewish emigration movement will not hinder the liberation of my people. My friends know how I wanted to exchange activity in the emigration movement for a life with my wife, Avital, in Israel. For more than 2,000 years the Jewish people, my people, have been dispersed. But wherever they are, wherever Jews are found, every year they have repeated, "Next year in Jerusalem." Now, when I am farther than ever from my people, from Avital, facing many arduous years of imprisonment, I say, turning to my people, my Avital, "Next year in Jerusalem." Now I turn to you, the court, who were required to confirm a predetermined sentence. To you I have nothing to say.
>
> —Anatoly Shcharansky, at his trial

Natan Sharansky, a very bright young mathematician and computer programmer, requested permission to **emigrate** from the Soviet Union to Israel in April 1973. Like most other Soviet Jews, he was not granted permission, and he became a "refusenik"—he refused to obey the illogical and arbitrary rules of the Soviet system. He was harassed and followed by the Soviet secret police, the KGB. He applied again for an exit visa one year later, along with his fiancée, Avital (Natalia) Stiglitz. He was again refused, and he was imprisoned for trying to "weaken" the Soviet state. Once Avital left for Israel, the day after they married, he threw himself into the struggle for **human rights** and the right of Jews to leave the Soviet Union where they were harassed, prevented from practicing their religion, and generally treated as second-class citizens. When he was sentenced in 1978 to thirteen years behind bars, he became one of the **dissidents** best known in the West, along with Nobel Prize–winning physicist Andrei Sakharov. Avital fought for Sharansky's release, pressuring Western governments to force the Soviet state to honor human rights in return for trade and good relations. When Mikhail Gorbachev became the leader of the Soviet Union in 1985, he agreed to release Sharansky in exchange for better relations with the United States. Sharansky moved to Israel, where he was given a hero's welcome, and has lived ever since.

Sharansky was born in a Ukrainian coal-mining town near the Black Sea. His parents were Jewish, but he knew very little about Judaism. Natan grew up unaware of the **anti-Semitism** that filled Soviet society. His father, a filmmaker and journalist, and his mother, an economist, instilled in Natan a love of learning. He won a gold medal for his scholarship in high school, and by the age of fourteen he was the town's chess champion. At the age of eighteen, he went to Moscow to study at a special mathematics school. It was in Moscow that he first became aware of his Jewish heritage, and how it could be held against him. During an argument, his best friend called him a "yid," a nasty word for "Jew." Sharansky recalled, "I think it was then that I decided [the Soviet Union] was no place for me."

The Six-Day War of 1967, in which Israel defeated its many Arab opponents within a few days, brought a surge of pride to the Soviet Jewish community. Sharansky, along with many others, began studying Hebrew, Jewish culture, and the **Nazi Holocaust** and made plans for a future in Israel. All this was forbidden by the Soviet state, officially atheist (a belief that no God exists). **Nationalist** culture of any kind threatened the Soviet state, which ruled over many different nationalities. Furthermore, if Jews were allowed to leave, then others in the Soviet Union would also want to. In a country with very little freedom and very few comforts, the **emigration** of millions of people was a very real possibility. Sharansky applied for an exit visa in April 1973, after finishing his studies at the Moscow Physical-Technical Institute with a special degree in cybernetics (the science of communication and control theory). He was refused. The Soviet officials explained that his schooling and his new job with the Moscow Research Institute for Oil and Gas had given him "access to classified material." This was a common reason for many Jews to be refused permission to leave the country. His work, supposedly classified for military reasons, was for an "open" institute, and his thesis at school had been on teaching computers to play chess.

Sharansky, as a refusenik, was now harassed by the state. He organized public protests as his friends in the dissident movement were arrested. In October 1973, at a protest rally, he met Avital Stiglitz, whose brother was a refusenik spending time in prison. The couple fell in love and decided to marry the following spring. They both applied for exit visas, but only Avital's was granted. They put off their wedding, while Natan spent the month of June 1974 in prison to prevent his contacting U.S. President Richard M. Nixon, who was visiting Moscow. On July 4, the day he was released from prison, Natan and Avital were married, and she left for Israel the following day, believing that he would soon follow. It would be almost twelve years until they would see each other again.

Sharansky was infuriated at being separated from his wife. He traveled all over the Soviet Union, gathering information on the mistreatment of dissidents. He was often assigned a number of KGB agents to watch him. The information he collected helped convince the United States to link improvements in U.S.–Soviet relations with increased Jewish emigration from the Soviet Union. When the Soviet Union signed the Helsinki accords on human rights in August 1975, Sharansky and a few other dissidents, including Andrei Sakharov and Yelena Bonner, formed the Moscow Helsinki Watch. They collected information about Soviet abuses of human rights and passed it on to the embassies of countries that had signed the Helsinki accords. Sharansky was fired from his job and was threatened and watched by the KGB. Once when he was talking with a group of journalists in his Moscow apartment, he was asked what it was like to be always watched by the KGB. Sharansky put on his coat, told the reporters to do the same, and walked out of the apartment. When they got to the elevator, two KGB men squeezed in with them. When the group reached the lobby, more KGB men joined them. Sharansky was led to a car that was waiting for him, while the reporters were blocked from accompanying him.

In March 1977, Sharansky was arrested and accused of being a Central Intelligence Agency (CIA) spy. U.S. President Jimmy Carter announced that Sharansky had no ties to the CIA, but it did not matter. Sharansky's true "crime" was his work drawing the world's attention to the human rights abuses by the Soviet Union. His trial began on July 10, 1978. No reporters were allowed into the courtroom, but Sharansky's brother, Leonid, was there, and he told the outside world what was going on in the courthouse. Sharansky defended himself, but was forbidden to call his own witnesses, and was limited in what he was allowed to ask his accusers. On the fourth day of the trial, he was convicted and sentenced to three years in prison, followed by ten years of hard labor.

Sharansky spent the first three years alone, in solitary confinement, at Chistopol prison. He had to put forth great efforts not to go crazy. He played countless games of chess in his imagination. (Later, he joked with a reporter that at least he always won.) He outlined a book that he planned to write, and he sang Hebrew songs at the top of his lungs. He tried to remind himself that the world had not forgotten him. In fact, although he did not know it, his wife, mother, and brother were working hard for his release. International Jewish organizations put pressure on many world governments to convince the Soviet leaders to release Sharansky.

Once he was moved to Perm 35, a labor camp, he had more contact with the outside world. He was encouraged by the occasional bits of news that got past his **censors**; one magazine contained a letter from U.S. President Ronald Reagan to Sharansky's wife. Convinced that the only way he would survive was to resist the system, Sharansky refused to obey prison rules. He would not work unless he was allowed to keep a Jewish prayer book and Sabbath candles in his cell. He went on a hunger strike to protest the guards' not giving him his mail. The terrible conditions, hard labor, and hunger strikes caused serious medical problems. He nearly became blind, and he suffered from heart problems as well. Avital increased her pressure campaign, fearing that her husband might die if he were not released. President Reagan insisted that the Soviet Union release Sharansky and fellow prisoner Andrei Sakharov before the United States would work to improve relations between the two countries.

When Mikhail Gorbachev became head of the Soviet Union in 1985, he worked with Reagan to end the Cold War between the two superpowers. one of the first steps in this warming of relations (known as "glasnost") was the release of Sharansky. The United States insisted that he be released before the Soviet and U.S. spies who had been captured by the other side. On February 11, 1986, Sharansky was escorted by Soviet secret service agents to the plane that was to fly him to East Berlin. The agents took away his book of Psalms, a present from Avital. He lay down in the snow and refused to move until it was returned to him. Once in East Berlin, he was told by the Soviet agents to walk in a straight line across the Glienecke

Bridge. Refusing to accept even this last command, Sharansky zigzagged across the bridge to the Western officials who were waiting to meet him.

Sharansky was reunited with his wife, and the couple flew to Israel, twelve years after their wedding. They were given a wild welcome and were met at the airport by Israeli Prime Minister Shimon Peres and a large crowd. They have settled into life in Israel, and have been joined by Sharansky's mother and his brother and his family. Sharansky has gotten involved in a few political battles in Israel, but he prefers to stay out of the spotlight. When he was criticized for some of his political views, he was asked how he felt about it. He answered, "That's the beauty of democracy." *See* BONNER, YELENA; SAKHAROV, ANDREI

Shiva, Vandana

(1953-   )

INDIAN PHYSICIST, FEMINIST, AND ENVIRONMENTAL ACTIVIST

> Across the world, women are rebuilding connections with nature, and renewing the insight that what we do to nature, we do to ourselves. There is no insular divide between the environment and our bodies. Environmental hazards are also health hazards . . . Pesticides do not merely pollute fields, they end up polluting our bodies. Destruction of biodiversity does not merely impoverish nature, it impoverishes tribal and peasant societies. These links exist in the real world even though they have been denied by fragmented and divided worldviews.
>
> The granting of patents in the North for products developed from Third World resources using Third World knowledge and preventing free use by the Third World, is a most obscene form of racism. This trade in genetic material is the slave trade of this era. How can I patent something that is living? The idea itself is abhorrent.
>
> —Vandana Shiva, on the connection between all aspects of life and nature

Vandana Shiva has spent her career teaching people that everything in life is connected. As someone concerned with the well-being of women, she argues, she might be concerned about the state of the environment. As an **environmentalist**, she is an **activist** who has gotten involved in world trade issues. She has also fought for the rights of **indigenous** (original native) peoples and peasant societies to maintain their traditional ways of life. She was honored with the 1993 Right Livelihood Award for her work in preserving the diversity of life on earth by collecting and storing seeds.

Shiva grew up in the Himalayan mountains. Her father worked for the forest service, and her mother composed songs about nature and sang them to her children. Shiva grew to love the forests and the mountains, and she spent her childhood trekking in the mountains near her home. She excelled in science, and after earning two master's degrees (M.A.s) in physics at the Punjab University in India, she traveled to Ontario, Canada, to earn two more degrees, including a Ph.D. in quantum physics in 1978. Even when she was studying in Canada, Shiva returned to India each summer to trek in her beloved Himalayas. While in Canada, she met Indian scientist Jayanto Bandopadhyay, whom she married. He wanted to stay in Canada, while she felt a great urge to return to India. She left Canada, taking her son with her, and the long-distance marriage eventually fell apart. She felt "materialistically rich but still highly impoverished" in the West. Highly critical of Western science for the way it divided the world into separate fields and ignored the connections, she explained, "I felt I would be socially **illiterate** and scientifically educated if I chose to stay on in the West."

Back in India in 1979, she worked at the Indian Institute of Technology, in Bangalore. During the next two years, she formulated her views on the connections between environmental destruction, **colonialism** (political and economic control of an area by another state), and the oppression of women. In 1982, she started her own institute—The Research Foundation of Science, Technology, and Natural Resource Policy—in the city of Dehradun. The institute's first location was a cow shed on the property her mother had left her. At the same time, she volunteered to help the Chipko movement, a crusade of peasant women of the Himalayas to prevent timber companies from replacing their mixed forests with pine tree monocultures (only one species). This combination of scientific learning with social action has become a central theme in Shiva's life: "I gave up an academic career for a dream to build an independent research initiative to generate a different kind of knowledge which would serve the powerless, rather than the powerful, which would not get all its cues from

Western universities and international institutions, but would also be open to the indigenous knowledge of local communities; which would break down the artificial divide between experts and nonexperts and subject and object." Rather than scientists treating the entire world as the object of their experiments, she feels that scientists must recognize that they themselves are part of the world and need to use their knowledge to make the world a better place.

Shiva worked on projects to clean up polluted water and to preserve the diversity of plant species in forests. As she saw it, one threat to **biodiversity**, or the existence of many different species of plants and animals in an ecosystem, was the creation of monocultures. In addition to being bad for the soil, replacing many species of trees with just pine trees meant that if a disease struck the pine trees, the entire forest would be wiped out. The problem becomes even more serious when the monoculture is a food crop. If millions of acres of different crops are replaced with one genetically identical crop, then the entire food supply is in danger of being wiped out.

Shiva wrote many books and articles on the causes and dangers of monocultures. One of the main reasons that monocultures exist is because the patent laws that govern world trade. If a Western biotechnology company takes the genetic material from an Indian plant and alters the DNA (its specific biological makeup) slightly, then that company now "owns" the new plant. If it buys lots of land, and replaces other crops with the new, "patented" plant, then it holds a monopoly and stands to make a huge profit. According to Shiva, this process goes against nature, which has produced ecosystems based on many different living things all depending on one another for their existence. She called the desire to replace diversity with uniformity a "monoculture of the mind," which she defined as a condition that "treats all diversity as a disease, and which creates coercive structures to model this biologically and culturally diverse world of ours on the privileged categories and concepts of one class, one race, and one gender of a single species." In other words, just as upper-class white men from the West colonized the **Third World** and exploited its citizens through violent domination, the patented species of plants and animals that these upper-class white men "own" are coming to dominate the planet. As an example, she pointed to what happened with the neem trees, a species with many different uses. Once the Western world discovered that an Indian tree called the neem provided a safe pesticide to be used on food crops, the price of neem seeds went from three hundred rupees to four thousand rupees per ton. Indian farmers could no longer afford to buy the seeds. Shiva warned, "The tree, which is today accessible to all, will become the private property of Western corporations."

Shiva has been one of the Third World's leading spokespeople in the debate over "free trade," which she sees as another method that the West is using to exploit the Third World. She created the concept of eco-**feminism**, which states that women have a special role to play to preserve the health of the earth. Her institute has always worked with local women, as well as with internationally respected scientists, to make and implement its policies. In 1991, Shiva started a project to save the seeds from thousands of species of plants that are disappearing from the world because of monocultures. Her first community seed bank began with two varieties of rice. Since 1991, two additional banks have been set up in India, and together they have managed to save four hundred of the one hundred thousand varieties of rice that once grew in India. Not only are the seeds stored, but they are made available to local farmers to use for their plantings. The seed campaign, which she named "Seed Satyagraha," after Gandhi's nonviolent campaign against the British, was launched at a farmers' rally in 1992. One year later, half a million farmers attended the campaign's first-birthday celebration in Bangalore.

Shiva continues to organize, write, and speak out against monocultures of all kinds, of plants and of thinking. The connections that she has made between how human beings look at and treat one another and how we look at and treat the environment have inspired millions of people, in the West as well as the Third World, to take action to save the earth from becoming a monoculture of humans. When Shiva received the Right Livelihood Award in 1993, she expressed her hope and her faith that the powerless and the weak will save the human race.

Slovo, Joe

(1926-1995)

SOUTH AFRICAN ACTIVIST AND POLITICIAN

> The people's patience is not endless. The time comes in the life of
> any national where there remain only two choices: submit or fight.
> That time has come to South Africa. We shall not submit and we
> have no choice but to hit back by all means within our power in de-
> fense of our people, our future, and our freedom.
>
> —Manifesto of Umkhonto We Size, 1961

Joe Slovo, the leader of the South African Communist Party, helped
convert the African National Congress (ANC) into a **terrorist** organization in its battle against **apartheid** (the strict separation of people
based on race). He was called "Public Enemy Number One" by the
South African government, and was one of the most hated and feared
enemies of apartheid. His wife, Ruth First, was killed by a letter
bomb allegedly planted by agents of the South African government.
Slovo maintained optimism throughout his life that the struggle
against apartheid would succeed, and that he would return to South
Africa as a free man. With the fall of apartheid in 1994, Slovo was
named interior minister in the government of President Nelson Mandela, a post that he held until his death from cancer in early 1995.

Slovo came to South Africa from Lithuania when he was nine
years old. His father, a van driver, could not make enough money to
support his family. Slovo left school in sixth grade in order to make
money for his family. He got a job as a warehouse assistant in a
chemical plant. He joined the union for warehouse distributors, then
became a union leader. He left the plant during World War II, and he
fought with the South African army in Italy. When the war ended, he
enrolled in Witwatersrand University, in Johannesburg, and excelled
as a law student. While at the university, he became active in revolutionary politics and joined the **Communist** Party of South Africa.
The party was banned in 1950, after the Nationalist Party won the
1948 election and put apartheid firmly into place. Slovo married journalist Ruth First in 1949, and the two of them helped re-form the

Communist Party as the South African Communist Party (SACP), which was banned in 1960.

In the years following the **Nationalist** Party's control of the government, Slovo was "banned" (forbidden from meeting with others or taking part in politics) numerous times. He was working as a lawyer, defending political **activists** who were being harassed by the government, and when he was banned, he continued his work underground. In 1955, a number of anti-apartheid organizations drafted a revolutionary document, the Freedom **Charter**. Slovo was not allowed to attend the Congress of Democrats meeting where the charter was adopted. Instead, he watched the meeting five hundred feet away, on the rooftop of a building, through binoculars. Shortly after the Congress meeting, Slovo and 155 others were arrested by the government for treason (crimes against the nation). Because he was banned, Slovo had to get special permission even to attend his own trial. He defended himself in court and succeeded in getting all charges against him dropped in 1958. Two years later, the SACP and the ANC were banned, and sixteen hundred people were arrested. Slovo was kept in jail without trial for five months.

Following the government crackdowns against their organization, ANC leaders decided that nonviolent struggle was not enough to end apartheid. Peaceful protests just made the government angrier, and they increased the oppression by nonwhites in South Africa. In 1961, Nelson Mandela asked Slovo to help form a military wing of the ANC. At Liliesleaf Farm, their secret hideout in a suburb of Johannesburg, Slovo and a few others formed Umkhonto We Size (the Spear of the Nation). They decided that they would limit their violent resistance to sabotage (destruction) of government and business property, rather than engaging in terrorism, **guerrilla** warfare, or outright revolution. Sabotage, they reasoned, would cause the least violence against people, while attacking the economy of South Africa. In the next year and a half, Umkhonto committed 150 acts of sabotage, while being careful not to hurt people if they could avoid it.

Slovo was out of the country when the South African police raided Liliesleaf in 1963, capturing most of the ANC leaders. Ruth First was arrested a month later. The ANC had been crippled by the arrests. South African blacks were afraid to talk about the ANC due to government action they feared they would be taken against them. Slovo set up the ANC headquarters in **exile** in Dar El Saawadi Salaam, Tanzania, an East African country. Without much money, the "headquarters" consisted of a couple of run-down rooms, and one typewriter. Slovo convinced the Soviet Union to help rebuild the ANC. He bought weapons and set up training camps, and he turned the ANC into a fighting organization by 1969. Slovo was named to the ANC Revolutionary Council, which was dedicated to full-scale guerrilla warfare against the South African government. ANC revolutionary fighters infiltrated South Africa from neighboring Mozambique and Angola, bringing with them weapons and knowledge of warfare. In 1976, riots broke out in Soweto, a black township outside Johannesburg. About twelve thousand South Africans left the country following the uprising, with eight thousand of them joining the ANC in exile. Slovo, as the architect of the campaign of violence, was largely responsible for the growth and increased success of the ANC.

The South African government fought back, sending commando units into Mozambique to find and kill Joe Slovo. In 1981, South African soldiers disguised themselves as Mozambique soldiers, crossed the border, and killed thirteen ANC leaders, including one white man mistaken for Slovo. In 1982, Ruth First was killed by a letter bomb in her office in Mozambique. South African diplomats tried to turn world opinion against Slovo by accusing him of the murder of his wife. Slovo sued the newspaper that ran the story, the *Johannesburg Star*, in a London court. He won over $50,000, but the paper refused to obey the court, and never paid him.

In 1985, Slovo became the first white to sit on the ANC's National Executive Council. He helped expand the number of "acceptable targets" of ANC violence, now including hamburger chain restaurants, art galleries, shopping malls, and rugby stadiums. The violence, coupled with an international boycott of South Africa, helped convince many South Africans that it was time to negotiate with the ANC. Nelson Mandela was released from prison in 1990, and democratic elections were held in 1994. When Mandela was elected president of South Africa, he appointed Slovo as one of his cabinet ministers. Slovo had thus become one of the leaders of a government that he had spent his whole life trying to overthrow. He remained in the ANC–led government until his death, in early 1995. *See* FIRST, RUTH; BIKO, STEVEN; MANDELA, NELSON

Smythe, Ethel

(1858-1944)

ENGLISH COMPOSER AND SUFFRAGETTE

Dame Ethel Smythe was one of the most colorful and determined women involved in the women's **suffrage** (right to vote) movement. She overcame opposition from her own family and the musical world to become a successful composer, and she threw herself into the movement to win the right to vote with creativity and courage.

Smythe was raised in a family that took very seriously its connections to the English army, navy, and church. She wanted no part of these institutions, and instead she announced, to the displeasure of her family, that she wanted to become a musician. She left England to study music at the Leipzig Conservatory in Berlin, and she was praised and encouraged by the composer Johannes Brahms. Although she was very talented, the public was not eager to accept that a woman could be a composer. She did not have her compositions played in public in England until 1890, when she was thirty-two years old. Three years later her *Mass in D* was performed at the Albert Hall, and she began to win some recognition as the first great English woman composer. She found that the German public was more interested in her work than was the English public, so she wrote operas that were performed in Germany from 1898 to 1906. Her third opera, *The Wreckers*, was her most famous, and was conducted by Bruno Walter in London in 1910.

The discrimination that Smythe faced led her to join the suffragist movement (to win women the vote) in England. In 1911, she wrote a song, *March of the Women*, which was sung by women throughout London. She joined the Pankhursts in throwing stones at a cabinet minister's window, and she was arrested and sent to jail. In what became her most famous act, she led the arrested women in singing *March of the Women*, conducting the song with a toothbrush from her cell in Holloway Prison.

Smythe wrote many other pieces, and she conducted the Metropolitan Police Band at the unveiling of a statue of Emmeline Pankhurst. She also wrote entertaining autobiographical works, describing her own musical life, and also the friendships she had made with many other famous women, including the English novelist Virginia Woolf. Smythe was made a Dame of the British Empire in 1922. *See* PANKHURST FAMILY

Szilard, Leo

(1898–1964)

HUNGARIAN-BORN ATOMIC PHYSICIST AND PEACE ACTIVIST

> On March 3, 1939, Dr. Walter Zinn and I . . . completed a single experiment to which we had been looking forward rather eagerly. Everything was ready, and all we had to do was to lean back, turn a switch, and watch the screen of a television tube. If flashes of light appeared on the screen, it would mean that neutrons were emitted in the fission of uranium, and that in turn would mean that the liberation of atomic energy was possible in our lifetime. We turned the switch, we saw the flashes, we watched them for about ten minutes—and then we switched everything off and went home. That night I knew that the world was headed for sorrow.
>
> —Leo Szilard, on the dangers of the nuclear era

Leo Szilard, an atomic physicist and one of the creators of the technology that led to the atomic bomb, spent his later life fighting against the military use of nuclear weapons and organizing scientists to work for world peace. He felt that after the United States dropped two atomic bombs on Japan at the end of World War II, the nations of the world could not be trusted with nuclear weapons. He favored the formation of a world government, and he organized conferences between Soviet and American scientists at a time when the two nations were locked in a bitter and dangerous Cold War. He formed the Council for a Livable World, a Washington, D.C., lobby that supported peace candidates for the U.S. Senate.

Szilard was born into a Jewish family in Budapest, in the Austro-Hungarian Empire, in 1898. He was a sickly child, and could not attend school due to his illnesses. His mother tutored him at home until he was well enough to go to elementary school. He later said that one of the most important influences on his life was a book that he read at the age of ten, Imre Madách's *The Tragedy of Man*. In the book, the earth is doomed because the sun is dying, and only Eskimos are left. Szilard said that the book taught him to concentrate on a "narrow margin of hope," even after the most awful prophecies are made. Many years later, after he helped to build the most destructive weapon known to humankind, he was to remember this lesson.

Szilard attended the Budapest Institute of Technology, planning to be an engineer, like his father. His studies were interrupted by World War I, during which Szilard fought in the Austro-Hungarian army. When the war ended, he enrolled in the Technical Institute of Berlin, and he soon met some of the most famous physicists in the world, including Max Planck and Albert Einstein. Szilard became interested in their work, and he gave up engineering to study theoretical physics. A brilliant and creative scientist, he became a regular visitor to Einstein's home, and the two of them patented several inventions, including a heat pump that would later regulate the temperature of nuclear reactors.

Szilard fled Berlin for England as soon as Adolf Hitler's **Nazi** regime came to power in Germany. He set up an organization that helped other European scientists who became refugees from Hitler. As it appeared that war would be likely, Szilard turned his attention to practical uses of his work on the structure of the atom. He received a secret patent in 1934 for his plans for a nuclear fission chain reactor, a device that, if he was correct, could produce the most powerful explosion ever created by human beings. In 1939, in the United States, he learned that German physicist Otto Hahn had split uranium atoms. He feared that this discovery would lead to Hitler's developing a bomb that used the released energy from the atomic nucleus to create a chain reaction—in other words, a nuclear weapon. Szilard and a colleague repeated Hahn's experiment, and they saw the flashes on the television screen that meant that the atom had been split. He knew then "that the world was headed for sorrow."

Szilard found himself in the uncomfortable position of trying to develop this weapon of destruction before the enemy did. He and three other physicists convinced the scientists working in the field of nuclear fission not to publish their work in scientific journals, so that the Nazis would not be able to develop nuclear weapons. One scientist, Frédéric Joliot-Curie, misunderstood Szilard's request and published his results. Now it was a race between German and American scientists to develop an atomic bomb. The United States government, however, did not take an interest in this research. Szilard feared that the government's lack of understanding would mean that the Nazis would develop nuclear weapons first, and perhaps win the war. Szilard and Albert Einstein approached President Franklin D. Roosevelt with a description of their work and its military uses. At first the president decided that the research would best be carried out by scientists at private universities, but Szilard, Einstein, and fellow physicist Enrico Fermi continued to pressure the government. Finally, in the summer of 1940, the atomic energy work was made part of the National Defense Research Committee of the United States. Szilard and Fermi were in charge of the first project, at Columbia University. In 1942, the project was moved to Chicago, where Szilard and Fermi created the world's first controlled nuclear chain reaction in a squash court underneath the football stadium at the University of Chicago. Soon after this, the Manhattan Project was begun in Los Alamos, New Mexico. This was an all-out attempt by the United States to develop a working atomic bomb. Szilard remained in Chicago and was responsible for extracting the plutonium that was needed for fueling the weapon.

In 1945, Szilard realized that the United States would win the race to develop an atomic bomb. His fears shifted from what Germany would do with such a weapon to what the United States would do with it. He and Einstein tried to convince President Harry S. Truman to demonstrate the power of the atom bomb to Japan in a way that would not harm people, but Truman decided to drop two bombs on Japanese cities, one each on Hiroshima and Nagasaki. Szilard felt that the United States could not be trusted as the only country in the world with nuclear capabilities. He led a movement of scientists to defeat the army's plan to keep nuclear technology as a military secret. The scientists helped to pass the MacMahon Act, which established the Atomic Energy Commission, a civilian agency, to control atomic research and testing.

In 1946, Szilard sent an open letter to the Soviet premier, Joseph Stalin, and U.S. President Truman, asking them to reassure the other country's people that they would try to control the spread of atomic weapons. He contributed to a book, *One World or None*, which was a collection of writings by scientists trying to wake up the public to the dangers of the new technologies. He saw with sadness and fear the nuclear arms race that swept through the U.S. and Soviet Union, and he became a crusader for disarmament. He **lobbied** (attempted to influence and convince) politicians, gave speeches, wrote books, and organized associations of scientists to take responsibility for the technology that they had created, which threatened to destroy the world. After his work on the Manhattan Project, Szilard gave up physics and devoted the rest of his scientific career to biology, the study of life. His work in physics, he felt, had produced nothing but death.

Szilard felt that the existence of nuclear weapons meant that the world could no longer afford war. He became a peace **activist**, and although he disapproved of the policies of the Soviet Union, he argued that the U.S. had to learn to deal with its rival through negotiation, rather than conflict. Each new weapon that either side built to defend itself from the other brought the world, in Szilard's opinion, one step closer to mass "suicide and murder." In 1957, he organized the Pugwash movement, a series of regular meetings between scientists from all over the world to discuss issues of international affairs. In 1962, he embarked on a lecture tour of U.S. colleges and universities, and was encouraged by the support that he felt from the students. Inspired by them, he established a permanent lobbying organization in Washington, D.C., that supported candidates for the U.S. Senate who pledged to work for world peace and understanding. By the end of his life, Szilard believed that only a world government would keep nations from destroying one another. He argued that national loyalty was dangerous, and that people would have to see themselves as "citizens of the world," rather than as Americans or Russians. He spent the years before his death in 1964 educating the world about the "narrow margin of hope" that existed even in the face of nuclear weapons.

Ten Boom, Corrie

(1892–1983)

DUTCH RESISTOR TO NAZISM

> I believe that God delights to use His children in the fulfillment of
> His plans for the world. I am sure He loves to use small people to
> do great things.
>
> —Corrie ten Boom, on her powerful belief in God's love

Corrie ten Boom was forty-eight years old when the German army invaded Holland in World War II. She and her family converted their home into a hiding place for Jews and other refugees fleeing the **Nazis**. The family was arrested in 1944, and Corrie and her sister were taken to Ravensbruck concentration camp. Corrie was released due to a clerical error just before all the women of the camp were murdered. She devoted the rest of her life to helping war refugees and displaced persons, and teaching the Christian message of service to others.

Corrie grew up in the Dutch town of Haarlem, the daughter of Casper and Cor ten Boom. Casper was a jeweler and watchmaker, and Corrie became a licensed watchmaker herself after involving herself in a romance that did not lead to the marriage she was hoping for. She was the first woman watchmaker in Holland. Although the family was poor, their strict Calvinist faith (which emphasized the importance and power of God) led them to offer food, shelter, and money to anyone in need. The house was always filled with visitors, some of whom stayed for years. Casper instilled his religious faith in Corrie and her sister, Betsie, and he taught them his love and respect for Jews, whom he called "God's ancient people."

Even while Corrie attended high school, she was always studying and teaching the Bible. After she became a watchmaker, she would work during the day, and then Bible discussions and care for her sick mother and aunts in the evening. She also helped take care of the many children of German war refugees and Christian **missionaries** that her father would take in. Their house on Barteljoris Street was known as the "Beje," and it became well known as a haven for those in need. Some of the children grew to adulthood in the Beje, raised by

Corrie, her father, and sister. Corrie also taught Sunday-school classes to retarded children, and taught Bible studies in public schools. She convinced some wealthy people in Haarlem to donate money so that she could organize girls' clubs. The clubs not only gave religious instruction, but taught the girls music, singing, dancing, gymnastics, and handicrafts.

In 1940, the German army invaded Holland and conquered the entire country in just five days. When the Jews were forced to identify themselves by wearing black armbands with yellow stars of David, Casper was so upset that he decided to wear one, too. Corrie and Betsie had to convince him that it would be a dangerous gesture, and that there was more important work to be done. They used the Beje as a hiding place for resistance fighters and Dutch Jews. Some of those hiding from and fighting the Nazis stopped off at the Beje on their way to somewhere else, and a few stayed on for years. The ten Booms built a secret room under Corrie's closet where people could hide when the Nazi secret police, the Gestapo, came looking for them.

The ten Booms could not provide shelter in the Beje to all the people who needed aid. Corrie helped to set up a network of houses like the Beje all over Holland. Many Dutch Jews were hidden in these houses for years. On February 28, 1944, the Gestapo raided the Beje and arrested thirty-five people, everyone they could find. They missed six people, who hid for several days in Corrie's secret room.

Casper, at eighty-four years old, died only ten days after being taken into custody. Corrie was sent to prison and grew ill with bronchitis. When she recovered, she was put to trial. The judge who heard her case was so impressed with her courage and her faith that he destroyed documents that the Gestapo had found in the Beje. Corrie was reunited with Betsie in June 1944, at the Vught concentration camp. The sisters led prayer and Bible study groups, using a Bible that Corrie had smuggled into the camp in her clothes. As the Allied armies advanced on Germany, the Nazis shot the men and boys at the camp, and they sent the women to Ravensbruck concentration camp to work as forced laborers. The conditions were terrible, and Betsie died in December 1944. Just before she died, she told Corrie of a dream that she had had: A home would be established to help all the people who had suffered during the war. This home would be a place for them to rest and recover before getting on with their lives.

Corrie was released on New Year's Day 1945, the result, she

learned later, of a clerical error. All the women who weren't released were later killed in Ravensbruck's gas chambers. Corrie went back to Holland, where she began working toward fulfilling Betsie's dream. She collected money and worked with friends to build a rehabilitation center for refugees and former prisoners of war, and she began traveling around the world spreading her message of love and courage. By 1977, when she was eighty-five, she had visited almost seventy countries. She gave up traveling due to poor health and settled in California, where she died in 1983, on her ninety-first birthday.

Thich Nhat Hanh

(1926–   )

VIETNAMESE MONK AND POET

> Happiness is not an individual matter. You cannot be happy individually. Let's talk of a married couple, for instance. How can one person in the couple be happy if the other is not happy? It's very clear. The only way to be happy is to make the other person happy, and then you will be happy, too. Our situation in the world is like that. People know quite clearly that if the Third World collapses and cannot pay its debt, then the whole monetary system will collapse, and the First World will collapse also. So taking care not to exploit the Third World and trying to help them stand on their own feet also helps the First World..
>
> Happiness is not an individual thing. Many people have seen that. Only, how can we practice it? We must sit together to find ways to educate ourselves, to educate our friends and our children.
>
> —Thich Nhat Hanh, from his Buddhist teachings

Thich Nhat Hanh is one of the most important and influential teachers of **Buddhism** in the West. He has written many books of poetry, has been involved in social and educational reform in his native Vietnam, and was nominated for the Nobel Peace Prize by Dr. Martin Luther King, Jr.

Thich Nhat Hanh, known to his friends and disciples as Thay (pronounced "tie"—the Vietnamese word for teacher), was born in a village in central Vietnam in 1926. He credited his loving mother with providing a happy childhood for him. When he was sixteen, he and four of his best friends all became Buddhist monks. He was given the name Thich (the Buddha's family name, and the name given to all Vietnamese monks) Nhat Hahn (meaning "one action"). As a monk, Thich Nhat Hanh studied mindfulness, or performing every action and thinking every thought fully conscious of the present moment. He used meditative techniques and short verses to help him to remember to focus on the present. He became frustrated at some elements of his training in the monastery, however, and suggested that the curriculum include modern Western thought, science, and literature. The monks who ran the monastery did not agree. Thich Nhat Hanh and some friends moved to Saigon, the capital of Vietnam, and lived together in an abandoned temple. During this time Thich Nhat Hanh wrote a huge amount of material. He edited several magazines about Buddhism, and wrote four books before he was twenty. Even though at the monastery he was forbidden from reading novels, he wrote novels and short stories. He also wrote two books of poetry.

The French ruled Vietnam during Thich Nhat Hanh's childhood and youth. They set up a **colonial** system of education that raised young Vietnamese boys in the Western style. Many Vietnamese feared that unless they sent their sons to these schools, the boys would not be successful under French rule. Thich Nhat Hanh founded Vietnam's first Buddhist high school, in the 1950s. He also founded his own monastery in central Vietnam, and he turned it into a center for spiritual renewal for monks, nuns, and laypersons alike. The curriculum that was offered in both places soon impressed the leaders of the Vietnamese Buddhist church, and they invited Thich Nhat Hanh to help set up Van Hahn Buddhist University in Saigon.

Thich Nhat Hanh wanted to learn more about the rest of the world, especially the world's other religions. In 1961, he traveled to the United States, where he studied comparative religion at Princeton University and Columbia University. He studied and taught, and he enjoyed his time in the United States very much. After two and a half years, however, monks in Vietnam asked him to return to his country and help them work for peace. In 1963, the regime of Vietnamese dictator Ngo Dinh Diem was toppled, and fighting was breaking out all across the country. The Soviet Union was supporting the **communist** forces, while the United States began, at first in a small way, to help the anticommunist fighters. Meanwhile, the Vietnamese people themselves were suffering because of the fighting. Thich Nhat Hanh immediately began leading a nonviolent resistance movement to the war and to the rulers who were oppressing the Vietnamese people. He wrote a book, *Engaged Buddhism*, which laid out the path of nonviolent work for peace and justice as the true pursuit of Buddhist enlightenment. Rather than choosing between meditating in their monasteries or going out and helping people who needed aid, Buddhist monks had to do both at the same time. Service, Thich Nhat Hanh wrote, was a form of meditation, if practiced in the right spirit.

The war raged on, however, and the United States actually entered the fighting. In 1964, Thich Nhat Hanh founded the School of Youth for Social Service, which was known to American reporters as the "little Peace Corps." Young people interested in rebuilding Vietnam went out into the countryside to build schools and health clinics. Later, as the war grew more fierce, they rebuilt villages and took care of the wounded. By the time of the fall of Saigon, in 1975, more than ten thousand Vietnamese were part of this work. Also in 1964, seeing that Vietnam had been divided into a North Vietnam and a South Vietnam, and the two governments were enemies, Thich Nhat Hanh tried to spread his message of peace by founding a publishing house, La Boi Press. As the editor of the official publications of the Unified Buddhist Church, Thich Nhat Hanh called on the participants in the war to lay down their arms and settle their differences peacefully. Neither government was interested in seeking peace at that time, however, and his writings were **censored** by both of them.

Many people in the United States were opposed to the U.S. involvement in Vietnam. One antiwar group, the Fellowship of Reconciliation, joined with Cornell University to invite Thich Nhat Hanh to come to the United States and describe the suffering of the Vietnamese people. He met with many important people, including Secretary of Defense Robert McNamara, Trappist monk Thomas Merton, and Dr. Martin Luther King, Jr. He and Dr. King became friends, and soon after their meeting King broke with other black leaders by saying that the United States should not be fighting in Vietnam. In 1967, Dr. King nominated Thich Nhat Hanh for the Nobel Peace Prize. Merton also wrote in favor of peace in Vietnam after meeting Thich Nhat Hanh. Following the American visit, Thich Nhat Hanh went to Europe, where he met with Pope Paul VI and heads of a number of European countries.

In 1969, the Paris Peace Talks were set up to try to end the war in Vietnam. The Unified Buddhist Church of Vietnam asked Thich Nhat Hanh to organize the Buddhist delegation to the talks. The talks led to a peace agreement in 1973, and when Thich Nhat Hanh tried to return to Vietnam after that, he was not allowed to enter the country. He remained near Paris and set up a small community, which he named Sweet Potato. He got involved in an effort to save Vietnamese people who had been sent away from their country in leaky boats, but he found that the neighboring countries of Thailand and Singapore were unwilling to help them. He returned to Sweet Potato, where he meditated, read, gardened, bound books, and saw a few visitors. He did not leave Sweet Potato for five years.

During this time, he received much information on **human rights** abuses in Vietnam, and he encouraged many people to fight against the injustice and abuses. His writings, although banned in Vietnam, were circulated there illegally, and he was seen as a source of inspiration to many people who opposed the government. The Vietnamese government viewed him as such a threat that twice it spread rumors that he had died. The first time, Vietnam was trying to set up its own Buddhist Church in 1982. The second time, the government was preparing to arrest Buddhist monks, nuns, and writers who opposed the "official" church.

In 1982, Thich Nhat Hanh came to the United States for a conference. He realized that there was a great hunger among many Americans for information about Buddhism. He arranged to lead retreats and give lectures in America, and he tried to build bridges of healing and trust between Vietnam and the United States. He has continued to speak out in favor of peace and justice. He teaches that only through mindfulness, through living in the present and finding joy in the unity of all life, can human beings live together in peace. In his most famous poem, "Call Me by My True Names," Thich Nhat Hanh explains the connectedness of all humans, and the suffering that comes when we forget that we are all brothers and sisters. He continues to be an inspiration to many who seek peace and justice through understanding, compassion, and forgiveness.

Timerman, Jacobo

(1923–)

ARGENTINIAN JOURNALIST

The journalist Jacobo Timerman founded and edited the newspaper *La Opinión* in Argentina beginning in 1971. He used the newspaper to criticize the Argentinian government for its campaign of terror against its own citizens, and he published stories about *desaparacidos,* or people who "disappeared" (and were actually killed) after being taken by extreme right-wing elements in the Argentinian military. He criticized government corruption and exposed government **anti-Semitism** (hatred of Jews). He fought against extremism of the left as well as the right in Argentina, and he received numerous death threats from both sides. He was kidnapped from his home in April 1977, and he spent thirty months in prison and under **house arrest** without ever being charged with a crime. When he was released in September 1979, he was stripped of his Argentinian citizenship and put on a plane to Israel. As a reporter in Israel, he was the center of controversy over his criticism of the Reagan administration's **human rights** policies, and the Israeli invasion and occupation of Lebanon.

Timerman was born in 1923 in the village of Bar, in the Ukraine, which was then part of the Soviet Union. His parents, Eva and Nathan, were poor, but were very involved in the struggle for rights for the Jewish people. Anti-Semitic feelings in the Ukraine were strong in the 1920s, and they often spilled over into violent organized attacks on Jewish villages, in which many people were slaughtered. These **pogroms**, as they were called, caused the Timerman family to flee to Argentina, in South America, when Jacobo was five. Seven years later, Nathan Timerman died, and Eva had to support Jacobo and his brother by herself. She sold clothes as a street vendor, and the family was allowed to live in a one-room apartment in exchange for performing janitorial duties in the building. Jacobo went to school during the day, and in the afternoons he worked as a messenger boy. He remembered his mother always discussing with him and his brother the fate of the world's Jews, especially during the **Nazi Holocaust** during World War II. He was attracted to the philosophy of

Zionism, or the movement to build a Jewish state, largely due to his mother's dream of a place where Jews could be safe. He attended **Zionist** youth group meetings, and he found himself attracted to **socialist** Zionists, who dreamed of a Jewish state that would abolish the differences between rich and poor among its citizens.

During World War II Timerman became an anti-Nazi **activist**. He was turned down by the English and American embassies when he asked to help fight against Adolf Hitler, but he turned his attention to Nazis closer to home. He was arrested for leading a group of young people on an attack of a Nazi newspaper in Buenos Aires, Argentina's capital. He was also arrested for attending a film festival for human rights in 1944.

Although he attended engineering school, Timerman quickly found that he was a natural reporter. After writing articles for many different papers during the 1940s and 1950s, he took a job as a staff writer for *La Razón*, a large Buenos Aires paper. He followed the Argentinian president-elect, Arturo Frondisi, on a tour of other Latin American countries, and he reported in depth about what the new president was planning. He became a well-known political commentator.

Timerman moved into television, radio, and magazine publishing. He founded a number of successful publications, and in 1971 he published the first issue of a liberal, intellectual newspaper called *La Opinión*. A friend of Timerman's recalled that the paper was an immediate success: "It was a breath of fresh air in Argentine life." The paper supported Israel, covered the arts, accepted no advertising, took courageous political stands, and allowed its writers to sign the articles that they wrote.

Timerman published *La Opinión* from 1971 to 1977, a period of extreme political instability and violence in Argentina. Both the left and right wings of Argentinian politics engaged in acts of terror and violence, and *La Opinión* criticized them equally. A terrorist group that wanted to restore to power the deposed dictator Juan Perón bombed Timerman's house in July 1972. Timerman refused to be intimidated. He answered many of the death threats that he received in front-page editorials in *La Opinión*, and he joked that he wondered which of his enemies would end up with his corpse. In his attacks on injustice and corruption, he angered the left and right equally. He attacked the Soviet Union for persecuting its citizens who disagreed with government policy, while he supported the **Marxist** government of Salvador Allende in Chile. He condemned right-wing actions by Israel's government, and he attacked the Palestine Liberation Organization (PLO) for its use of **terrorism** and **guerrilla** tactics against Israel.

Lieutenant General Jorge Videla overthrew the Argentinian government in March 1976 and encouraged the military to dispose (get rid of, even by killing) of his left-wing enemies. *La Opinión* was the only Spanish-language newspaper in Argentina to report on and oppose the disappearances, and the paper called for fair and open trials of people accused of treason (state crimes) against the government, rather than secret killings. Timerman's friends urged him to save his own life by fleeing Argentina, but he replied, "I am one who belongs to Masada," referring to the mountain in Israel where Jewish rebels fighting against Roman armies in ancient times chose to kill themselves rather than surrender to the Roman forces.

Timerman was asleep in his home at 2 A.M. on April 15, 1977, when twenty men in street clothes burst into his house and, brandishing weapons, took him away. The men were acting on orders of the Argentinian government. Timerman's wife and children did not know what had happened to him for six weeks, until they found out that he had been taken to prison. He was kept in solitary confinement, beaten, given electric shocks on his genitals, and interrogated brutally. His captors tried to humiliate him in every possible way. Timerman wrote about his experiences in his 1981 book, *Prisoner Without a Name, Cell Without a Number*. International groups like **Amnesty** International and the Organization of American States (OAS) fought for his release, as did individuals like Soviet author Alexander Solzhenitsyn and U.S. diplomat Henry Kissinger. Timerman was released from prison in July 1978, but he was kept under **house arrest** until September 1979, when he was forced to leave Argentina and go to Israel.

Timerman published his book in 1981 and won worldwide admiration and sympathy, but he quickly found himself in the midst of controversy in Israel. He wrote in Israeli newspapers that the Reagan administration criticized human rights abuses in left-wing countries but ignored them in right-wing countries. He compared Jewish leaders in Argentina who had refused to speak out against his imprisonment to the Jews who had helped the Nazis exterminate their own communities. After a short trip to the Arab nation of Lebanon with some Israeli army units, he wrote a controversial book criticizing the Israeli invasion and occupation of Lebanon. He has received numerous awards from human rights and journalistic organizations, and he continues to wield his mighty pen against those who, in his eyes, abuse their power.

Trocmé, André

(1901–1971)

FRENCH PASTOR AND RESISTOR TO NAZISM

André Trocmé, the **pacifist** pastor of the Protestant Church in the small French town of Le Chambon sur Lignon, inspired the towns-people to risk their lives to save Jews from the **Nazis**. The entire town hid Jews, forged false passports for them, and smuggled them to safety in the neutral country of Switzerland. When asked after World War II why they took such risks to save strangers, the people of Le Chambon appeared confused by the question. It never occurred to them *not* to help, thanks to the incredible leadership of Trocmé.

Trocmé spent his early life in the town of St. Quentin. His father was a successful lace manufacturer, but unlike his brothers, Trocmé did not join the family business. Instead, he was inspired by his family's love of religion and acts of **humanitarianism** to join the Protestant church. During his teenage years he participated in an organization of Protestant young people, the Union of St. Quentin. The group performed acts of kindness to those in need, such as giving food to Russian prisoners of war during World War I. After receiving a degree at St. Quentin University in 1918, he traveled to Paris and studied religion at the prestigious Sorbonne for six years.

During this time he began to develop his ideas about **pacifism** and Christianity. He helped found the French chapter of a pacifist group, the Fellowship of Reconciliation (FOR). But it took an incident in the French army to turn him into a complete pacifist. He was drafted into the French army, and he volunteered to be a member of a geographical survey unit, in the hopes that he could avoid carrying a gun. The unit went to Morocco, in North Africa, where a rebellion was taking place. For their own protection, the men were given rifles and ammunition. Trocmé secretly gave them back and traveled unarmed with his unit. His commanding officer discovered this during an equipment inspection, and he asked for an explanation. The officer said that he understood why Trocmé felt this way, but that Trocmé should have thought about it before joining a group of twenty-five men who were obligated to defend one another. Trocmé got the message. From that moment on, he became a true **conscientious objector** (CO) to war.

After graduating from the Sorbonne, Trocmé wanted to attend a religious school that stressed social action as much as theology (the study of religion). He studied at Union Theological Seminary in New York in 1925. Although he was disappointed by the school, he did meet Magda Grilli, an Italian woman whom he married upon his return to France in 1926. His first position as pastor was in Mauberge, but he remained there for only one year. In 1928, he took a job as pastor at the Reformed Church in Sin-le-Noble, a poor mining village in the north of France. He soon got into trouble with the local police for his preachings on pacifism and nonviolence. He attended pacifist meetings, hosted pacifist youth groups, and testified at trials of people who did not want to serve in the army because of their religious beliefs. The national leaders of the Reformed Church had forbidden pastors to preach about nonviolence, and Trocmé decided to take his message to a smaller village, where it would be less noticed.

He chose a village in the Cévennes region of France. He and Magda moved there in 1934. Le Chambon had provided a refuge for Huguenots (French Protestants) fleeing persecution by Catholics in the seventeenth century, and Trocmé felt that it would be a good place to set up a pacifist Christian high school. He was joined by a fellow conscientious objector and friend from his University days, Edouard Théis, and in 1938 they founded the Collège Cévanol. Soon the school had attracted 350 students, and it was known internationally as well as inside France. Trocmé managed to split his time between the school and the townspeople of Le Chambon, peasants and shopkeepers who responded to his message of love and nonviolence and duty.

In 1940, Nazi Germany invaded France and set up a puppet French government in the northern part of the country. Led by Trocmé, the entire staff of the Collège Cévanol refused to pledge their loyalty to the head of the Vichy regime, as it was known. Trocmé met with leaders of the American Friends' Service Committee, a Quaker organization dedicated to helping victims of violence around the world, and he decided that Le Chambon would become a **sanctuary**, or safe haven, for Jews and others persecuted by the Nazis. The students and teachers at the Collège Cévanol joined with the townspeople in forging identity documents for the refugees, hiding them in their own houses, shops, and farms, and smuggling them to safety across the border into Switzerland. They saved more than two thousand Jews during the Nazi occupation.

Trocmé and Théis were visited in 1943 by officers of the Vichy government. After dining with the pastors in their own homes, the officers arrested them for their illegal activities to save Jews. While in prison, they taught Bible classes to hundreds of **communists,** who had also been arrested by the government. Because so many people were angry at the arrests of Trocmé and Théis, they were released after less than two months, even though they refused to promise to follow the law.

After Trocmé's return, he found out that the Gestapo (Nazi secret police) were planning to kill him in revenge for the murder of a French person who was helping the Nazis. Trocmé escaped into the woods and lived in hiding for almost a year, spending his nights with one sympathetic farmer after another. Magda Grilli also showed heroism during this time. She took a job as a waitress in a hotel that the Gestapo had taken over to use as a detention center for people about to be killed. She received their last wills, and even helped one to escape.

Le Chambon was liberated from Nazi domination in 1944. Trocmé came out of hiding and became the pastor once again. He became the traveling secretary of the FOR, and he organized food and clothing and medical supplies for eleven million refugees in southern Germany. He also tried to rebuild the German pacifist movement, which had been all but destroyed by the Nazis. He also resumed his quest to make it legal in France to become a CO. He helped form the Committee of Spiritual Resistance, an organization that encouraged French soldiers fighting in the North African country of Algeria not to fight against the Algerian people. He also led demonstrations against nuclear war, and in the 1960s he turned his attention to the creation of peace groups in Italy. He lived in Le Chambon during this time, and died in Geneva in 1971.

One of the Jewish children rescued by the villagers of Le Chambon, Pierre Sauvage, grew up and became a filmmaker. He returned to Le Chambon to interview Trocmé and the villagers in order to find out what had motivated them to risk their lives for him and his fellow Jews. His film, *Weapons of the Spirit*, showed that the pastor, his wife, and the townspeople felt that they were acting in the only possible way human beings could behave. Sauvage wrote in 1983:

> The late pastor of Le Chambon lived his life, his eloquent pacifist's life, as a demonstration of Christian faith. Yet, in his unpublished memoirs, he confided that his faith was, ultimately, in the possibility of good on earth, "without which," he added, "the theoretical existence of God doesn't interest me."

Tutu, Desmond Mpilo

(1931–   )

SOUTH AFRICAN ARCHBISHOP AND ACTIVIST

Archbishop Desmond Tutu won the Nobel Peace Prize in 1984 for his courageous work in the struggle against **apartheid** (strict separation of people based on race) in South Africa. The first black ever elected archbishop in the Anglican Church, he has devoted his life to ending apartheid through nonviolent means.

Tutu was born on October 7, 1931, in Klerksdorp, a gold-mining town west of Johannesburg, the largest city in South Africa. As a child, he was exposed both to the world of English language and culture, and to his native African languages and traditions. His father taught in a Christian **missionary** school, and his mother did laundry to make enough money to feed the family. As a child, he accepted the fact that whites and blacks in South Africa were kept separate from each other. He believed that this was the way God had created the world.

When he started attending school, he began questioning the world around him. He met Father Trevor Huddleston when he was twelve, in a poor black neighborhood of Johannesburg. Huddleston had taken a vow of poverty, and had been assigned to the parish of black Christians in the area where Tutu was living. Huddleston's work to help the blacks made Tutu see that things could be different. Huddleston preached that apartheid was un-Christian. Tutu began to feel the humiliation of being a second-class citizen.

After receiving a teaching degree from the University of Johannesburg in 1954, Tutu became a teacher at Madibane High School, an Anglican school for blacks. The Anglican Church closed the school when the South African government forced the mission schools to teach only black culture and languages. Tutu understood that it was the government's desire to keep the blacks as an uneducated source of cheap labor. He continued teaching in a high school in a black township near his parents' house. He married Nomalia Leah Shenxane in 1955. When the law forbidding the teaching of "white" subjects to blacks went into effect in 1957, Tutu resigned from the high school and studied to become a priest in the Anglican Church. He was ordained in 1961, and then he traveled to London to study divinity and theology at King's College. He returned to South Africa in 1966.

As a priest, Tutu fought for the rights of blacks in South Africa. He became general secretary of the South African Council of Churches (SACC). He took stands against government policy, and helped organize scholarships for young blacks who wanted but could not afford an education. He gradually turned the SACC into a powerful voice of protest against apartheid. He became a bishop in 1976. In 1980, the prime minister of South Africa, P.W. Botha, insisted that Tutu condemn the African National Congress (ANC), the largest organization dedicated to ending apartheid. Tutu refused, and he demanded that

Botha end white rule in South Africa (apartheid meant that blacks were not allowed to vote in elections, even though they made up more than 70 percent of the population of South Africa).

By 1984, when Tutu stepped down as head of the SACC, he was practically the only black leader in South Africa who was not in prison. He continued to speak out, and he did not let himself become discouraged. His efforts paid off—on October 16, 1984, he was awarded the Nobel Peace Prize. He traveled to Oslo, Norway, to receive the award, and he made a speech that focused the world's attention on South Africa. He continued to preach nonviolent resistance to people of the blacks of South Africa. In 1994, South Africa held its first-ever free elections, in which people of all races voted. Nelson Mandela, the ANC leader who had spent more than twenty-seven years in prison, was elected the country's first black president. Tutu continues to work for peace and justice in South Africa and around the world.

Villa, Pancho

(1878–1923)

MEXICAN REVOLUTIONARY AND GUERRILLA LEADER

Francisco "Pancho" Villa, the son of a field laborer in San Juan de Río, became one of the most feared and beloved men in Mexican history. He was orphaned at a young age, and he took it upon himself to protect his parentless family. He committed his first act of violence and rebellion when he killed one of the owners of the estate where he worked because the man had assaulted his sister. Villa escaped to the nearby mountains, where he lived as a fugitive during his teenage years. He joined Francisco Madero's uprising against the **dictator** Porfirio Díaz in 1909, and he soon distinguished himself as a gifted soldier, organizer, and military leader. Villa had learned to read and write despite having had no formal schooling, and he put his talents to good use in the rebellion, which toppled Díaz in 1911. Villa was extremely popular with the people of northern Mexico, and he knew the land intimately, having made the outdoors his home for years. He led a division of soldiers who fought for Madero and helped him become Mexico's leader.

One of Madero's generals, Victoriano Huerta, distrusted Villa and sentenced him to death, but Madero ordered that Villa not be killed, but instead placed in prison. Villa escaped from prison in 1912 and went to the United States. Huerta had Madero assassinated, and he took power for himself. Villa crossed back into Mexico and formed a large military force known as División del Norte (Division of the North). He joined forces with another rebellious military leader, Venustiano Carranza, and deposed Huerta by 1914. Villa was made governor of the state of Chihuahua. Carranza and Villa became bitter rivals once there was no one left to fight, and they began fighting against each other. Villa was forced to flee Mexico City, where the two had been ruling together, and he joined up with the revolutionary Emiliano Zapata in December 1914. Carranza defeated the two men and their armies, and Villa fled into the mountains of northern Mexico. Villa wanted to show the people of the north that Carranza was not in charge there. He demonstrated this by executing seventeen United States citizens at Santa Isabel in 1916. Following this gesture, Villa crossed the border with his troops and attacked the New Mexican town of Columbus. U.S. President Woodrow Wilson sent Brigadier-General John J. Pershing and his forces to capture Villa, but the outlaw was too popular with the Mexicans of the region to be turned in. Villa knew the terrain better than Pershing, and the Mexicans resented the U.S. army presence in their country. Villa continued his **guerrilla** actions and **terrorism** and rebellion against the Mexican government as long as Carranza was in power, until 1920. When Carranza was overthrown, Villa was granted a pardon. He was given a ranch in Chihuahua on the condition that he never again take part in Mexican politics. He agreed, and he settled down to a quiet life working his own ranch. Politics did not leave him alone, however. In 1923, Villa was assassinated while on his ranch. *See* ZAPATA, EMILIANO

Waite, Terry

(1939–   )

ENGLISH HOSTAGE NEGOTIATOR AND HOSTAGE

> The approach I always take in negotiation is to try to build trust and
> to bring out the best side in people. If you give them a chance to
> display the best side, they sometimes take it. This is fundamental to
> this work.
>
> —Terry Waite, on hostage negotiations

Terry Waite seemingly performed miracles of negotiation in winning the release of **hostages** (people, military or civilian, captured
and used as bargaining chips) around the world in the 1980s. As the
assistant to Archbishop of Canterbury Robert Runcie, the spiritual
leader of the British Anglican Church, Waite persuaded Iranian
leader Ayatollah Khomeini, Libyan ruler Muammar el-Qaddafi, and
leaders of Nigeria to release the Western hostages they had captured.
In 1985 and 1986, he worked to free American hostages held in
Beirut, Lebanon, by a **terrorist** organization called Islamic Jihad
("Holy War"). After meeting with partial success, he returned to
Beirut to continue negotiations in January 1987. Instead of meeting
with the captors, he himself was kidnapped. The world did not know
whether he was alive or dead until another hostage was released in
August 1991 and reported that Waite was in captivity and still alive.
Waite won his own freedom in November 1991, after spending al-
most five years in terrible conditions.

Terence Hardy Waite was born in the village of Styal, in Cheshire,
in northern England. His father was a local policeman, and the Waite
family lived a comfortable, middle-class life. Terry left high school at
age sixteen because of a great urge to travel and see the world. He
first joined the Grenadier Guards of the British army, but he resigned
after less than a year because he was allergic to the khaki dye in the
uniforms. His next move was to join the Church Army, an international organization similar to the Salvation Army. He combined his
love of travel with a sense that he wanted his job to matter, to be
something that he truly loved to do.

Waite finished his high school degree at Wilmslow School in Cheshire, and then studied at Church Army College in London. He also attended private schools in Italy, France, and the United States. He married fellow student Helen Frances Watters in 1964, and he began serving the bishop of Bristol as a lay (not religiously ordained) training assistant. He traveled widely throughout Africa and the United States, and he loved the excitement of relief work in the African nation of Sudan. In 1968, the Waites moved to another African nation, Uganda, where Terry became an advisor to the archbishop. In 1972, the couple were held at gunpoint during **dictator** Idi Amin's expulsion of all Asian people living in Uganda.

From 1971 to 1980, Waite worked for the Vatican, as a consultant on international **missionary** work. When the archbishop of Canterbury offered Waite a similar position within the Church of England in 1980, Waite accepted. His first test came on Christmas Day 1980, when he flew to Iran to try to persuade the dictatorial ruler, Ayatollah Khomeini, to release three Anglican missionaries who had been accused of spying. Waite made a memorable impression—he clothed his 250 pounds and six-foot-seven body in religious robes to emphasize that he represented the Church of England, and not the British government. He brought a personal message to Khomeini from the archbishop, and gifts for the hostages. After secret negotiations, the missionaries were released in early 1981. Waite was hailed as a national hero. He was made a knight of the British Empire, an award he accepted while on crutches because of a biking accident.

In 1984, Waite succeeded in convincing Libyan dictator Muammar el-Qaddafi to release four British citizens who had been taken hostage while working in Libya. Although Waite arrived in Libya in November, he was only granted a meeting with Qaddafi on Christmas Day. The pair met for two hours, during which time they discussed Qaddafi's interest in Greek philosophy and modern religion. Waite gave Qaddafi a book about Aristotle's influence on Arab thought, and he even joked with the Libyan leader about the state of the Libyan postal service. When they finally got around to discussing the hostages, Waite learned that Qaddafi believed that Libyan citizens in London were being harassed by the police. Waite assured Qaddafi that this was not the case, and he immediately offered to set up a Church of England "hot line" for Libyans to call if they had complaints about their treatment. After two months of slow negotiations, Qaddafi released the hostages in exchange for Waite's word that the hot line would be set up.

Waite was now flooded with requests for his "miraculous" gifts as a hostage negotiator. He refused most of them, agreeing to try only if he felt there were a real chance that he could help. He enjoyed his media attention as a British "superhero," but he tried to explain to people that he was simply trying to establish a relationship of mutual trust and respect between the parties to the negotiation. Friends said that his secret was to be self-confident, and at the same time to make the person he was negotiating with feel important as well.

Waite's most difficult missions occurred in Beirut, Lebanon, a city ruled by armed militia, units that had ties to many different countries and **guerrilla** organizations. Waite was sent in 1985 to try to win the release of four Americans—Lawrence Jenco, Terry Anderson, David Jacobsen, and Thomas Sutherland—captured by the terrorist organization Islamic Jihad. Although Waite had once told a reporter that Beirut was the only city he feared, he agreed to go. Well aware of the possible danger to himself, he wrote a note asking that if he were kidnapped, no ransom should be paid. The negotiations were long and complex. Waite traveled back and forth between Beirut and England, and he finally won the release of Jenco in August and Jacobsen in November 1986. Because the negotiations were utterly secret, many journalists discussed theories that Waite was a pawn of United States President Ronald Reagan or White House aide Oliver North. Rumors were spread that Waite had won the release of the hostages by assuring Islamic Jihad, who were armed and funded by Iran, that the United States would sell weapons to Iran to use in its war against its neighbor, Iraq. Waite was furious at these charges. He denied them and said that they threatened to lose him the trust that he had worked so hard to win, and endangered his own life. His words proved true. In January 1987, Waite met with Islamic Jihad members to negotiate the release of the last two hostages. He asked to be taken to see the remaining hostages, Anderson and Sutherland. Instead, Waite himself was taken captive. The world knew only that he had disappeared; his captors did not reveal whether he was alive or dead.

Finally, another kidnapped British citizen, John McCarthy, was released in August 1991. He informed the world that Waite was still alive. Waite himself was released on November 18, 1991, on day number 1,763 of his captivity. Waite later stated that he was kept in complete isolation and darkness for most of that time, chained to a wall. He was beaten often, and his guards occasionally pretended to execute him.

Rumors over Waite's possible involvement with the United States's decision to sell arms to Iran surfaced again upon his release. When the Iran-Contra scandal broke in 1987, it was revealed that Oliver North, and perhaps many other high officials in the Reagan administration, had sold arms to Iran in exchange for the release of American hostages in Lebanon, with the profits from that sale illegally going to the Contra rebels in Nicaragua, in Central America. Waite denied any knowing involvement in this affair. He said, "People are playing games and governments are playing games all the time. You are just walking through a minefield and one day you may tread on a mine. I treaded on a mine. That's about it."

Wallace, Catherine

(1952–   )

NEW ZEALAND ECONOMIST AND ENVIRONMENTALIST

> Besides, all else aside, Antarctica is enormously important as a symbol that there is one place we will not just go rape and pillage. Preserving it as a wilderness is a sign that there's a little bit of the globe that we'll leave to itself. I simply believe that nature does have rights and that humanity has got some obligation to be a good neighbor on the planet. I really reject the idea that the whole planet is put here for us to use. But I do have quite strong faith in the general populace. When things are explained to them, they really do make the hard decisions.
>
> —Catherine Wallace, on saving the Antarctic environment

Catherine Wallace is a New Zealand economist and **environmental activist** who has led the international movement to preserve Antarctica from human development. She was awarded the Goldman Environmental Prize in 1991. Antarctica, the ice continent at the southern tip of the earth, has traditionally been off limits to human settlement, mining, and industry. In the 1980s, however, many countries began exploring Antarctica, and they negotiated treaties dividing up the continent's land and natural resources.

Wallace was born in the New Zealand research center of Hamilton. Both of her parents earned doctoral degrees (Ph.D.'s) in the sciences from the University of Cambridge in England. She credits her mother with teaching her respect for all living things. While studying at Victoria University, Wallace became active in the civil rights movement. This work gave her the experience and confidence she needed to fight and win against a mining company that tried to take her family's farm in 1979. That experience led her to form a **grass-roots** (local-level) organization that successfully amended the Mining Act of 1981 to prevent other farms from being threatened.

Her group became involved in international issues, as well as local ones. One of the main concerns of environmentalists in the 1980s was the secret negotiations among many countries for the rights to mine minerals found in Antarctica. Among other things, environmentalists worried about the effects of a large oil spill in the seas around Antarctica. They saw this as a likely event because of the many icebergs that could puncture a tanker's hull. Wallace's group, the Antarctic and Southern Ocean Coalition (ASOC), had tried to get publicity for their cause without much success until 1983. In that year, ASOC managed to obtain a secret United States document that was the basis for the U.S. negotiations on Antarctica. ASOC members published a summary of the document, along with their explanations of what it meant. The leader of the U.S. delegation denied everything. ASOC then retyped the entire document, to prove that it was genuine. Wallace did not want to release the actual document, in order to hide the identity of whoever in the negotiations had passed it on to them.

Wallace and her fellow activists were not allowed to participate in the negotiations, but they rented rooms in buildings near the negotiation sites, and they ran to talk to the negotiators during coffee breaks and recesses. They explained complex issues to many of the negotiators, and they showed how heavy use of Antarctica would hurt their countries' economies. Eventually the activists were allowed to participate in the negotiations as **lobbyists** (those who conduct activities aimed at influencing public officials). They convinced two countries with veto power over the treaty, France and Australia, to refuse to allow oil drilling in Antarctica. The prime minister of Wallace's own country, New Zealand, was furious at her. Many of her colleagues at

Victoria University, where she lectures in economics, disapproved of her activities. She refused to let personal attacks prevent her from speaking what she believed was the truth. Finally, the prime minister came out publicly in favor of permanent protection for Antarctica.

In 1989, as the Antarctica convention came to a close without achieving its goals of opening the continent up to development, the *Exxon Valdez* oil tanker ran aground in Alaskan waters and released millions of gallons of crude oil into Prince William Sound, which had been a magnificent, unblemished environment. Not only was the water fouled by the massive spill, but thousands of animals and many species of plants were killed. In October 1991, the countries negotiating the Treaty on Antarctica signed a Protocol on Environmental Protection that banned all mining in Antarctica for fifty years unless all twenty-six nations signing the treaty agreed to lift it. Wallace continues to fight for protection of Antarctica. She notes that the ban does not go into effect until all twenty-six countries ratify the treaty, which has still not happened. She continues to teach people a simple economic truth—much of the damage humans have done to the environment is due to wasted energy. She proposes economic solutions to reduce the demand for energy, and she remains confident that the world's citizens will make the right decisions when they have all the facts.

Wallenberg, Raoul

(1912–1947?)

SWEDISH DIPLOMAT AND RESCUER OF JEWS

> When there is suffering without limits, there can be no limits to the methods one should use to alleviate it.
> —Raoul Wallenberg, expressing his humane view of life

Raoul Wallenberg saved thousands of Hungarian Jews from being killed by the **Nazis** during World War II. He went to Hungary as a Swedish diplomat and gave Swedish passports to hundreds of Jews. He hired hundreds of Jews as embassy staff members, a position that automatically made them safe from deportation to death camps. He used bribes, flattery, lies, forgeries, and threats to save as many Jews as he could. He disappeared following the Soviet invasion of Hungary in January 1945. The Soviets refused to state what happened to him until 1957, when they issued a statement claiming that he was imprisoned in Moscow, and had died of a heart attack in 1947. The Soviets provided no evidence of this, however, and Wallenberg's family and the Swedish government did not believe it. Some believe that he may have remained alive in Soviet prisons for many more years. The truth about what happened to this hero is still not known.

Wallenberg was born in 1912, into one of Sweden's wealthiest families. They were known as the "Rockefellers of Sweden." He traveled and studied abroad for much of his life, graduating from the University of Michigan in 1935. He then traveled for business purposes, and wound up in Haifa, the main port city of Palestine. During the 1930s, many Jews had escaped from Adolf Hitler's Germany and had settled in Palestine, and they were working to turn it into a Jewish homeland. Wallenberg met many of these refugees, and he became aware of the Nazi persecution of the Jews. He gained a special interest in the fate of the Jews of Hungary when he went to work for an export company owned by Hungarian Jews. The owners were afraid to travel to the central European countries that Hitler had conquered. They sent Wallenberg in their place, and the young man soon became aware of the dangerous position of Hungary's Jews.

The man that Hitler charged with the responsibility of exterminating (murdering) all the Jews of Europe, Adolf Eichmann, arrived in Hungary in the spring of 1944. Jewish organizations and the United States government War Refugee Board appealed to Sweden, a neutral country, to allow one of its diplomats to work secretly to rescue Hungarian Jews. As a Swedish diplomat, the rescuer would be protected from attack under international law. Wallenberg was mentioned as the perfect choice. He is reported to have said, "If I can help, if I can save a single person, I will go." He insisted on his own terms before accepting, however—he would have the independence to do whatever it took to save Jews, including offering bribes to Hungarian and German officials. Sweden reluctantly agreed.

Wallenberg entered Budapest, the capital of Hungary, on July 9, 1944. His first step was to get in touch with his friends: embassies of neutral countries in Hungary, including the Vatican, Switzerland,

Spain, and Portugal, and Hungarians known to be opposed to Nazism. With large amounts of money, he recruited spies within the Budapest police force and the Hungarian **Fascist** Party, and so was able to learn about plans to exterminate Hungarian Jews. He formed relationships with important Nazis, including Eichmann himself. He used every means available to try to save Jews. He even threatened that Eichmann would be prosecuted for war crimes.

Other diplomats in Hungary were shocked at Wallenberg's tactics. He gave protective Swedish passports to hundreds of Jews. He rented thirty-two buildings in Budapest and declared that they were "extensions" of the Swedish embassy. The people inside those buildings were therefore entitled to diplomatic protection. More than twelve thousand people moved into those houses. But Wallenberg's tactics were not keeping pace with the brutal extermination program. He had to get even bolder. He once chased after a group of Jews being marched to their deaths toward the Austrian border. He pulled hundreds of them out of line and got their German officers to release them into his custody. He forged more passports and jumped on top of a train filled with Jews that was bound for the extermination camp of Auschwitz. He handed the passports to whomever could physically reach them. After he was unable to forge more passports, he gave out food and medical supplies, and he was one of the only people who treated the Hungarian Jews with respect. One survivor recalled, "He gave us the sense that we were still human beings. . . . He talked to us and showed us that one human being cared about what was happening to us."

In October 1944, the Hungarian government was overthrown by an even more brutal one. The new fascist government tried to speed up the process of extermination of the Jews, and refused to honor Wallenberg's diplomatic immunity. Wallenberg continued his work on the run, hiding in one safe house (a special place where a person could take refuge) after another. In January 1945, the Russian army invaded Hungary and officially put an end to Wallenberg's mission of saving Jews from the Nazis. Wallenberg did not want to leave Budapest while the city was in ruins. He had developed a plan to rebuild the city and resettle the refugees, and he wanted to discuss it with the Soviet conquerors. The Soviets were suspicious of Wallenberg, however. They knew he was wealthy, and they were aware that he had been in contact with the Nazis, the Hungarians, and the Americans, all enemies or soon-to-be enemies of the Soviet Union. The Soviets invited Wallenberg to army headquarters for questioning. He disappeared for two days, then came back to Budapest accompanied by Soviet soldiers. Although Wallenberg told a friend at the time that he wasn't sure if he was the Soviets' guest or prisoner, he did believe that his diplomatic immunity would protect him. He returned to the Soviet army headquarters for another meeting on January 17, and he was never seen by the people in the Swedish embassy again.

The Swedish government, not wanting to harm relations with the Soviet Union, gently requested information about Wallenberg's location and fate. Soviet officials claimed that he had been kidnapped by Hungarian Nazis. But reports by released Soviet prisoners saying that they had seen Wallenberg in different Moscow prisons began to filter to the West. Wallenberg's family pressured the Swedish government to find out more, but their reluctance to press the Soviets led to no information. In 1957, following the rise of Nikita Khrushchev as premier of the Soviet Union, the Soviet government released a statement that Wallenberg had died of a heart attack in a Moscow prison on July 17, 1947. The Soviet government did not provide proof, and reports of sightings of Wallenberg continued from the 1960s to 1987. Many people in England, the United States, and Israel, along with Wallenberg's own family, are still fighting to find out the truth of what happened to this brave and heroic saver of lives.

Williams, Betty (see Corrigan, Mairead)

Yunus, Muhammad

(1943–   )

BANGLADESHI ECONOMIST

> If you worry about food, that worry is so overwhelming, you can-
> not think about anything else . . . Banks reject a particular class of
> people. Their fundamental belief is that banking can only be done
> on the basis of collateral. That means the more you have, the more
> you get . . . Handouts put people to sleep. There is no challenge.
> You get the money, eat, and become a vegetable. But humans thrive
> when they're challenged.
>
> —Muhammad Yunus, expressing his economic theories

Muhammad Yunus was born in Bangladesh, India, on June 28, 1940, and was educated as an economist. In 1976, Dr. Yunus was a professor of economics at Chittagong University in Bangladesh, teaching the latest economic theories about **capitalism**, banking, and wealth. As he started to meet the poor villagers who lived near the university, he began to doubt what he was teaching. He asked them why they were poor. They explained to him that because they owned nothing, no bank would give them a loan. Without money to start a business, the peasants were forced to borrow raw materials from the traders who bought their finished products. The traders charged so much interest that the peasants could barely save enough money to eat, let alone put money aside to buy their own raw materials. Yunus asked how much money it would take for a peasant to start a business. The answer—about $30—astounded him. He loaned a group of vil-lagers a total of $30, and thus began the Grameen Bank.

Yunus formally opened the Grameen Bank in 1983. His idea was one that had never been tried before—lending money to the poorest people in one of the world's poorest countries. Less than one percent of the population of Bangladesh had ever received a bank loan. Banks refused to lend to people who were poor, who couldn't read, or were women. Yunus set out to change all that. The Grameen Bank does not require collateral, or some property that the lender has to give up if he or she cannot repay the loan. Instead, five borrowers come together to form borrowing groups. They all promise to help one another make the weekly payments on the loans. First, the poorest two people in the group receive a loan. If they make five weekly payments on time, then the next two in the group receive their loans. If all four continue to repay, then the fifth gets a loan as well. All of them work very hard to make sure the others succeed.

Yunus discovered very early in the life of the bank that women were much better at using the loans wisely than men. He established a policy of lending mostly to women. He explained, "Women paid far more attention to the children, to the households, to the future. Men try to enjoy it now. Women are very efficient managers of scarce resources, because when times are bad, the woman is the one who suffers the most." By 1988, 50 percent of Grameen's borrowers were women. By 1995, that number had risen to 94 percent. During the time that the bank has operated, its repayment rate has been 98 percent. Yunus explained how the systems works: "If you give a person a loan worth about $75 to buy a cow, then she can start selling the milk. She might make 100 taka [about $2.50] a week. Her installment payment on the loan would be about 20 taka [50 cents] a week." In a country as poor as Bangladesh, a profit of two dollars a week is a big achievement.

A study conducted in the mid-1990s showed that more than one-third of all Grameen borrowers no longer live in poverty. Among those who had been borrowing for a few years, 75 percent were either out of poverty or close to leaving. Grameen has given loans to more than two million people, and the bank continues to grow. In 1994, the bank lent its billionth dollar, and it continues to lend about $30 million per month, in amounts that average $100 each. The money is important, but it is not the only part of the Grameen strategy to get people out of poverty. Along with lending money to women, Yunus insisted that the women be protected from the laws in Bangladesh that give men control of their women. In order to receive a housing loan, the title to the plot of land must be in the woman's name. That way, if the man wants to divorce his wife, he, not she, must leave the house. Good housing is important in Bangladesh because the peasant huts often get destroyed by the winds and rains of the yearly monsoon (flood) season. Grameen provides money for houses with four cement pillars against the wind, tin roofs against the rain, and sanitary latrines against infection and disease. The housing loans are repaid over a ten year-period.

Grameen's women borrowers are encouraged to help one another.

Yunus described one visit he made to a village in which Grameen had made a number of housing loans. Yunus met a man who was living in a new house. Yunus asked the man if he was happy. The man replied that he was, that his wife was working very hard, and that finally they had enough food to eat. He hesitated, and then offered one complaint: "I used to enjoy beating my wife, but the last time I beat her I made a pact with myself that I would never do it again because the other women in her borrowing group came to me, and they argued with me and shouted at me. When I beat my wife before, no one said anything; no one cared. This is no longer true with the women in her borrowing group."

Yunus established Grameen centers all over Bangladesh. These centers are headed by women, and they run the operations of the bank in the villages. Along with the obligation to repay the loans, the center-chiefs wrote down a list of "Sixteen Decisions" that all Grameen borrowers are expected to follow. Visitors to Grameen villages have reported that the women sometimes get together and chant the decisions out loud. Some of the decisions are about living with discipline, unity, courage, and hard work, bringing prosperity to families, building sturdy houses, growing vegetables all year long, planting trees, keeping families small and healthy, educating the children, building pit latrines, not inflicting injustice on others, helping one another, not practicing child marriage, and not giving or receiving dowries (special gifts) in weddings. Many of these decisions are designed to break the cultural barriers to women's equality and success in Bangladesh. Recently, Yunus and the Grameen Bank have come under attack by Muslim **fundamentalists** in Bangladesh, who believe that women must be controlled and owned by their husbands. Grameen women are often the wage earners in their families, and they have gotten more power than the men.

The Grameen model has spread throughout the world, including the United States. Community banks in Arkansas and Illinois lend money to poor people in inner cities based on the same principles of empowerment of women and group responsibility. U.S. President Bill Clinton has been a supporter of Yunus since the two men met in Arkansas while Clinton was that state's governor. Yunus was in Arkansas to set up the Good Faith Fund in Pine Bluff. American economists said that the idea would not work in this country, because Americans wanted loans of tens of thousands of dollars, not a few hundred. Yunus replied that if Americans wanted loans that big, then there were no poor people in America. People in Arkansas who came for loans told him that they could start a business with as little as $375. Yunus reflected, "The academicians have their ideas about the world, and the reality is so different." Yunus should know; the economics professor has built one of the strongest and most successful banks in the world doing what his own academic theories said was impossible. The poorest people in the world have turned out to be the best loan risks. When he accepted the 1994 World Food Prize, Yunus declared, "I believe in the capacity and capability of human beings. The more we can free each individual from the barriers in society, the better off society will be and the better off the individual will be."

Zapata, Emiliano

(1877?–1919)

MEXICAN LEADER OF PEASANT REVOLT

> The land belongs to those who work it.
>
> —Emiliano Zapata, on peasants' rights

Emiliano Zapata inspired Mexican peasants in the state of Morelos to revolt against a system of rule that was taking away their land, their way of life, and their self-respect. He battled both wealthy landowners who were stealing the peasants' land by keeping them in debt, and a corrupt government that turned its back on its most needy citizens. His influence remains so strong that in 1994, seventy-five years after his death, another peasant revolt in Chiapas, Mexico, took its name, the Zapatista rebellion, from him.

Zapata was born in Anenecuilco, a small village near the center of Morelos state. He was of mixed Spanish and Indian blood. Most of his nine brothers and sisters did not survive into adulthood, despite the fact that the Zapata family was better off than most of the villagers. Zapata's father raised horses and cattle, and so the family did not have to work as laborers at the **haciendas**, or large estates, of the wealthy landowners. For most of the nineteenth century, the people of Anenecuilco lived as their Indian ancestors had for centuries. Most of the land was owned by the community, rather than by individuals, and all members of the community had a say in what was planted, as well as a share in what was harvested. But when the dictator Porfirio Díaz came to power in 1876, he tried to modernize the system of agricultural production of Mexico. The old way seemed very wasteful to him. Large *haciendas* could produce food and goods not only for the local people, but for export (sale outside the country) as well. Food production was less profitable than crops for export, such as sugar. Wealthy Mexicans bought land in the Morelos region and bribed officials to receive the titles to lands they could not buy legally. Sugar replaced all the other crops, and during bad harvests only the largest and wealthiest farmers could survive. The others had to sell their land to buy food to eat.

All this was happening as Zapata grew to adulthood. He saw how cruelly Díaz dealt with villages that tried to resist the changes. He saw his friends and neighbors become slaves on rich people's sugar plantations. He saw villages disappear as the government encouraged the growth of the sugar industry.

When he was sixteen, both his parents died. Zapata had to support his family. He worked on the family horse farm, farmed for *hacienda* owners, and trained horses. Word about his skill as a horseman spread throughout the area. He was hired to train the horses of a local *hacienda* owner who happened to be Díaz's son-in-law. He had firsthand experience with the greed of the *hacienda* owners. When one of his animals wandered onto *hacienda* land, the owner often made him pay a fine to get the animal back, or kept it outright. Zapata joined a village defense committee that stood up to the *hacienda* guards. When he was eighteen, he got into a fight with some guards. They called for the local police, who arrested him and started to take him away. His older brother and some friends rode after them, and they forced the police, at gunpoint, to release Zapata.

In 1909, at the age of thirty, Zapata was elected leader of the Anenecuilco village council. He was chosen because, as a known "warrior," he would defend the village lands against the *haciendas* that were growing larger and closer every day. After his election, he went to Mexico City, hired a lawyer, and met with Díaz's political opponents. To stop Zapata, the Mexican government drafted him into the army. Díaz's son-in-law, remembering Zapata's excellent work with his horses, requested that Zapata be released from duty. When Zapata returned to Anenecuilco, he learned that a neighboring *hacienda* had seized most of the village's remaining land. He and about eighty armed villagers occupied the land and waited for government troops to come. They never did. The Mexican government was dealing with unrest elsewhere in the country and did not want to provoke an uprising in Morelos. Two neighboring villages joined with the fighters from Anenecuilco to form a large peasant army. They knocked down *hacienda* fences and reclaimed land for their villages. Zapata led raids like this all over Morelos state, while the police stood back in fear of the rebellious and heavily armed band. Peasants from all over adored and trusted Zapata, who did not forget his roots. He wore the clothes of a village leader, not a fancy leader, and never compromised on his goal of land reform.

In 1911, the corrupt Díaz regime was toppled by Francisco Madero, a wealthy Mexican who had actually defeated Díaz for president in 1910, but was jailed after winning the election. He escaped to Texas, and led a revolt in March 1911. Zapata and his followers saw this as the opportunity to begin their revolt as well. Díaz saw that he could not win, and he fled the country. When Zapata and Madero met, the peasant leader agreed to support the wealthy politician in exchange for real land reform. Madero agreed, and he told Zapata that he had to disband his revolutionary army. Zapata refused, saying that he did not trust the federal army of Mexico. He demanded that the land be returned to the peasants right away, and he invited Madero to visit Morelos and see the situation for himself.

Madero had no intention of carrying out the type of land reform that Zapata wanted. He had to think of his supporters among the wealthy classes of Mexico. He offered to give Zapata a large ranch in thanks for his service during the revolution. Zapata took his rifle butt and thrust it against the ground. He roared, "Señor Madero, I did not join the revolution in order to become a *hacienda* owner; if I am worth anything, it is because of the confidence and trust which the farmers have in me. Well, they believe that we are going to fulfill the promises that we have made to them, and if we abandon these people who have made the revolution, they will have every right to turn their guns on those who have forgotten their promises." Madero promised to do what he could.

When Zapata returned to Morelos, he learned that the new governor appointed by Madero was to be a wealthy landowner. Madero assured Zapata that land reform would go forward, as long as all but four hundred of his supporters turned in their weapons. Zapata was to be named chief of police. After the weapons were turned in, Zapata applied for weapons for his police force. The governor refused to give them to him. Madero explained apologetically that the *hacienda* owners had opposed Zapata's nomination as police chief. Zapata was given an escort of fifty armed men and was told to retire to his village.

Zapata was looking forward to returning to Anenecuilco to become a farmer. He planned to marry and raise a family, and had had enough of fighting and politics. But he was not allowed to rest for long. Madero sought to unify the country by calling for free elections. He resigned in favor of a temporary government that would carry out the elections. The temporary government, rather than calling for elections that would unite all Mexicans, was torn by a power struggle between supporters of Madero and supporters of Díaz. During Zapata's wedding celebration, news came that federal troops loyal to Díaz had invaded Morelos. The country was now locked in a civil war. Zapata reassembled his army and prepared to fight. Madero returned to Mexico City, where he was expected to win the upcoming election, while Zapata and his followers took to the hills. The federal troops marched on Morelos, and they "pacified" the rebellious region with guns and bayonets. Zapata fought battles from the hills, often ambushing the federal soldiers. Over the next few years, he led the peasants of Morelos to oppose government after government, as long as the promised land reform did not materialize. When Zapatista forces captured government troops, they disarmed them and let them go, unlike the government forces, which usually murdered their prisoners of war.

In 1914, Zapata and his rebel army marched on Mexico City. His main opponent, the wealthy northern landowner Venustiano Carranza, was ousted from power by another revolutionary, Pancho Villa. Villa was the only other powerful figure in Mexico, aside from Zapata, who favored land reform. The armies of the two men converged on Mexico City in November 1914, to the dread of the residents. Villa and Zapata did not get along; however, Zapata and his men returned to Morelos at the end of 1914, confident that land reform was finally about to take place. They enacted a sweeping land reform act, and in 1915 Mexicans enjoyed one of the best harvests they had ever had. The peasants in Morelos saw Zapata as their father and their savior. He was called upon to settle local disputes, and he was hopeful that the example of his state would soon spread to other states in Mexico as well.

The good times lasted only a short while, however. Carranza rebuilt his army, and in June 1915 he defeated Villa and regained control over Mexico City. The federal troops treated the Mexican peasants brutally, stealing their cattle and horses, and jailing and killing hundreds of people. Zapata reassembled his army and fought against Carranza's men. But the civil war was bloodier than any that had gone on before. Villagers who aided the Zapatistas were shot, and entire villages were punished for their loyalty to their hero. By 1919, Carranza controlled every section of Mexico except for Morelos. Zapata was an embarrassment to the leader, who tried to show the world that he was in charge of Mexico. For his part, Zapata could only look upon his beloved Morelos in anger and sorrow. The fighting had transformed it into a wasteland. Almost half of the population was gone, either dead or having escaped to a safer area. The land reform was destroyed.

Zapata heard of a serious disagreement between two of Carranza's military leaders, and he tried to divide them further. He wrote to the younger officer, Colonel Guajardo, and asked him to join the Zapatistas with all his troops. The commanding officer, González, intercepted the letter and threatened Guajardo with a court-martial unless the colonel played along and led Zapata into a trap. Guajardo agreed, and he wrote to Zapata telling him of his desire to join the Zapatistas. Although Zapata and his generals did not fully trust Guajardo, they were desperate, and they needed the ammunition that he offered to bring with him. On April 10, 1919, Zapata was killed in an ambush. His body was dumped in the town square of a village near Anenecuilco, but the stunned peasants at first refused to believe it was him. Other Zapatista leaders kept the rebellion going, and they succeeded in bringing about small land reforms over the years.

When peasants in the Chiapas region of Mexico rebelled against the federal government on January 1, 1994, they honored the fallen leader by referring to themselves as Zapatistas. His memory and his inspiration continue to live in the hearts of the Mexican peasants.

Zassenhaus, Hiltgunt

(1916–   )

GERMAN-AMERICAN RESISTOR TO NAZISM

> I wanted to demonstrate that the most dangerous wall in human relations is the wall of indifference. We must get involved even if our own interests are not at stake. We must recognize that history is not made by governments but by our own daily actions.
>
> —explanation of why Hiltgunt Zassenhaus wrote her autobiography

Hiltgunt Zassenhaus was born in Hamburg, Germany, to Julius, a historian, and Margret Zassenhaus. She made her first protest against the **Nazi** government in Germany as a high school student in 1933, at the age of seventeen. Students in her school were required to give the Nazi salute and say "Heil Hitler" every morning. Zassenhaus refused every time, until school authorities finally forced her to make the salute. Rather than follow their orders, she stuck her hand through a glass window, breaking the window and bloodying her arm.

Zassenhaus attended the University of Hamburg, where she got a degree in Scandinavian languages. Despite her earlier protests, she was trusted by the Nazi government and was assigned the job of reading the mail of Danish and Norwegian resistance fighters captured by the Germans in World War II. She was ordered to **censor** this mail (cross out any writing that might be used to hurt the Nazi war effort). In her 1974 memoir, *Walls: Resisting the Third Reich—One Woman's Story*, she recounted how she began smuggling medicine, food, clothing, and mail to the prisoners whose mail she was supposed to censor. She also kept her own private files on the whereabouts of these prisoners, when they were moved from Hamburg prison to anywhere else.

In 1945, Zassenhaus was chatting with a prison guard when she learned that Adolf Hitler had ordered that all political prisoners in Germany were to be killed. Zassenhaus immediately contacted a Norwegian minister, and the two of them got in touch with Count Folke Bernadotte of the Swedish Red Cross, a neutral **humanitarian** organization. They persuaded Bernadotte to negotiate with the head of the Gestapo (the Nazi secret police), Heinrich Himmler. Himmler agreed to release all the prisoners that the Red Cross could find. He did not know that Zassenhaus had kept records of all these prisoners, and he probably assumed that the Red Cross would find it nearly impossible to locate any of the prisoners. With Zassenhaus's help, however, approximately 1,200 prisoners were rescued. Zassenhaus herself was never caught by the Nazis. After the war, she moved to Copenhagen, Denmark, where she completed the medical studies she had begun in Germany. In 1948, she was honored with the medals of both the Danish and Norwegian Red Crosses. She has been honored many times since then for her heroism, including being nominated for the Nobel Peace Prize in 1974. In 1954, she moved to Baltimore, Maryland, in the United States, where she established a medical practice.

Zetkin, Clara

(1857–1933)

GERMAN FEMINIST AND COMMUNIST LEADER

Clara Zetkin became a leader of the German Social Democratic Party (SDP) at a time when women were not allowed to vote, run for political office, or even participate in party politics. She fought for the rights of women and combined her **feminist** ideals with a powerful belief that only the overthrow of the **capitalist** system would make life better for working men and women. She opposed World War I, and she founded what became the German **Communist** Party when the SDP supported Germany's entry into the war. In 1932, one year before her death, she convened the German Reichstag (parliament) and gave a speech attacking Adolf Hitler and **Nazism**.

Zetkin was born Clara Eissner in Wiederau, a small town near

Leipzig, in the Saxony region of Germany. Most of the townspeople were textile workers and farmers. Her father was the local schoolteacher and church organist, while her mother, who had been previously married to a doctor, founded a women's education society. She believed that all people, including women, were equal, and that women should have the same rights, economic and political, as men.

Zetkin's father retired when she was twenty-five years old, and the family moved to Leipzig so that she could attend the Van Steyber teachers' academy. From 1872 to 1878, she read **socialist** newspapers and writings and attended meetings of German feminist groups. She became involved in the SDP in 1878, although as a woman she was not allowed to join officially. A young immigrant from Odessa, Russia, Ossip Zetkin, who was a member of the SDP, introduced Clara to the writings of political and social philosopher Karl Marx, and he explained to her the idea of **scientific socialism**: a means of organizing the **proletariat** (working class) to overthrow the capitalist system. With Ossip, Clara gave up her middle-class life and began to live like a member of the working class. This caused a break with her family. Clara and Ossip traveled to Russia, where they met revolutionaries who impressed Clara very much. From that time on she devoted herself to a life of **activism** to teach the working classes to rise up in revolution.

Ossip was expelled from Germany following the German government's passage of the Anti-Socialist Law. Clara also left, first to teach factory workers in Linz, Austria, and later to write propaganda for the SDP in Zurich, Switzerland. In 1882, Clara and Ossip were reunited in Paris. They were never married officially, because Clara feared that she would lose her German citizenship, but she took Ossip's last name, and the couple had two sons within three years. During her years in Paris, Clara worked to improve the conditions of workers, and especially proletarian women. She believed in total equality for men and women, even if it meant that women had to work and bear children, and could be employed in dangerous occupations. She felt that only the end of capitalism would mean the beginning of a better life for women. As long as women toiled under capitalism, all their work simply made rich people richer, and did nothing to help their own families.

Both Clara and Ossip developed tuberculosis (a disease affecting the lungs) during their years in Paris, due to the extreme poverty they had chosen to endure to show their solidarity (sympathy) with the working poor. Clara returned to Leipzig, where she made up with her family, who nursed her back to health. Ossip had no such support, however, and he died of his disease in January 1889. Clara had little time to mourn, because of the important socialist congress that was to meet in Paris on the one hundredth anniversary of the French Revolution (July 14, 1889). The Second International Congress, as it was called, gave her a chance to make her radical views on women and revolution known to a wide audience. She was given the responsibility at the congress for recruiting more women into the SDP, in spite of the fact that it was against the law for women to join.

In 1890, the Anti-Socialist Law was struck down by the German parliament. Zetkin moved to Stuttgart, Germany, where she became editor of the SDP's women's newspaper, *Die Gleichheit* ("Equality"). She edited the paper for twenty-four years, and she responded to criticism that it was too theoretical (of no practical use) by adding popular supplements for housewives and children. *Die Gleichheit* reached a circulation of 125,000 by 1914. Although Zetkin never had much time for a personal life, she was remarried in 1899, to the painter Georg Zundel. She was forty-two at the time, while he was only twenty-four. They remained together for about fifteeen years, and were officially divorced in 1927.

While women were not allowed to belong to the SDP, they were able to join trade unions that were closely linked to the Socialist Party. Zetkin threw herself into the effort to encourage union women to become politically active in the socialist movement. She gave hundreds of speeches, printed handbills that were distributed on factory floors, and collected money to be used by striking workers. As a result of working with the union women, her own views shifted. Zetkin came to believe that working women needed special protection in order to fulfill the two roles of worker and mother. In 1908, when women were finally allowed to join political parties in Germany, Zetkin fought to keep the socialist women's movement independent of the men's. She felt that the men would not act with the best interests of women in mind, and that women socialists would be more radical, and less likely to compromise their beliefs. Instead of seeing working men and women as equal, Zetkin came to understand that proletarian women had different needs, and needed different representation, than proletarian men.

Zetkin and the Polish-German revolutionary Rosa Luxemburg were almost alone in opposing Germany's entry into World War I. The rest of the SDP felt that it would be disloyal to oppose the war. Zetkin and Luxemburg and a few others called for a mass strike of German workers to protest the war. Without permission of the SDP, Zetkin organized a women's antiwar conference in 1915. She was jailed by the German government for writing against the war in *Die Gleichheit*. The SDP fired her as editor of the paper in May 1917, because of her opposition to the war and her support of the Russian Revolution.

Zetkin left the SDP and formed, along with Luxemburg and two others, the Spartacus League, which became the German Communist Party in November 1918. She was a delegate to the Reichstag from 1920 to 1932, although she spent much of that time in the Soviet Union working with that newly formed nation's first premier, Vladimir Lenin, and Alexandra Kollontai, a Soviet diplomat. Despite her failing health, she continued to fight against the persecution of women, and she spoke out against **fascism** and **racism**, in Germany and around the world. In 1932, as the oldest living member of the Reichstag, she was given the privilege of convening the body for what would be its last year of independence. She used the occasion to attack Adolf Hitler and the Nazi movement, and she called for a United Front of Workers, men and women together, to fight against Nazism. Not long afterward, the Nazis burned down the Reichstag and blamed the communists, paving the way for Hitler's rise to dictatorship of Germany in 1933. Zetkin moved to the Soviet Union, where she died on June 20, 1933. She was mourned by the leaders of that country, including Joseph Stalin; Lenin's widow, Nadezhda Krupskaya; Kollontai; and Eastern European communist leaders as well. She was buried in the Kremlin (center of Soviet government) wall. *See* LUXEMBURG, ROSA

Glossary

activism positive and direct action to achieve change in human society.

activist a person who takes positive and direct action to achieve change in human society. Often an activist works by empowering and inspiring others.

amnesty a government's granting of forgiveness for a crime. Prisoners who receive amnesty are released from prison.

annex to incorporate conquered land into one's own country.

anti-Semitism hatred and persecution of Jewish people.

apartheid the system of racial segregation in South Africa that existed until 1994. Non-whites were oppressed under apartheid laws that denied them the right to live and work in most of the country; literally meaning, in Afrikaans, "apartness."

asylum governmental protection of a person from a different country. Soviet **dissidents** often sought asylum in the U.S. during the Cold War between the two superpower nations.

autonomous self-governing.

autonomy limited ability of a people to govern themselves.

biodiversity a variety of living things in a place or region.

Buddhism an Asian religion and philosophy founded in the sixth century B.C. by Buddha, based on the belief that self-denial and goodness will enable the soul to reach Nirvana, a state of perfect blessedness.

capitalism an economic system in which companies, factories, and land are privately owned and in which goods are distributed in a competitive market, their prices determined by supply and demand.

capitalist one who supports or participates in the economic system of capitalism.

caste one of the ranked groups in Hindu India. Caste members are born into their classes, and may not marry outside of them.

censor to remove or prohibit undesirable ideas from printed matter, films, television programs, and speeches. Governments that try to control the opinions of their citizens often censor material that is threatening to the existing social framework.

charter a document granting certain rights to a group of people or establishing a set of powers and responsibilities for a new organization or institution.

civil disobedience a strategy of social protest in which a group or individual refuses to follow laws thought to be unjust. The goal of civil disobedience is to change the laws without resorting to violence.

collective farm a farm on which all work is shared, all equipment and property are commonly owned, and where the profits and losses are shared equally by all the residents.

colonialism political and economic control over an area by a state, some of whose people have inhabited the area. Modern European colonialism over much of Africa, Asia, and Latin America has also involved exploitation of native populations and **missionary** activity to spread Christianity.

communism the economic and political system in which all private property is outlawed, and all property is held in common. European communism also included the belief in the need for violent revolution to bring the system into existence.

communist one who espouses the ideas of **communism**.

conscientious objector one who refuses to serve in a military unit for religious or moral reasons; often referred to as CO.

contraception any given method of preventing pregnancy. These include birth control pills, condoms, other devices, and natural methods.

cooperative a business or other venture which the workers own and manage collectively for the common good.

coup short for **coup d'état**.

coup d'état a forceful overthrow of a government or ruler by a small group of people with some political or military power; literally, in French, a "blow to the state."

depression (economic) an economic crisis in which unemployment is high and poverty is widespread.

desaparacidos opponents of Latin American **dictators** who were secretly killed by government death squads; literally, in Spanish, "the disappeared."

dictator an absolute ruler of a country who controls the military and does not have to stand for reelection. If a dictator wishes to remain in power, he or she can be removed only by force.

diplomacy a method by which countries and ethnic groups achieve foreign policy goals by bargaining with each other.

dissident a Soviet citizen who opposed the Soviet government.

emigrate voluntarily move away from one's country.

emigration the act of voluntarily moving away from one's country.

environmentalist a person who acts to protect the environment from human destruction. The environmental movement aims at maintaining the world's ability to support many forms of life. Environmental concerns include clean air, clean water, the richness of soil, and preventing the extinction of entire plant and animal species.

exile (n.)   a person who has been forced to leave his or her country by the government, or who has voluntarily left his or her country for a prolonged period of time. The state of not being allowed in one's country is also called exile.

exile (v.)   to force someone to leave his or her country.

fascism   a political and social movement that places the state above the individual and stresses obedience to a **dictator** rather than independent thinking.

fascist   one who believes in the doctrines of **fascism**.

female circumcision   an operation that occurs in some Islamic countries, in which a young girl's clitoris is removed to prevent her from enjoying sexual relations.

feminism   a social reform movement of the nineteenth and twentieth centuries, also called the women's rights movement. The goal of the movement is equal rights for women in all aspects of human life.

feminist   one who believes in or participates in the women's movement for equal rights.

fundamentalism (religious)   the belief that one's holy book is the literal word of God. Fundamentalists tend to be intolerant of the views and actions of others, especially those who believe in modern culture, science, or human knowledge.

genocide   the murder of an entire ethnic, national, or religious group.

grass-roots activism   a movement for social change that comes from ordinary people, instead of established organizations and leaders.

guerrilla   a fighter who opposes an established army, usually by using surprise attacks on military targets.

hacienda   a large Central American plantation on which poor peasants work for a wealthy landowner.

Hindu   a follower of **Hinduism**.

Hinduism   the religious beliefs and practices of the majority of the people of India. Hinduism is one of the world's oldest religions, and contains such concepts as reincarnation, caste (strict adherence to social class), vegetarianism, and karma.

Holocaust   the Nazi program to murder six million Jews and five million others, including Gypsies, nonwhites, homosexuals, socialists, and Jehovah's Witnesses, because they were considered unfit to live. The Holocaust took place from 1933–1945.

home rule   the phrase used by Irish Nationalists of the nineteenth and twentieth centuries to describe their goal of self-government, and independence from British rule.

hostage   a person taken prisoner, often by a terrorist group or enemy nation.

house arrest   the detention of a political prisoner within his or her own home.

human rights   the basic rights that all human beings deserve, including the right to live, to be safe from violence, to have enough to eat, to travel freely, to privacy, to participate in making decisions that affect them, and so on.

humanism   the philosophical outlook that regards human achievement and human values as the main concerns of life.

humanitarianism   devotion to helping humanity, especially in relieving pain and suffering.

illiterate   unable to read or write.

immigrate   to go to another country or homeland after leaving one's place of birth.

indigenous   native to an area. Indigenous people have lived on their lands for thousands of years. When European settlers traveled around the world, the changes they brought often made it impossible for indigenous people to continue with their traditional lifestyles.

internationalism   the belief that national boundaries cause wars and hatred, and that one world government is necessary to establish peace on Earth.

kibbutz   a cooperative farming and manufacturing settlement in Israel. All production activities and profits are shared equally by all members of the kibbutz.

lesbian   a woman who engages in sexual activity with women instead of men.

libel   a false public statement intended to expose a person to public ridicule or hatred, or to ruin a person's reputation.

liberation   freedom. Movements of liberation seek to free people from the domination of other people.

liberation theology   a movement among Catholic priests in Latin America, in which the story of Jesus is used to justify revolution to help the oppressed masses.

lobbyist   a person who represents a special interest group and tries to influence government policy.

malnutrition   hunger and disease as a result of not getting enough healthy food.

Marxism   the theoretical system of Karl Marx, which became the basis for **socialism** and **communism**. Another name for Marxism is scientific socialism.

Marxist   one who follows the theories of Karl Marx.

missionary   a person sent by a religious organization to spread that religion, usually to a foreign country.

nationalism   identifying strongly with one's own national or ethnic group. When a group does not enjoy self-determination, nationalism often involves fighting for independence. When a group has its own state, nationalism often involves believing that one's group is better than other groups and has a right to rule over them.

nationalist   one who defines his primary loyalty and duty to his nation or country, sometimes glorifying his own nation and regarding it as superior to others.

nationalization   a state takeover and operation of a private company or business.

Nazi   a member of the racist and **fascist** National Socialist German Workers' ("Nazi") Party, led by Adolf Hitler from 1919 to 1945. Members of similar parties, and people who share Hitler's views, are also called Nazis.

négritude   a literary and philosophical movement of African and Caribbean writers living in Paris in the 1930s, 1940s, and 1950s. It criticized Western culture and European domination of African peoples and extolled African history, culture, and religions.

nonproliferation   stopping the spread of weapons, especially nuclear bombs, into countries that do not yet have the technology to manufacture them.

pacifism   the belief that all violence is wrong. Many pacifists combat injustice through nonviolent protest, such as refusing to follow certain laws.

paramilitary   a group of people that acts like a small army.

pogrom   a government-organized persecution or massacre of a minority group. Literally, in Russian, "to shake from a tree," the word was first used to refer to the attacks on Jews in czarist Russia in the nineteenth and twentieth centuries.

proletariat   the working classes of society who do not own the factories, farms, and businesses in which they work. In socialist theory, the proletariat is encouraged to rise up against the owners of capital and take control and ownership over their places of work.

promiscuity   having many sexual partners.

racism   the belief that humans of some races are better than those of others. Most racists hate people physically different from themselves and believe them to be inferior.

sanctuary   a place of refuge or safety, often offering immunity from the law, e.g., a church or another country.

scientific socialism   the theory, first espoused by Karl Marx, that **socialism** will replace **capitalism** because of laws of economics and human nature. Scientific socialism teaches that human history is simply the history of class struggle between rich and poor.

self-determination   the ability of a people to rule themselves.

socialism   a system of government in which the state owns the means of production, including companies, factories, and farm lands. Under socialism, people receive goods and services according to their needs, rather than their ability to pay for them. It is an attempt to eliminate the gap between rich and poor. In contrast to **communism,** socialism assumes a slow evolution from **capitalism**, rather than sudden revolution.

Spanish Civil War   the conflict which occurred from 1936 to 1939, in which **fascist** and traditionalist forces in Spain combined to overthrow the democratically elected second Spanish republic.

subsistence   an economic condition in which people make only enough money to live but cannot save anything or improve their lives.

suffragist movement   the social and political movement to win the right to vote for women. Women who participated in this movement were called **suffragettes**. The right to vote is known as **suffrage**.

terrorism   the use of violence against civilians to bring about change in a government's policy. Terrorists blow up buildings, hijack airplanes, and commit other acts of violence to create a climate of fear.

theologian   a religious thinker.

Third World   countries not aligned in the Cold War either with the developed, **capitalist** West or the **communist** Eastern Bloc. Third World nations typically are in the Southern Hemisphere, and their populations are primarily people of color. Most people of the Third World live in poverty.

totalitarianism   a form of government that first appeared in the twentieth century, in which the state attempts to control all aspects of human existence, including politics, economics, daily living, opinions, religions, and thoughts. Individual obedience to the state is the main goal.

Western Hemisphere   the half of planet Earth that includes North and South America.

Zionism   the political movement in the nineteenth and twentieth century to reestablish a Jewish state of Israel.

Zionist   one who worked to reestablish, or now supports, the Jewish national state of Israel.

Sources and Further Reading

ADAMS
  Current Biography Yearbook—1994. New York: H.W. Wilson, 1994.

ARAFAT
  Stefoff, Rebecca. *Yasir Arafat*. New York: Chelsea House, 1988.
  World Book Encyclopedia. Chicago: World Book Inc., 1992.

ARISTIDE
  Current Biography Yearbook—1991. New York: H.W. Wilson, 1991.

ARIYARATNE
  Ingram, Catherine. *In the Footsteps of Gandhi*. Berkeley, CA: Parallax Press, 1990.

ASHRAWI
  Current Biography Yearbook—1992. New York: H.W. Wilson, 1992.

AUGUSTE
  Reebok Foundation Press Release.

AWAD
  Ingram, Catherine. *In the Footsteps of Gandhi*. Berkeley, CA: Parallax Press, 1990.

AYLWARD
  Uglow, Jennifer S., ed. *The International Dictionary of Women's Biography*. New York: Continuum, 1982.

BADEN-POWELL
  Current Biography Yearbook—1946. New York: H.W. Wilson, 1946.
  Uglow, Jennifer S., ed. *The International Dictionary of Women's Biography*. New York: Continuum, 1982.

BENENSON
  Blue, Howard. "The First Year." *Amnesty International U.S.A.*, May 1981.
  Winner, David. *Peter Benenson: Taking a Stand Against Injustice*. Milwaukee, WI: Gareth Stevens Publishers, 1991.

BIKO
  Bigelow, Barbara Carlisle, ed. *Contemporary Black Biography*. Detroit: Gale Research, 1993.

BLUM
  Bronner, Stephen Eric. *Léon Blum*. New York: Chelsea House Publishers, 1987.
  Contemporary Authors. Detroit: Gale Research, 1987.
  Current Biography Yearbook—1940. New York: H.W. Wilson, 1940.

BONHOEFFER
  American Academic Encyclopedia Online, 1994.
  World Book Encyclopedia. Chicago: World Book Inc., 1992.

BONNER
Current Biography Yearbook—1987. New York: H.W. Wilson, 1987.
Facts on File: Weekly World News Digest. New York: Facts on File, January 6, 1995.
Uglow, Jennifer S., ed. *The International Dictionary of Women's Biography.* New York: Continuum, 1982.

BOOTH FAMILY
Uglow, Jennifer S., ed. *The International Dictionary of Women's Biography.* New York: Continuum, 1982.

BREYTENBACH
Current Biography Yearbook—1986. New York: H.W. Wilson, 1986.

BUKOVSKY
Current Biography Yearbook—1978. New York: H.W. Wilson, 1978.

CALDICOTT
Browne, Ray B., ed. *Contemporary Heroes and Heroines.* Detroit: Gale Research, 1990.
Current Biography Yearbook—1983. New York: H.W. Wilson, 1983.

CARDENAL
Browne, Ray B., ed. *Contemporary Heroes and Heroines.* Detroit: Gale Research: 1990.

CASSIN
Hess, John L. "Peace Prize Goes to French Jurist." *The New York Times,* October 10, 1958.
Magill, Frank N., ed. *Great Lives from History: Twentieth-Century Series.* California: Salem Press, 1990.

CHAI
Browne, Ray B., ed. *Contemporary Heroes and Heroines.* Detroit: Gale Research, 1990.

CHATTOPADHYAY
O'Neill, Lois Decker, ed. *The Women's Book of World Records and Achievements.* Garden City, NY: Anchor Press, 1979.
Uglow, Jennifer S., ed. *The International Dictionary of Women's Biography.* New York: Continuum, 1982.
Utne Reader, March/April 1992.

CHAUDHARY
Reebok Foundation Press Releases.

CHAZOV
"Doctors' Group Wins Nobel Peace Prize." *The Washington Post,* October 12, 1985.
Marquand, Robert. "Détente of a Different Sort: U.S.–Soviet Physicians Find That Cooperation Wins the Prize." *Christian Science Monitor,* October 15, 1985.
Thatcher, Gary. "Senior Soviet Official Is Rare Dove in Globe's Antinuclear Dovecote." *Christian Science Monitor,* February 26, 1984.

CORRIGAN

Current Biography Yearbook—1978. New York: H.W. Wilson, 1978.

Uglow, Jennifer S., ed. *The International Dictionary of Women's Biography.* New York: Continuum, 1982.

COUDENHOVE-KALERGI

Current Biography Yearbook—1948. New York: H.W. Wilson, 1948.

COURTNEY

Uglow, Jennifer S., ed. *The International Dictionary of Women's Biography.* New York: Continuum, 1982.

DAW AUNG SAN SUU KYI

Newsmakers: The People Behind Today's Headlines. Detroit: Gale Research, 1992.

DIMITROVA

Katzarova, Mariana, "Bulgaria's Poet by Profession, Vice–President by Duty." *Ms. Magazine,* July/August 1992.

DOLCI

Contemporary Authors, First Revision Series.

EL SAAWADI

Contemporary Authors, New Revision Series. Detroit: Gale Research, 1994.

O'Neill, Lois Decker, ed. *The Women's Book of World Records and Achievements.* Garden City, NY: Anchor Press, 1979.

Uglow, Jennifer S., ed. *The International Dictionary of Women's Biography.* New York: Continuum, 1982.

ENOKI

O'Neill, Lois Decker, ed. *The Women's Book of World Records and Achievements.* Garden City, NY: Anchor Press, 1979.

Uglow, Jennifer S., ed. *The International Dictionary of Women's Biography.* New York: Continuum, 1982.

FANG LIZHI

Current Biography Yearbook—1989. New York: H.W. Wilson, 1989.

FAWCETT

Uglow, Jennifer S., ed. *The International Dictionary of Women's Biography.* New York: Continuum, 1982.

FIRST

Contemporary Authors Online, 1994.

FREIRE

Brooke, James. "Leftist Plans Rebirth of São Paulo's Schools." *The New York Times.* May 28, 1989.

Freire, Paulo. *Pedagogy of the Oppressed.* New York: Continuum, 1993.

GANDHI

Bush, Catherine. *Gandhi.* New York: Chelsea House Publishers, 1985.

GARRETT

Meachem, Steve. "Pop's Mr. Politics." *Manchester Guardian,* May 3, 1990.

GELDOF
Moriarty, Mary, and Cathy Sweeney, *Bob Geldof.* Dublin: The O'Brien Press, 1989.

GONNE
Uglow, Jennifer S., ed. *The International Dictionary of Women's Biography.* New York: Continuum, 1982.

GUEVARA
Kellner, Douglas. *Ernesto "Che" Guevara.* New York: Chelsea House, 1989.

HAM SOK HON
American Friends Service Committee nomination of Ham Sok Hon for the Nobel Peace Prize, 1985.

HAMMARSKJÖLD
American Academic Encyclopedia Online, 1994.
Sheldon, Richard N. *Dag Hammarskjöld.* New York: Chelsea House, 1987.
World Book Encyclopedia. Chicago: World Book, Inc., 1992.

HEINEMANN
Current Biography Yearbook—1969. New York: H.W. Wilson, 1969.
World Encyclopedia of Peace. First edition. New York: Pergamon Press, 1986.

IBARRURI
Current Biography Yearbook—1967. New York: H.W. Wilson, 1967.
Uglow, Jennifer S., ed. *The International Dictionary of Women's Biography.* New York: Continuum, 1982.

ICHIKAWA
O'Neill, Lois Decker, ed. *The Women's Book of World Records and Achievements.* Garden City, NY: Anchor Press, 1979.
Uglow, Jennifer S., ed. *The International Dictionary of Women's Biography.* New York: Continuum, 1982.

JACOBS
O'Neill, Lois Decker, ed. *The Women's Book of World Records and Achievements.* Garden City, NY: Anchor Press, 1979.
Uglow, Jennifer S., ed. *The International Dictionary of Women's Biography.* New York: Continuum, 1982.

JOHN XXIII
Browne, Ray B., ed. *Contemporary Heroes and Heroines.* Detroit: Gale Research, 1990.
Current Biography Yearbook—1959. New York: H.W. Wilson, 1959.
Walch, Timothy. *Pope John XXIII.* New York: Chelsea House Publishers, 1987.

JOSEPH
Russell, Diana E. H. *Lives of Courage.* New York: Basic Books, Inc., 1989.

KERN
Hoose, Phillip. *It's Our World, Too!* Boston, MA: Little, Brown & Co., 1993.
Wallace, Aubrey. *Eco-Heroes.* San Francisco: Mercury House, 1993.

KHAAS

Rubin, Trudy. "A Light Goes Out in the Middle East." *Philadelphia Inquirer*, May 17, 1995.

KHAN (Abdul Ghaffar)

World Encyclopedia of Peace. First edition. New York: Pergamon Press, 1986.

KHAN (Begum Liaquat Ali)

Uglow, Jennifer S., ed. *The International Dictionary of Women's Biography*. New York: Continuum, 1982.

KLARSFELD

Newsmakers: The People Behind Today's Headlines, 1989 Cumulation. Detroit: Gale Research, 1989.

KOUCHNER

Current Biography Yearbook—1993. New York: H.W. Wilson, August 1993.

KÜBLER-ROSS

Current Biography Yearbook—1980. New York: H.W. Wilson, 1980.

LAING

Contemporary Authors, New Revision Series. Detroit: Gale Research, 1991.
Current Biography Yearbook—1973. New York: H.W. Wilson, 1973.
Newsmakers: The People Behind Today's Headlines, 1989 Cumulation. Detroit: Gale Research, 1989.

LEACH

Current Biography Yearbook—1994. New York: H.W. Wilson, August 1994.

LEFAUCHEUX

Uglow, Jennifer S., ed. *The International Dictionary of Women's Biography*. New York: Continuum, 1982.

LEFEBVRE

American Academic Encyclopedia Online, 1994.
Current Biography Yearbook—1978. New York: H.W. Wilson, 1978.

LUTHULI

Meyer, Edith Patterson. *In Search of Peace*. Nashville TN: Abingdon, 1978.
World Book Encyclopedia. Chicago: World Book, Inc., 1992.

LUXEMBURG

Magill, Frank N., ed. *Great Lives from History, Twentieth Century Series*. California: Salem Press, 1990.
Uglow, Jennifer S., ed. *The International Dictionary of Women's Biography*. New York: Continuum, 1982.

MAATHAI

Current Biography Yearbook—1993. New York: H.W. Wilson, 1993.
Wallace, Aubrey. *Eco-Heroes*. San Francisco: Mercury House, 1993.

MACBRIDE

Browne, Ray B., ed. *Contemporary Heroes and Heroines*. Detroit: Gale Research, 1990.

Current Biography Yearbook—1947. New York: H.W. Wilson, 1949.

Meyer, Edith Patterson, *In Search of Peace*. Nashville TN: Abingdon, 1978.

The New Encyclopedia Britannica. Fifteenth edition. Chicago, 1992.

MAKARIOS III

American Academic Encyclopedia Online, c.v. Makarios III, Archbishop, 1994.

Current Biography Yearbook—1956. New York: H.W. Wilson, 1956.

MANDELA

Bigelow, Barbara Carlisle, ed. *Contemporary Black Biography*. Detroit: Gale Research, 1992.

Browne, Ray B., ed. *Contemporary Heroes and Heroines*. Detroit: Gale Research, 1990.

Newsmakers: The People Behind Today's Headlines, 1989 Cumulation. Detroit: Gale Research, 1989.

MASIH

Reebok Foundation Press Releases.

MENCHÜ

Current Biography Yearbook—1993. New York: H.W. Wilson, October 1993.

MOTHER TERESA

Giff, Patricia Reilly, and Ted Lewin, *Mother Teresa, Sister to the Poor*. New York: Viking Kestrel, 1986.

Jacobs, William Jay. *Mother Teresa, Helping the Poor*. Brookfield, CT: Millbrook Press, 1991.

Newsmakers: The People Behind Today's Headlines, 1993 Cumulation. Detroit: Gale Research, 1993.

MYERS

Contemporary Authors, New Revision Series. Detroit: Gale Research, 1987.

Current Biography Yearbook—1993. New York: H.W. Wilson, 1993.

NASRIN

Anderson, John Ward. "Banned in Bangladesh." *The Washington Post*, December 11, 1993.

Baker, Deborah. "Exiled Feminist Writer Tells Her Own Story." *The New York Times*, August 26, 1994.

Schwartz, Amy E. "Cutting Edge of the Islamic Revolution." *The Washington Post*, September 16, 1994.

Sontag, Susan. "Nasrin: A Political Woman-Hunt." *Los Angeles Times,* August 17, 1994.

NEILL

Contemporary Authors, First Revision Series. Detroit: Gale Research, 1981.

Current Biography Yearbook—1961. New York: H.W. Wilson, 1961.

NGAU

Goldman Foundation Press Releases.

Newsmakers: The People Behind Today's Headlines, 1991 Cumulation. Detroit: Gale Research, 1991.

NIEMÖLLER

Current Biography Yearbook—1984. New York: H.W. Wilson, 1984.
World Encyclopedia of Peace. New York: Pergamon Press, 1986.

NOEL-BAKER

Current Biography Yearbook—1946. New York: H.W. Wilson, 1946.
Josephson, Harold, ed. *Biographical Dictionary of Modern Peace Leaders*. Connecticut: Greenwood Press, 1985.

PANKHURST FAMILY

Faber, Doris. *Petticoat Politics*. New York: Lothrop, Lee & Shephard Co., 1967.
Uglow, Jennifer S., ed. *The International Dictionary of Women's Biography*. New York: Continuum, 1982.

PÉREZ ESQUIVEL

American Academic Encyclopedia Online, 1994.
World Encyclopedia of Peace. New York: Pergamon Press, 1986.

PETHICK-LAWRENCE

Uglow, Jennifer S., ed. *The International Dictionary of Women's Biography*. New York: Continuum, 1982.

RAMA RAU

Contemporary Authors Online, 1994.
O'Neill, Lois Decker, ed. *The Women's Book of World Records and Achievements*. Garden City, NY: Anchor Press, 1979.
Uglow, Jennifer S., ed. *The International Dictionary of Women's Biograhpy*. New York: Continuum, 1982.

ROBLES

McQuiston, John T. "Alfonso García Robles Dies at 80; Shared Nobel for Atom Arms Ban." *The New York Times*, September 4, 1991.

ROMERO

Browne, Ray B., ed. *Contemporary Heroes and Heroines*. Detroit: Gale Research, 1990.

RUSSELL

Uglow, Jennifer S., ed. *The International Dictionary of Women's Biography*. New York: Continuum, 1982.

SADAT

Current Biography Yearbook—1986. New York: H.W. Wilson, 1986.

SCHINDLER

Keneally, Thomas. *Schindler's List*. New York: Simon and Schuster, 1982.

SEED

Clark, Hattie. "If a Tree Falls, John Seed Hears It." *Christian Science Monitor*, August 13, 1987.

SENESH

Atkinson, Linda. *In Kindling Flame: The Story of Hannah Senesh.* New York: Lothrop, Lee, & Shepard Books, 1985.

Cohen, Martha, translator. *Hannah Senesh: Her Life and Diary.* New York: Schocken Books, 1972.

SHARANSKY

Contemporary Newsmakers, 1986. Issue 2. Detroit: Gale Research, 1986.

Current Biography Yearbook—1987. New York: H.W. Wilson, 1987.

SHIVA

Cornerstones (Newsletter of the Right Livelihood Foundation). October, 1994.

Packet from the Foundation for Science, Technology, and Resource Policy.

SLOVO

Newsmakers: The People Behind Today's Headlines, 1989 Cumulation. Detroit: Gale Research, 1989.

SMYTHE

Uglow, Jennifer S., ed. *The International Dictionary of Women's Biography.* New York: Continuum, 1982.

SZILARD

Current Biography Yearbook—1947. New York: H.W. Wilson, 1947.

Josephson, Harold, ed. *Biographical Dictionary of Modern Peace Leaders.* Connecticut: Greenwood Press, 1985.

Shapiro, Michael. *The Jewish 100: A Ranking of the Most Influential Jews of All Time.* Secaucus, NJ: Carol Publishing Group, 1994.

TEN BOOM

Browne, Ray B., ed. *Contemporary Heroes and Heroines.* Detroit: Gale Research, 1990.

THICH NHAT HANH

Ingram, Catherine. *In the Footsteps of Gandhi.* Berkeley, CA: Parallax Press, 1990.

TIENSUU

Wallace, Aubrey. *Eco-Heroes.* San Francisco: Mercury House, 1993.

Hoose, Phillip. *It's Our World, Too!* Boston, MA: Little, Brown & Co., 1993.

TIMERMAN

Current Biography Yearbook—1981. New York: H.W. Wilson, 1981.

TROCMÉ

"Andre Trocmé." *Peace News.* London, May 4, 1949.

Josephson, Harold, ed. *Biographical Dictionary of Modern Peace Leaders.* Connecticut: Greenwood Press, 1985.

McKee, Elmore. "Light of Hope in Le Chambon." *The Christian Century,* April 30, 1947.

TUTU

Green, Carol. *Desmond Tutu: Bishop of Peace.* Chicago: Children's Press, 1986.

Hope, Marjorie, and James Young. "Desmond Mpilo Tutu: South Africa's Doughty

Black Bishop." *The Christian Century*, May 31, 1980.
Winner, David. *Desmond Tutu*. Milwaukee, WI: Gareth Stevens Publishers, 1988.

VILLA
The New Encyclopedia Britannica. Fifteenth edition. Chicago, 1992.

WAITE
Browne, Ray B., ed. *Contemporary Heroes and Heroines*. Detroit: Gale Research, 1990.
Current Biography Yearbook—1986. New York: H.W. Wilson, 1986.

WALLACE
Wallace, Aubrey, *Eco-Heroes*. San Francisco: Mercury House, 1993.

WALLENBERG
Browne, Ray B., ed. *Contemporary Heroes and Heroines*. Detroit: Gale Research, 1990.

WILLIAMS
Current Biography Yearbook—1979. New York: H.W. Wilson, 1979.
Uglow, Jennifer S., ed. *The International Dictionary of Women's Biography*. New York: Continuum, 1982.

YUNUS
MacFarquhar, Emily. "A Banking Lesson from Bangladesh." *U.S. News and World Report*. April 3, 1995.
Mammott, Mark. "Banker Breaks Barriers for Poor." *USA Today*. October 17, 1994.
Mann, Judy. "An Economic Bridge Out of Poverty." *The Washington Post*. October 14, 1994.
Munroe, Tony. "Tiny Loans, Big Return." *The Washington Times*. October 13, 1994.

ZAPATA
Ragan, John David. *Emiliano Zapata*. New York: Chelsea House Publishers, 1989.

ZASSENHAUS
Contemporary Authors Online, 1994.
O'Neill, Lois Decker, ed. *The Women's Book of World Records and Achievements*. Garden City, NY: Anchor Press, 1979.

ZETKIN
Magill, Frank N., ed. *Great Lives from History, Twentieth Century Series*. California: Salem Press, 1990.
Uglow, Jennifer S., ed. *The International Dictionary of Women's Biography*. New York: Continuum, 1982.

Index